Play, Drama & Thought

Fourth Edition, Revised

Other works by Richard Courtney

Arts Education

The Arts in Society (ed.) (Edmonton: Alberta Culture, 1974)
Teaching & the Arts (Melbourne College, Australia, 1979)
The Face of the Future (ed.) (Ottawa: Canadian Conference of the Arts, 1980)
Aesthetic Learning (Ottawa: Social Science & Humanities Research Council of Canada, 1985)
The Quest: Research & Inquiry in Arts Education (Lanham, Maryland: University Press of America, 1985)
Practical Research (Toronto: Bison Books, 1988)
Learning through the Arts (with Paul Park) (Toronto: Ontario Ministry of Education, 1981)

With David Booth, John Emerson & Natalie Kuzmich: *Teacher Education in the Arts* (Toronto: Bison Books, 1985); *Basic Books in Arts Education* (eds.) (Toronto: Bison Books, 1986); *No One Way of Being: Practical Knowledge of Elementary Arts Teachers* (Toronto: Ontario Ministry of Education, 1988)

Educational Drama

College Drama Space (ed.) (London University Institute of Education, 1964)
Drama for Youth (London: Pitman Books, 1964)
Teaching Drama (London: Cassell, 1965)
The School Play (London: Cassell, 1966)
The Drama Studio (London: Pitman Books, 1967)
The Dramatic Curriculum (London, Ontario: University of Western Ontario, 1981)
Re-play: Studies of Human Drama in Education (Toronto: Ontario Institute for Studies in Education Press, 1982)
The Rarest Dream: "Play, Drama & Thought" Re-Visited (London: National Association for Teaching of Drama, 1984)
Dictionary of Developmental Drama (Springfield, Illinois: Charles C. Thomas, 1987)
Drama Education Canada (Toronto: Bison Books, 1987)
Recognizing Richard Courtney: Selected Papers in Educational Drama (ed. D. Booth & A. Martin-Smith) (Markham, Ontario: Pembroke Publishers, 1988)

Therapy

Drama in Therapy. 2 vols. (ed. with Gertrud Schattner) (New York: Drama Book Specialists, 1982)

History

Outline History of British Drama (Totawa, New Jersey: Littlefield Adams, 1982)

Play

Lord of the Sky (Toronto: Toronto: Bison Books, 1988)

Poetry

Wild Eyed Girl (Ilfracombe, Devon: Arthur H. Stockwell, 1948)
Beasts and Other People (Toronto: Bison Books, 1987)
Tales of a Travelling Man (Toronto: Bison Books, 1987)
The Turning of the World (Toronto: Bison Books, 1988)

Richard Courtney

Play, Drama & Thought

Fourth Edition, Revised

The Intellectual Background to Dramatic Education

 Simon & Pierre
Toronto, Ontario, Canada

Design and Cover © 1989 by Simon & Pierre Publishing Co. Ltd. /
Les Éditions Simon & Pierre Ltée.

First published 1968
Second Edition October 1970
Third, revised and enlarged edition, 1974
Fourth Printing

Cassell & Collier Macmillian Publishers Ltd. 1968, 1974

1 2 3 4 5 • 93 92 91 90 89

Canadian Cataloguing in Publication Data

Courtney, Richard
    Play, Drama & Thought: The Intellectual Background to Dramatic Education

4th ed. rev.
Bibliography: p.
Includes index.

ISBN 0-88924-213-5
1. Drama in education.   2. Drama - Origin.
3. Drama - Therapeutic use.   I. Title.

PN3171.C68 1989   792'.07'1   C89-093910-1

Cover design by: Christopher W. Sears
General Editor: Marian M. Wilson
Editor: Peter Goodchild
Printer: Les Ateliers Graphiques Marc Veilleux Inc.

Printed in Canada

To order:
Simon & Pierre Publishing Company Limited
P.O. Box 280 Adelaide Street Postal Station
Toronto, Ontario, Canada M5C 2J4

for Rosemary

Acknowledgments

The author and publishers wish to thank the following for permission to reprint copyright material:

Addison-Wesley, Reading, Mass, for four extracts from "Role Theory" by T. R. Sarbin in *Handbook of Social Psychology, I*, edited by Gardner Lindzey (1954); George Allen & Unwin Ltd., for seven extracts from *Psychoanalytic Explorations in Art* by Ernst Kris, and for two extracts from "Psychoanalysis and Anthropology" by Géza Róheim in *Psychoanalysis Today*, edited by S. Lorand; Associated Book Publishers Ltd., for an extract from *Child Treatments and the Therapy of Play* by L. Jackson and K. M. Todd (Methuen & Co. Ltd.); Basic Books Inc., for nine extracts from *Creativity in the Theater* by Philip Weissman, and for five extracts from the *Collected Papers of Sigmund Freud*, edited by Ernest Jones, published in the United States of America by Basic Books Inc., New York, 1959; Dr. Gregory Bateson, Dr. Margaret Mead and the New York Academy of Sciences, for four extracts from *Balinese Character* by G. Bateson and M. Mead; Beacon House Inc., for fourteen extracts from *Psychodrama*, Volume I, by Dr. Jacob Moreno; The University of Chicago Press, for three extracts from *Language and Culture*, edited by H. Hoijer; William Heinemann Medical Books Ltd., for three extracts from *An Introduction to the Work of Melanie Klein* by Hanna Seaga; The Hogarth Press, for two extracts from *Developments in Psychoanalysis*, edited by Joan Rivière (1952), and for an extract from *The Riddle of the Sphinx* by Géza Róheim (1934); The Hogarth Press and International Universities Press Inc., for three extracts from "Psychoanalysis and Anthropology" by Géza Róheim in *Psychoanalysis and the Social Sciences*, I (*Imago*, 1947); Holt Rinehart & Winston Inc., for three extracts from "The Oedipus Complex, Magic and Culture" by Géza Róheim in *Psychoanalysis and the Social Sciences, II* (1950), for extracts from "Circuses and Clowns" by S. Tarachow in *Psychoanalysis and the Social Sciences*, III (1951), for two extracts from "A Psychoanalytic Study of the Fairy Tale" by E. K. Schwartz in *The American Journal of Psychotherapy* (1956, 10), for three extracts by Mark Kanzer from *The Journal of the American Psychoanalytic Association*, and for four extracts from *The Psychoanalyst and the Artist* by D. E. Schneider; Alfred A. Knopf Inc., for an extract from *Moses and Monotheism* by Sigmund Freud, published in the United States of America by Alfred A. Knopf Inc., New York; the Liveright Publishing Corporation, for an extract from *Beyond the Pleasure Principle* by Sigmund Freud, published in the United States of America by Liveright Publishers, New York; Norton & Company Inc., for extracts from *An Outline of Psychoanalysis* and

New Introductory Lectures by Sigmund Freud, published in the United States of America by W. W. Norton & Company Inc., New York; Penguin Books Ltd., for extracts from *Dreams and Nightmares* by J. A. Hadfield, and from *Group Psychotherapy* by S. H. Foulkes and E. J. Anthony; Prentice-Hall Inc., Englewood Cliffs, N.Y.; *The Psychoanalytic Quarterly*, for four extracts from "Psychopathetic Characters on the Stage (1904)" by Sigmund Freud, for an extract from "On Preconscious Mental Processes" by Ernst Kris, and for three extracts from "A Note on Falstaff" by Franz Alexander; the Rationalist Press Association Ltd., for two extracts from *Myth and Ritual in Dance, Game and Rhyme* by Lewis Spence (C. A. Watts & Co. Ltd); Routledge & Kegan Paul Ltd., and Norton & Company Inc., New York, for five extracts from *Play, Dreams and Imitation in Childhood* by Jean Piaget; Sigmund Freud Copyrights Ltd., Mr. James Strachey and the Hogarth Press Ltd., for extracts from *An Outline of Psychoanalysis (S.E. 23)*, *Beyond the Pleasure Principle (S.E. 18)*, *New Introductory Lectures (S.E. 22)*, *Moses and Monotheism (S.E. 23)*, *Collected Papers V, Humour (S.E. 21)*, *Collected Papers IV*, "Creative Writers and Day Dreaming" *(S.E. 9)*, in the Standard Edition of the *Complete Psychological Works of Sigmund Freud*; John Wiley & Sons Ltd., for four extracts from *Learning Theory and the Symbolic Process* by O. H. Mowrer, and for five extracts from *Learning Theory and the Symbolic Process* by O. H. Mowrer, for five extracts from *Thought and Language* by L. S. Vygotsky.

The extract from Lili E. Peller's "Libidinal Development as Reflected in Play" is reprinted from *Psychoanalysis*, Volume 3, No. 3, Spring 1955, through the courtesy of the Editors of *The Psychoanalytic Review*, and the Publisher, the National Psychological Association for Psychoanalysis Inc., New York, N.Y.

Contents

Diagrams

Preface

This fourth edition is virtually a new book. It was first written in 1966 and published in 1968, had three editions and many printings by 1974, and was translated into other languages. In 1984, the National Association for Drama Teachers (U.K.) invited me to write *The Rarest Dream: "Play, Drama & Thought" Re-Visited*, but the world had changed so much that, when the book later went out of print, I had almost decided to let it remain so. I have been persuaded, however, that a whole new generation of drama practitioners face new problems and that a new edition which addresses its concerns might be useful. Some issues are perennial, and so I have retained what is necessary. But I have also added much that is new and excluded some material that is now less relevant. I repeat my thanks to those named in previous editions, but I must add my gratitude to: the Dramatic Arts Consultants' Association of Ontario and other drama teachers' associations in Canada, the United States, Britain and Australia for workshops and other experiences which have kept me aware of contemporary problems; my colleagues Joyce Wilkinson, Howard Russell, and Walter Pitman (O.I.S.E.), David Booth (University of Toronto), John McLeod (Melbourne, Australia), Sue Martin (University of Windsor), Gisèle Barret (Université de Montréal), Bernie Warren (Concordia University), John Ripley (McGill University), Metin And (University of Ankara), Penina Mlama (University of Dar es Salaam) and Joseph Riheiro (University of Witwatersrand); and to many doctoral and thesis students in educational drama, including Judith Barnard, Bradley Bernstein, Robert Campbell, Jay Chen, Don Cordell, Elizabeth Dickens, Barbara (Severin) Gans, Robert Gardner, Poranee Gururatana, Belarie Hyman-Zatzman, Sandra L. Katz, Brenda Lamothe, Alistair Martin-Smith, Peter L. McLaren, Dennis Mulcahy, Brenda Parres, Laurence Sparling, Elizabeth Straus, Larry Swartz, Audley Timothy, Christine Turkewych, Bronwen Weaver and Nikki (DiVito) Wilson, for their helpful comments on various issues; and to my wife, Rosemary Courtney, for the new index.

Introduction

"Why do you teach my child to act?" asked a parent. "I don't want him to go on the stage."

"But nor do I."

"Then why don't you teach him something important — like math or how to write?"

Years ago, parental opposition of this kind to educational drama was considerable. It exists today, but hardly to the extent that it did forty years ago. It is based on misconceptions. The first is that standing over a child and forcing him to add up or write an essay is to provide him with an education. We must convince parents that math or writing is best learned by the child *wanting* to do them. If we can obtain the same intensity in the child in learning situations that he or she has in the playground, then this is the basis of a real and permanent education.

The second is that educational drama is "stage training." It isn't. Essentially, educational drama is a child playing dramatically. It takes place when children play "space travel" with each other or with a teacher in the classroom. Or the teacher beats a tambourine and asks 6 year old children what it reminds them of: trains, perhaps — so we're all trains, moving together, impersonating the movements and sounds of trains. With 12 year olds, we may ask them to create their own play (to improvise), but to concentrate on the climax. We still maintain the elements of dramatic play, but now they are channelled towards the creative use of form. With 16 year olds, perhaps, we may be working with a piece of script, but we still ask the student to play dramatically. When "theatre" enters, it docs so incidentally. We are not methodically teaching students stage technique. The teacher allows theatre to happen as and when the student requires it: by "reading" their needs, the teacher may introduce theatrical elements.

Educational drama is the use of dramatization for the purposes of students' learning. Depending on how it is used, it can promote one or more of at least four kinds of learning:

1 *Intrinsic Learning*: improvement of a person's qualities: perception, awareness, thought-style, concentration, creativity, self-concept, problem identification and problem solving, motivation, persistence, etc.

2 *Extrinsic Learning*: improvement of the non-dramatic themes and subjects used; e.g., history, literature, etc.

3 *Aesthetic Learning*: improvement of the quality of feeling (our responses) and thus the tacit level of insight, intuition, etc.

4 *Artistic Learning*: improvement of older students' skills in creating theatre.

We can also distinguish the following (organizational) stages of development in educational drama:

elementary, approx. 5-11 years: dramatic play

secondary, approx. 12-18 years: dramatic play mingling with theatre

tertiary, approx. 18+ years: theatre based on dramatic play

I have given a full description of terms in the *Dictionary of Developmental Drama*, but in this book we can distinguish the following:

Being	consciousness; the sense of Self as a human being; the total personality, including its effect on others
Being "as if"	the transformation of Being into something else; turning the *actual* into the *fictional* in order to work with it; as we live, both co-exist to us.
creative drama	spontaneous dramatic play for educational ends
developmental drama	the *study* of dramatic play/transformation
drama	the process of thinking/acting "as if"; transformation creates fiction parallel to actuality
dramatic play	play based on imagining
dramatization	making events dramatic (e.g., in narrative)
drama therapy	the use of drama/dramatic play for positive mental and/or physical health
educational drama	the use of dramatic play for learning
games	formalization of play into patterns with rules
imagining	thinking "as if"; metaphoric mode of possibility
improvisation	impromptu performance
play	1 activity pursued because we enjoy it 2 a script for theatre ("a play") 3 an attitude of mind ("the play world")

theatre	coding of play into performance to an audience
transformation	change from one thing to another, e.g.: 1 person into character (acting) 2 one idea into another (learning)

In the school situation, there are two major approaches to educational drama. Teachers vary in their approach, but the two have more similarities than differences. They are:

A *The Dramatic Method*

The use of dramatic activity for learning in parts of, or all, the elements of a school program ("drama across the curriculum").

B *Drama as such*

As a subject drama has specific elements: creative drama/improvisation, movement, speech/language and, with older students, theatre.

Essentially *we start with the learner* — not with the idea of where the activity will lead us (philosophic idealism), which imposes our ideas on the child. We begin with *these* students, observe their drama, and attempt to lead them on — at their pace and in their own time. The difference can be best seen with theatre. In the first approach, student are instructed in theatre skills: items are taught when the adult thinks they ought to be. In the second, students are introduced to theatre skills as they require them for their development. Such an *emergent approach* has evolved naturally from the mainstream of Western thought (see Part 1). It has its roots in contemporary psychology (Part 2), sociology and anthropology (Part 3), and it relates closely to modern concepts of mind and society (Part 4).

Unless otherwise indicated, the use of "he" in the text is meant to indicate both male and female.

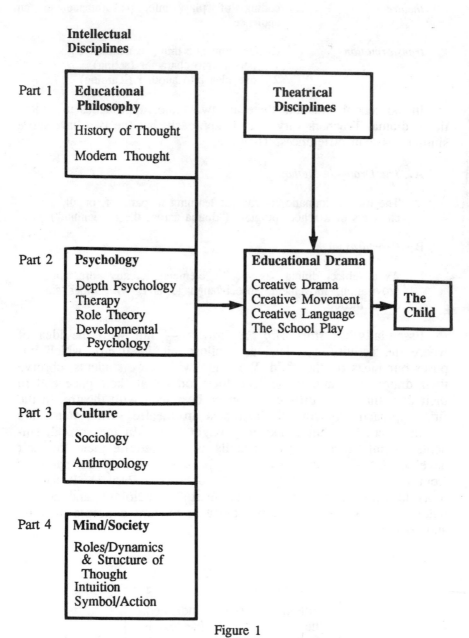

Figure 1

Educational Drama & Related Disciplines

Chapter 1
Educational Drama

The essential human characteristic is creative imagination. It enables us to master our environment, to overcome the limitations of our brain, our body, and the material universe. It is the "something more" that distinguishes us from the upper primates.

The creative imagination is essentially dramatic in character. It is thinking "as if." It is to see an event from two points of view, to see possibilities, to see the relations between two ideas and the dynamic force between them. The child's first year of life is mainly motor. Then, suddenly with some children, the change comes: they play, develop humour, and pretend to be themselves or someone else. Despite previous changes, this is the one that makes the difference between *Homo sapiens* and other species: to grasp things from another's point of view, to find the possibilities in the situation and the humour in the paradox, to work with the inherent qualities in two ideas and the possible double action between them. The child becomes a living metaphor: "a costumed player" — 2-in-1 and 1-in-3.

Imagining is inextricably linked to dramatic action. At about 10 months of age, pretending to be someone else grounds all later action. It is *"the primal act"*: the foundation of human experience. We pretend, physically and overtly, when we are very young; or we may do it internally when we are adults. But we are Being "as if" every day — whether we know it or not — with our friends, our family, strangers. The most common image for this behaviour is "the mask and the face": our real self is hidden by the many "masks" (roles) which we assume each day.

Acting is the way we live with our environment, finding adjustment in play. The young child, facing what is not understood, plays with it dramatically until it is. Alongside the actual world we create a dramatic (fictional) world, which allows us to work with the actual and master it. As this process is vital for the future of humanity, it lies at the centre of education. Without it we would merely be a mass of motor reflexes with scarcely any human qualities.

It is this living drama that is used by modern education for the purposes of learning. It answers a major need of our time. The increasing mechanism of our pseudo-scientific society does not focus on essential human qualities; as a result, people are becoming more dissociated from their human-ness. In contrast, "looking at things from someone else's point of view" is a dramatic act. It enables people to work together with trust, cultivates "the whole human being," and concentrates upon our creative potential. It destroys stereotypes and dissociation. If we wish our children to live and work in a human world in the next century, the dramatic imagination must be encouraged and fostered by schooling. Historically, however, there were major differences in the use of drama, according to the time and place in which it was used.

Drama in the History of Education

The Ancient World

Athenian education of the 5th century B.C. was based on three activities: (1) physical play, races, and games, while dancing was stressed — it required great skill and was central to all religious and dramatic ceremonies; (2) music, such as playing the flute and lyre, with the study of rhythm and harmony; and (3) literature, such as reading, writing and recitations from the poets (particularly Homer), using the full resources of inflection, facial expression and dramatic gesture. Wealthy citizens also trained the chorus of the Theatre of Dionysos, often poor boys, who went through a rigorous program of poetry, religion, singing and dancing to express the individual's harmony of thought. The Greek theatre was an educational instrument, disseminating knowledge to the populace for whom it was also the only literary pleasure available. The dramatists were viewed as teachers of equal importance to Homer; their works were recited in much the same way.

The earliest Roman education was minimal: rudimentary reading, writing, arithmetic, physical exercise and training for war. In the 3rd century B.C. schools emphasized Greek language and literature. By Augustus' reign, Latin grammar schools included rhetoric and dialectic, because the educational model was the "self-presentation" of the great orator.

The early medieval Church condemned drama and dance so there were none in schools. From the 4th century there was a strong musical tradition. By the 6th century the Benedictine monastery schools were the centre of learning with a tradition of education in the spoken word, and later some were part of the performances of Mystery Cycles. But schools were scarcely places to encourage dramatic activity.

Renascence Education

The discovery of classical books regenerated learning. The 15th century Roman Academy of Pomponius Laetus, an association of scholars, performed Latin plays and reintroduced Plautus into Italy. Members of the Italian academies became teachers, and their dramatic interests reached many children. Most famous was Vittorino da Feltra, whose Mantua school focused on games, play and physical exercises. He used imitation battles: the boys captured fortresses, set up camps and stormed trenches — dramatic play with a vengeance! He also discovered that those most eager in their play were the most zealous in both conduct and learning.

By the late 16th century, almost all schools used drama. Humanism emphasized the art of speaking, particularly in Latin and in dialogue, and reintroduced the study of ancient plays. The production of school plays became common; Tudor schools were famous for their singing and theatre traditions. In 1528, Wolsey's Statutes for Ipswich School emphasized drama for classical studies, speaking and appreciation. School drama was also used for developing the mother tongue, as exemplified by Nicholas Udall: his children, both at Eton and Westminster, performed in high places; and he created for them *Ralph Roister Doister*, the first English comedy of any note, where he wrote:

> For mirth prolongeth life and causeth health.
> Mirth recreates our spirits and voideth pensiveness,
> Mirth increases amity, not hindering our wealth,
> Mirth is to be used both of more and less,
> Being mixed with virtue in decent comeliness
> As we trust no good nature can gainsay the same:
> Which mirth we intend to use avoiding all blame.

This is a claim that comedy promotes relaxation, re-creation, spiritual health and morality. At Eton, Udall influenced two later headmasters: William Malim of Eton, who developed movement in plays; and Richard Mulcaster of Merchant Taylor's, who used the dramatic method for the learning of all subjects in the school. The Children of the Chapel Royal became so expert that in Shakespeare's time they rivalled the professional troupes.

Sir Thomas More enjoyed acting, particularly improvisation, at Christmas. Among his friends, Erasmus said that drama should refute vice, and Sir Thomas Elyot emphasized dramatic dancing as a learning method; his pupil, Roger Ascham, tutor to the young Elizabeth, used dramatic literature, play, recreation and physical exercise in education. Plays were popular in the universities of Oxford and Cambridge during Christmas. Among them were Interludes, Latin and English plays, and another early English comedy, William Stevenson's *Gammer Gurton's Needle*, which was performed by students. The first English tragedy, Norton and Sackville's *Gorboduc*, was played by the law students of the Inns of Court in 1562. By the end of the century, just prior to the plays of Marlowe, Lyly and the University Wits combined the academic drama and the popular theatre.

Drama was also used by the Jesuits. This Order, founded in 1534 by Ignatius Loyola, was devoted to developing Latin as an international language. To this end, schools used the presentation of plays, many written by the teachers or students. By the early 17th century, the plays were very didactic and had become magnificent displays.

17th & 18th Centuries

The Puritans in England, basing their beliefs on the Mosaic law that one sex should not wear the clothes of another (delightfully ridiculed by Ben Jonson through Zeal-of-the-Land Busy in *Bartholomew Fair*), attacked the theatre from the middle of the 16th century for the next hundred or more years. The result was a vast reduction in professional performances. Drama in schools they tolerated (just) if the plays were morally sound and in Latin. The Puritans' effect on education was not immediate as we can see from Ben Jonson's 1631 comment about teachers: "They make all their scholars playboys. Is't not a fine sight to see all our children made interluders? Do we pay money for this?" Even Milton loved the drama before he joined the Puritans. They could not stamp it out in schools.

By the 18th century, neo-classicism no longer encouraged school drama. Latin language rather than literature was stressed, reinforced by Locke's belief that education had to form habits of mind, and that the method, not the content, mattered. Dead languages were ideal to breed inner discipline and discourage plays. Girls' education was different. French royalty had long supported the drama. Mme de Maintenon, wife of Louis XIV, formed the convent of Saint-Cyr for poor but well-bred girls, who used dialogue and improvisation. They performed plays by Corneille, and Racine even wrote both *Esther* and *Athalie* for them. Associated with the school was Fenélon, Archbishop of Cambrai, who, in *Education of Girls* (1687) said, "Let them learn through play." Approving improvisation more than the repetition of texts, he influenced England: *Dido and Aeneus* (1689), by Henry Purcell and Nahum Tate, was first performed at a girls' school in Chelsea. In France, the girls of Saint-Cyr performed in front of Marie Antoinette. But school drama was suppressed even before the Revolution.

Despite Rousseau's clarion call for children's freedom, most schools remained deadeningly oppressive. The ideas of the Romantic writers took a long time to reach the classroom. Goethe and others made one clear distinction: the professional theatre had no place in education, but school plays and improvisation had great learning value: plays required considerable skills of memory, gesture and inner discipline; and improvisation shaped and expressed ideas while developing imagination. Schools did not alter much in the period, but ideas about them did. Rousseau's *Émile* (1762) was the open door through which, eventually, educational innovators such as Froebel, Pestalozzi, Montessori, Dewey and Caldwell Cook could march.

Basedow, a friend of Goethe, was inspired by Rousseau to start the Philanthropium in Hamburg, where work and play were synonymous. Pestalozzi followed Rousseau in developing what was "natural" to the child, while Froebel's purpose in establishing his kindergartens (later a model in Britain) was to provide simple ideas of self-activity and expression:

> Play is self-active representation of the inner — a representation of the inner from inner necessity and impulse. The plays of childhood are the germinal leaves of all later life; for the whole man is developed and shown in these, in his tenderest dispositions, in his innermost tendencies. The whole of later life of man, even to the moment when he shall leave it again, has its source in this period of childhood. [235]

The resuscitation of the school play began when the children of Queen Victoria and Prince Albert performed *Athalie* and other plays in their original languages. Increasingly grammar schools helped language learning by the performance of plays in those languages: Bradfield's triennial Greek play, first performed in 1881, continues today. There were also productions of plays by Shakespeare and others. By 1900 even my grandfather staged an annual school play in his small rural school.

The 20th Century

Doing vs. Dramatizing

Modern educational drama grew from Rousseau's "Consider the man in the man and the child in the child." It began from two ideas: "learning by doing" and "learning by dramatic doing."

In the United States, John Dewey's phrase "learning by doing" spawned a whole host of practical experiences in schools, only some of them dramatic. Dewey said that

> the primary root of all educative activity is in the instinctive, impulsive activities of the child, and not in the presentation and application of external material, whether through the ideas of others or through the senses; and that, accordingly, numberless spontaneous activities of children, plays, games, mimic efforts . . . are capable of educational use, nay, are the foundation stones of educational methods. [166]

Many schools experimented with practical methods, including Dewey's own Laboratory School; the Porter School, near Kirksville, Missouri, where Marie Harvey worked with groups on projects and included a little dramatization; and the Dalton School, New York, where the "learning by doing" often culminated in dramatic activity.

There was a different emphasis with "learning by dramatic doing." It began with H. Caldwell Cook's *The Play Way*, which gave its name to the whole movement. Working at the Perse School, Cambridge, before World War I, Cook used drama for many school subjects but particularly the arts. What Cook achieved in a British grammar school, Harriet Finlay-Johnson did slightly differently in an elementary state school. However, it was not just a British movement: John Merrill worked similarly at the Francis W. Parker School in the United States; and William Wirt developed the Gary, Indiana plan, whereby the school auditorium was used for the "work-study-play" concept, where drama stimulated oral communication.

Between Two World Wars

There followed a period of consolidation. Although dramatic play had been seen as important by thinkers as diverse as Plato, Rabelais, Rousseau and Dewey, putting it fully into practice had to wait. In the United States, Hughes Mearns' inspirational book, *Creative Power*, took Dewey's ideas towards the creative arts. This concept influenced the young Winifred Ward, who wrote *Creative Dramatics*, a foundational book in the field. From then on, most American workers linked story telling, children's creative playmaking, and children's theatre. At the same time Jacob Moreno, a trained psycho-therapist, arrived in New York from Vienna, where he had established a "theatre of spontaneity." In New York he developed psycho-drama and sociodrama, therapeutic methods based on improvisation, which helped education to widen its horizons.

In Britain school plays continued as an activity for seniors, while for other students the emphasis was more on drama as a method: as a way of learning. Sir Percy Nunn said in 1922, "Imitation is the first stage in the creation of individuality, and the richer the scope for imitation the richer the developed individuality will be." [461] In other words, personal rather than social development was stressed. By the 1920's and 30's, infant teachers were experimenting with free play for learning. Some, like E. R. Boyce, used it with "the project method," which was taken up in elementary schools. The Rose Bruford College (then a private school) began to produce speech and drama teachers, and the Society of Teachers of Speech and Drama began. Maisie Cobby and E. J. Burton were providing all kinds of drama services in Essex — as classroom activities and for amateur theatre. The play way approach continued quietly in a variety of schools: Mary Kelly in the south west created plays with adults, and Robert G. Newton used improvisation amongst the unemployed in the Depression.

The First New Wave

After World War II, there was a flurry of activity in British educational drama circles. A series of important meetings revealed a tension between drama teachers and theatre professionals over the place of drama in education. [114] The British government opened the first two state training colleges for teachers of drama and the arts (Trent Park and Bretton Hall). A number of drama advisers were appointed for specific educational jurisdictions — including Maisie Cobby, Peter Slade, T. E. Tyler, Jack Mitchley and others.

All agreed that children must be engaged in dramatic activity, to act "as if." But there were different views as to the best approach:

1   The majority advocated the dramatic method. Thus Maisie Cobby in London and most other drama advisers used drama for learning in schools with different emphases (e.g., for literature, for speech, and for movement); but they also worked with school plays and with adults in theatre.

2   Theatre people like George Devine, John Allen, and E. Martin Browne, supported by the British Drama League, advocated "theatre education": children were to be educated by being an audience.

3   Peter Slade, drama adviser for Birmingham, held a romantic view. There was already a strong "child art" movement (led by Cizek in Europe, Herbert Read in Britain, C. D. Gaitskell in Canada, and Viktor Lowenfeld in the USA) and Slade adapted this as "child drama," which was "an art form in its own right": this was natural, dramatic play used to express the personality; it was beneficial personally and socially, and revealing in a therapeutic sense.

These viewpoints came to characterize British educational drama for 20 years. Each used both spontaneous drama and theatre but with different emphases. In this period drama grew quickly in Britain. By the end of the 1960's, it was an activity in many (but not all) schools: with most 5-7 year olds, many 7-11 year olds, and some 11-18 year olds. By 1968 one third of all pre-service teachers could take educational drama as a main subject. Brian Way, who had previously worked with Slade, founded his Theatre Centre, London, where his companies initiated "participation plays": small audiences of children joined the actors in the dramatic action but under carefully controlled conditions. [614] At the same time, Way published *Development through Drama*, easily the most popular "how to do it" book for teachers which, although very practical, emphasized open-ended personal development in the manner of Maslow.

In the United States, creative dramatics continued, based on Ward's work. It was thus allied to children's theatre and in the universities (where most teacher preparation occurred) it came under Theatre as a discipline. The growth of creative dramatics, thus, was different from that in Britain. By 1955 there were 92 institutions offering courses in creative dramatics, but the teachers remained mostly in elementary schools. [553] Even more than Ward, they linked creative dramatics to theatre: Siks, for example, called it "an art for children." In secondary schools, the program was almost universally "theatre arts" and staged the latest Broadway play or musical.

The Second New Wave

By the early 70's the world had changed. There were now many experienced drama teachers so a pioneer's romantic statements did not always meet their need for detailed educational rationales. This need was met by Dorothy Heathcote, and by Gavin Bolton, who was severely critical of the pioneers. Both worked in the tradition of the dramatic method ("drama across the curriculum" or "an educational medium") but with some differences: Heathcote saw herself as a teacher first and a drama teacher second (i.e., drama techniques were universally applicable). She advocated the use of the "teacher-in-role," where, at key moments, she joined the improvisation; both she and Bolton encouraged the children to "live through" experience in the "here and now" rather than re-play previous experience. Both used themes similar to theatre: contrasts, tension, rhythm, etc.

A new growth was the Theatre-in-Education (TIE) teams, trained as both actors and teachers (first practiced by Brian Way), which used curriculum ideas for classroom performances, many participational. Some TIE teams were politically left-wing, and many drama teachers who used drama to inculcate such political ideas later suffered in the Thatcher years when drama funds were drastically cut. Another change was the growth of improvisation based on the methods of Viola Spolin and/or Keith Johnstone. Indeed, these "theatre games" became so popular that, alongside activities taken from Brian Way's book, they became the backbone of drama work in classrooms all over the world.

Creative dramatics in the USA was not subject to such great changes, although "the radical 60's" had changed theatre irrevocably. Pressured by "scientific" educators, leaders tried to justify creative dramatics in objective terms: e.g., Siks changed her rationale to a "process-concept structure approach" — the dramatic process of the players reveals to the teacher an inherent conceptual structure of the activity. Nellie McCaslin, always eclectic, provided a rationale in the educational mainstream. Virginia Koste, in reaction against behavioural attitudes, and as an artist, emphasized play as both growth and an art. Traditionalists, however, found themselves in the rearguard facing an onslaught from those using theatre games. Another change was the growth of genuine educational drama research in North America.

For years educational drama in the Commonwealth had followed the UK and USA. From the mid-1960's these countries produced their own leaders and quickly progressed. In Australia there was excellent pre-service teacher education in Melbourne, which, with the Drama Resources Centre of Victoria, was a power-house influencing other States. In Canada all education is controlled provincially so educational drama was different in the 10 provinces and 2 territories: e.g., speech-oriented in Newfoundland but theatre-based in British Columbia. Ontario focused on drama teacher education as "method" (pre-/in-service/M.A./Ph.D.) and, in 20 years, produced hundreds of high-calibre teachers working with tens of thousands of students. Quebec's Francophone traditions led to "expression dramatique" as an alternative approach which, through its leader Gisèle Barret, affected work in Canada, the USA, Spain, France, Portugal, etc.

The budget cuts by political conservatism in the 1970's and 80's had severe effects in Britain, the United States and Australia. These were less in Canada, which forged ahead and, in many instances, filled the leadership gap. By the late 70's, educational drama had spread to Europe and, by the 80's, to many Third World countries: e.g., Penina Mlama at the University of Dar es Salaam used similar approaches to resuscitate tribal rituals in the downtown core of the city. Educational drama had made great progress since Cook began his play way.

Perspectives on Educational Drama

Today there are various views about educational drama. But they are not diametrically opposite: they are similar, yet different. All of them are based on the "as if" bond between creative imagination and dramatic acts. All regard theatre as important, some more, some less. Where they differ is in their fundamental assumptions about human beings; these assumptions affect *how* they do *what* they do. Many of these assumptions are tacit: basic, unconscious beliefs that may not be directly revealed in what advocates of educational drama say. *Contemporary educational drama as a field is characterized by a plurality of views*: a series of perspectives which, if taken together, make up its theory and practice. A display of these perspectives is given in Figure 2.

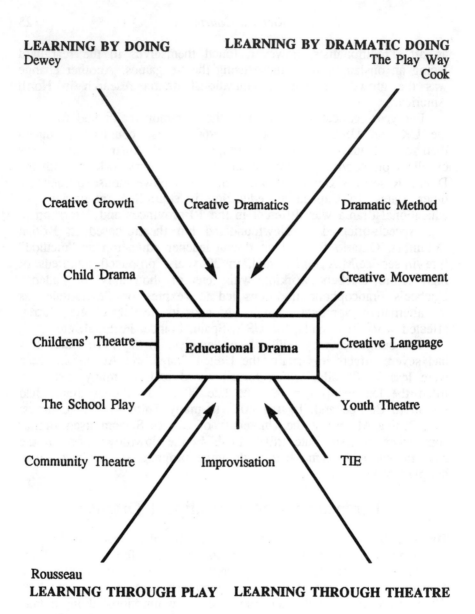

LEARNING BY DOING
Dewey

LEARNING BY DRAMATIC DOING
The Play Way
Cook

Creative Growth   Creative Dramatics   Dramatic Method

Child Drama   Creative Movement

Childrens' Theatre — **Educational Drama** — Creative Language

The School Play   Youth Theatre

Community Theatre   Improvisation   TIE

Rousseau
LEARNING THROUGH PLAY   LEARNING THROUGH THEATRE

Figure 2

The Plurality of Educational Drama

While the earliest *theory* about educational drama was that of Edmond Holmes (1911), the earliest *practical* statement about using drama for general learning was that of Caldwell Cook. Previously the school play had been the sole drama activity in education. Cook changed this; acting was a sure way to learn. In history, the facts became the basis for a story which the children then improvised: by experiencing it, they really understood it. Cook's play way was founded on three basic principles:

1   Proficiency and learning come not from reading and listening but from action, from doing, and from experience.

2   Good work is more often the result of spontaneous effort and free interest than of compulsion and forced application.

3   The natural means of study in youth is play. [118]

Play teaches us how to learn: for Burton it is "an approach to, and a method of dealing with, the business of life." It is "a means of widening experiences," says Heathcote, and a teacher's job is "how to negotiate so that people go through a process of change." The players learn, Bolton states, because they separate and objectify an event after which, say Slade and Way, the actor builds a new whole. The actor's devotion to and persistence in the dramatic task, and inherent trust in both the task and the other actor, embeds the learning in the actor's consciousness and memory.

Child Drama

For Slade, drama is a powerful learning tool, but he emphasizes that it as an activity in its own right, because, even with the baby, it is an art where "sucking a finger whilst at table and describing a circle with a wet finger on the table is more obviously Art. Clenching the wet fist and banging the table with meaning (e.g., 'more food') is more obviously Drama." [557]

Like any art, dramatic play has its own significant space: the toddler begins to move in a circle; by about eight years old in a horse-shoe shape and, with adolescence, in an end shape. Child drama also has an emotional value; it provides catharsis — "spitting out evil in a legal framework" — which makes it an effective therapy. Theatrical values, only of secondary importance, are introduced to children as they are old enough to absorb them. As there is a kind of drama for every child at a particular age, a teacher must provide each with an appropriate experience.

Drama as Growth

Brian Way is committed to personal inner growth through drama in a very practical, even anti-intellectual, manner. He is famous for the adage, "Begin from where you are," that is, the mental state and context of the player. His goal is to develop the concentration, sensory awareness, imagination, physical self, speech, emotion and intellect of each individual. These can be approached in four stages: the discovery of resources; personal release and mastery of resources; sensitivity to others within the discovery of the environment; and enrichment of other influences within and outside the personal environment. In his tacit assumptions, he is a holist of a naturalist bent, with links to Slade, Maslow and Gestalt therapists. He has worked with teachers and actor-teachers in participational theatre in Britain, Europe and North America.

Creative Dramatics

Superficially there appears to be little difference between the methods of Burton, Heathcote, Slade and Way, and creative dramatics. It is a little more structured, particularly in the use of storytelling, but otherwise similar activities are used. The difference is in an attitude of mind, which pervades all that occurs. From Dewey creative dramatics teachers assume a philosophic idealism: they always have an end-in-view, which is "a given." From Mearns they assume that this end-in-view is the art of theatre. Thus the close link of creative dramatics and children's theatre consists of a *duality*, separate but linked, which contrasts with the *emergence* of theatre in the dramatic method. Their ends are different and so the means vary.

Creative Movement

From Asclepius onwards, dance had been viewed as a component of education, with several notable exceptions. In the 20th century it was generalized to spontaneous and creative movement, pioneered by Peter Slade from the 1930's as a functional expression of children. More structured was the work of Rudolf Laban, whose scheme included six movement elements and eight basic efforts. These in various combinations made up movement sequences: the skills from which spontaneity could develop expression. Laban's work is continued at the Movement Studio, Addlestone, Surrey. Various teachers have combined creative drama and Laban-style creative movement in exciting ways, but no one more successfully than Alan Garrard. [633] Working with adolescent boys, he developed their creativity towards dance drama and theatre. Nancy King combines the dramatic method, dance and other arts in *Giving Form To Feeling*, a multi-media approach based on (aesthetic) feeling directed towards general learning.

Creative Language

The dramatic method is tied to creative language: listening, speaking, reading and writing. More conservative teachers continued "speech training" and elocution. Others emphasized "language flow" like Slade, talk like Arthur Wise, and creative language like Marjorie Hourd. When Jacques Derrida said, "Speaking is life but writing is death," [162] he meant that speech and dramatic acts (self-presentation, like Socrates) were the media closest to consciousness. Similarly, Cecily O'Neill says language is the heart of the drama process, and David Booth shows that drama and talk are intertwined for they jointly create our world view and our view of ourselves: "Drama is a medium for out-loud thought . . . the child in drama is inside language, using it to make meaning, both private and public, in the 'here and now' dynamic, with the potential of abstract reflective thought at any given moment." [67] But there is also a close relation to "dialoguing," in the sense used by Bakhtin. Two persons, attempting to understand one another, create the fiduciary contract of trust, [258] and attempt to see things from the other's viewpoint (a dramatic act); then dialogue is a genuine dramatic inter-change.

Theatre Education

Theatre as an educational medium has a variety of forms. The popularity of the school play continues today. Normally an out-of-school activity in Britain and the Commonwealth, it can be tied to theatre arts in American secondary classrooms. Play choice has widened from the traditional Shakespeare to virtually everything, formal and informal. But fewer young children perform as teachers become aware that they might suffer psychological damage.

Three theatre activities that arose in the 1960's and 70's were TIE, Youth Theatre and Improvisational Theatre. The first two were successful in Britain and Australia, but not in North America: TIE groups working with curriculum materials in schools have, more recently, suffered setbacks due to politics and cost; Youth Theatre, however, continues as small, unified groups of teenagers with dedicated leaders who explore all kinds of dramatic action. But Improvisational Theatre has been a great success everywhere, particularly when relying on the skilled training of Spolin and Johnstone, and in every aspect of educational theatre.

Children's theatres are mostly professional companies performing specifically to audiences of children. Their numbers increased in the United States in mid-century, but more recently they have retained conservative standards in the face of an ever-changing society. America has produced some specialized dramatists for this form (e.g.,

Charlotte Chorpenning, Jonathan Levy, Susan Zeder), and some companies specialize in spectacular staging. In Britain the movement began in London under Sir Ben Greet in 1918, while Bertha Waddell founded her Scots company in 1927. After World War II, Caryl Jenner kept the form alive, and it continues fitfully. In Canada, Holiday Playhouse in Vancouver (with Joy Coghill and Myra Benson) kept the torch burning for many years. Their example, together with two national tours by Brian Way, brought forth a rash of small anglophone and francophone troupes, many participational, in the 1960's. Some, like Regina's Globe Theatre, directed by Ken Kramer (most recently assisted by Brian Way), have enviable reputations by taking participational theatre by Jeep to remote prairie communities in the depth of a Canadian winter. Léon Chancerel initiated children's theatre in France. The best Russian companies are very lavish, and there have been a variety of experiments elsewhere in Europe. [114] In addition, educational drama receives various kinds of support from community theatres, which are valuable resources. They have a long history in Europe while, in North America, some are associated with universities.

Conclusion

With the increasing speed of change in society, people require improved abilities in human relations, inter-action and negotiation — precisely what educational drama teaches. Our successors will have to face an increased demand for educational drama and, more problematically, answers to questions that have yet to be asked. Much more research and scholarship are going to be needed. This book attempts to provide the necessary intellectual background: Part 1 deals with educational philosophy; Part 2 with psychological issues; Part 3 with questions of culture; and Part 4 with matters of consciousness and society.

Part One

Play, Drama & Educational Thought

Chapter 2
Drama in the History of Thought

Play is a medium. It is a "thing between," a dynamic that relates our consciousness to the world and so creates meaning. In play the medium is, indeed, the message.

Dramatic play is so all-inclusive that those who define it find it has slipped between their categories. Play is not an object: it is something people do. But it means different things in different times and places. What it meant to the Greeks is not exactly what it meant to the Victorians. The significance of the dramatic act always varies with the context of the player. Whenever play has been regarded as Being "as if," thinkers have regarded play as vital to learning.

Ancient Thought

Thinking and acting "as if" are at least as old as *Homo sapiens*. There are pebbles with markings that resemble faces from c. 3,000,-000 B.C., while red ochre was spread on graves "as if" it was blood, from c. 2,500,000 B.C. Paleolithic carvings on bone or deep in caves are calendars [405] that dramatized the seasons (telling when the buffalo will rut, emigrate, etc.), to go alongside the rituals, where hunters acted "as if" they were buffalo, wolves and other spirits. The actual and fictional co-existed. A tribal priest, or shaman, controlled spirit life in rituals (just as modern African witch doctors "doctor" witches), and, when initiated, his secular self was "killed" by the ancestor spirits, who then "resurrected" him with a new personality having "power." Impersonating a spirit through possession was to use the "as if" to maintain social order.

The ancient Near Eastern agricultural civilizations understood themselves and their world by enacting ritual-myths in seasonal festivals. Just as the crops had their annual cycle, so the cosmos and humanity were dramatized in an annual death-and-resurrection in the person of the King. The life of the gods and human beings were mirror images of each other: one was "as if" it was the other — what happened in one, happened in both. In Egypt, the cosmos and life were created by the "breath" of the god Thoth, a shadowy figure best known for taking the roles of others. In addition the idea of "the double" was inherent in Egyptian thought: there were two Egypts (Upper and Lower), two crowns (red and white), two of everything — even the pharaoh had to perform "the dance of the land" twice. In other words, life rested on the use of roles and self-presentation. In the Abydos ritual, the priest playing Horus was also Osiris and represented the pharaoh: personality was multiple with a number of "souls."

Ancient Greece

The invention of writing by the Phoenicians split the myth from the ritual. When a myth was written down it became objective: it could be compared with "the facts" and found to be "false." The *Iliad* was a war-game between the gods, in which the Greeks and Trojans were their playthings: the play of the gods was as wilful as that of children, and destiny was a matter of chance. Play was an *agon*, or contest: human competitiveness was a dramatic act — people were "as if" gods competing with one another. What Homer implied, Hesiod explicitly stated: humans acted "as if" they were gods. The pre-Socratics went further: for them, play was Being "as if." Heraclitus said that life itself was play: "Lifetime is a child at play, moving pieces in a game." [340] Xenophanes even doubted the existence of the gods but said that human beings must act "as if" they believed in them. [207] In other words, only in dramatic fiction can we understand reality.

Socrates

Plato in his dialogues made his old master, Socrates, the protagonist of the dramatic disputes. Socrates took the role of an ignorant person (which he was not), always asking questions and never giving answers. This is the famous "Socratic irony": by acting "as if" he knew nothing, he drew from others the truths they had not realized before. The Socratic method was of dialogue and direct play: he presented himself in a fictional role and in direct speech, and the others also presented themselves in direct speech. Where the essence of life for Thoth was "breath" and roles, for Socrates it was "speech" and the drama of self-presentation.

Plato

Plato was a philosophic idealist: there was an abstract, ideal Ultimate, which he called the Ideas, or Forms (the "Good," "Beauty," etc.), that were eternal; each object in the universe was a manifestation (imitation) of its Ideal. This was the basis for his famous attack on tragedy, the arts and literature in the *Republic*. They were two degrees removed from truth: the truth was the eternal Ideas; the reality we live in was an imitation of that truth; while play and the arts were imitations of that imitation.

Plato distinguished two kinds of play: the irrational, which is "bad" mimesis; and the rational, which is "noble" mimesis. But in the less-than-perfect state he describes in the *Laws*, "noble" mimesis can be used: "Man is created to be the plaything of the gods; and therefore the aim of everyone should be to pass through life, not in grim earnest, but playing at the noblest pastimes." [489] "Noble" play, whereby humans imitate the divine, is rational, the highest expression of human freedom, and is closely linked to education. In the practical world of education: "Children from their earliest years must take part in all the more lawful forms of play, for if they are not surrounded with such an atmosphere they can never grow up to be well educated and virtuous citizens." [490]

In the *Symposium*, the Idea of Beauty is the ultimate aim of education, and it appears in a flash of intuition. Intuition produces the only kind of art of which Plato approves, and in the *Ion* he states that both acting and poetry can reveal divine truth through inspiration. Play and aesthetic experience are the foundations of education. Thus

> the young of all creatures cannot be quiet in their bodies or in their voices, they are always wanting to move and cry out; some leaping and skipping, and overflowing with sportiveness and delight at something, others uttering all sorts of cries. . . . Shall we begin then, with the acknowledgement that education is first given us through Apollo and the Muses [for] he who is well-educated will be able to sing and dance well. [489]

Plato's goal for education was to develop the natural abilities of each person in order to make a good and useful citizen. Girls and boys should have the same curriculum and be encouraged to express themselves freely, thus disclosing their potential abilities, and play should be the basis of all education until about the age of 10.

In the *Laws* he took over Xenophanes' view of play. The arts create "as if" fiction, which has value in acquiring knowledge: it is "the useful lie" because it provides practical (not rational) knowledge. Yet in the *Phaedrus*, Plato went much further: the *logos* is unified with Thoth, Hermes and Socrates: it is a vital process embodied in a person who is a transformer, or shape changer — "one who puts play into play."

Aristotle

Play's purpose is to realize potential, to create order, to provide meaning. Aristotle did not accept the separate existence of Plato's World of Forms. For him, change is time, movement and Becoming; matter is potentiality, making the possible actual; the energy in matter tries to organize it in some order, which is the goal (*telos*) of the process — a concept remarkably like the modern idea of DNA as stored information. Play and the arts are practical and useful to education; they "should be neither illiberal, nor too laborious, nor lazy." Introduced for relaxation "as a medicine" (catharsis), they are means to an end — to realize potential. Art should be based on practical skills but not to the level of professional performance: "they should study only so far as to be capable of feeling delight." Their function "is to describe, not the thing that has happened, but a kind of thing that might happen" — it is to learn the value of possibility. [16]

Aristotle's *Poetics* is short and incomplete. Play as Being "as if" disappears. Plato said it gave practical knowledge, but for Aristotle truth only comes from nature (*physis*). He uses "mimesis" as near to "copy" and, as Spariosu says, [563] this is to confine the "as if" to 2,000 years of mimicry. The success of "as if" to Aristotle lies in whether it is "plausible":

> It is Homer who has chiefly taught other poets the art of telling lies skilfully. The secret of it lies in a fallacy. For assuming that if one thing is, or becomes, a second thing is or becomes, men imagine that, if the second thing is, the first likewise is or has become. . . . For the mind, knowing the second to be true, falsely infers the first. . . . Accordingly, the poet should prefer probable impossibilities to improbable impossibilities. [16]

Aristotle answers Plato's attack on the theatre. Imitation gives the actor the skills to imitate the essence of the thing. Characters are not presented like life: tragedy makes them worse, comedy makes them better.

> Imitation is natural to man from childhood, one of his advantages over the lower animals being this, that he is the most imitative creature in the world, and learns first by imitation. . . . It is also natural for all to delight in works of imitation. . . though the objects themselves may be painful to see, we delight to view the most realistic representations of them in art [because] to be learning something is the greatest of pleasures, not only to the philosopher but also to the rest of mankind, however small their capacity. [16]

This leads to his theory of catharsis, whereby tragedy "purges" emotions.

> A tragedy . . . is the imitation of an action that is serious and also, as having magnitude, complete in itself, in language and pleasurable accessories, each kind brought in separately in the parts of the work; in a dramatic, not in a narrative form; with incidents arousing pity and fear, wherewith to accomplish its catharsis of such emotions. [16]

His full text is not extant. Aristotle likely thought the emotions aroused by tragedy purged the soul like a medicine: impure emotions were experienced so that the noble emotions of pity and fear could be improved. This view of emotion strongly influenced Kierkegaard, Freud, Moreno and Peter Slade.

Roman Thought

Through Roman authors ancient ideas reached the Middle Ages. For Cicero, art was Aristotle's imitation, while theatre was "a copy of life, a mirror of custom, a reflection of truth" (an idea which Shakespeare used in "to hold, as 'twere, the mirror up to nature"). But most Romans agreed with Horace that drama must "unite information with pleasure." [295] Education was functional: to develop self-presentation through the skills of oratory. The great orator was a role model, Cicero in particular. Well educated persons dramatized the role model in actions to promote rational order, finding merit in different views and making a compromise without surrendering basic ideals. Plotinus represented Plato's thought and was influential up to the 12th century. Quintilian affected the late medieval period and early Renascence. His *Training of an Orator* was Ciceronian, influencing such diverse people as Petrarch, Erasmus, Luther, Disraeli and John Stuart Mill.

The Middle Ages

The Church attacked dramatic dance, but it survived. The Biblical dance tradition helped: David danced in the temple, and, in the *Apocrypha*, the Mother of God danced before the temple, and Christ danced with his disciples. In the 7th century, St. Isadore composed a sacred ritual dance — a rare event as a Christian theatre tradition of Arius in the 3rd century had been declared the Arian heresy. Gregory the Great counselled Augustine not to oppose the pagan's possessed dances but subtly adapt them to church rituals. Thus Europe was Christianized and the "as if" kept alive for, as Mikhail Bakhtin tells us, carnival was a form of revitalization, a participation in the life/death forces of Nature.

Yet the Church was full of drama. A Christian lived *in imitatio* of Christ. For Augustine the world was a theatre (mortals acted out their lives before God and Heaven), and Amalarius saw the Mass as a drama. The atonement was a dramatic conflict (Christ vs. Satan) for Anselm. Honorius' works (c. 1100), with the Mass a drama in the theatre of the Church, were widespread. [277] In consecrating a new church, Psalm 24 had dramatic force: as the Bishop rapped on the door, a hidden priest ("as if" the spirit of evil) rushed wildly out (a mix with the pagan scapegoat), still a church ritual today. The medieval church drama began, and Aquinas approved play and social amusements (for relaxation and social cohesion) and professional acting "for man's consolation."

The Renascence

The "As If" of the Artist

Being "as if" grew with the creative artists of the Renascence. The novels of Rabelais spread the idea of play as humanist freedom. He provided Gargantua with a wide curriculum including play, the creative arts, dancing and 316 games to exercise the mind and body. Rabelais broke the medieval world view, creating a humanistic one built on laughter, unusual logic, time measured in creative acts, and Being "as if" as growth. He influenced many including Montaigne, Shakespeare, Cervantes and Rousseau.

Montaigne, the French essayist and sceptic, understood the play metaphor. He saw the innate "as if" quality of himself as a writer: "I owe a complete portrait of myself to my public" is a Renascence parallel to the modern entertainer, Sammy Davis, Jr., who said, "Every morning when I open my front door, I'm on, baby, I'm on!" For Montaigne, dramatic play was essential for education: the child "shall not so much repeat as act his lesson." Play was not "mere pretence": "children's plays are not sports and should be deemed their most serious occupations." [437]

"All the world's a stage" was an ancient metaphor used by Pythagoras, Augustus Caesar and Wyclif. Shakespeare made it uniquely his own. His early plays talk of life being "as if" theatre, and he delights in terms like "a part," "to play," and so on. He changes the metaphor's meaning during his working life. Many of his characters are "deep dissimulars," false actors like Richard III and Iago. Many comedies have "a play within a play" to question reality and illusion. The metaphor questions kingship: Richard II is a symbol of royalty and so is an actor. At the end of his life, Shakespeare changed the metaphor from theatre to drama. In *The Tempest*, the actor and the person dissolve into one:

> We are such stuff
> As dreams are made on; and our little life
> Is rounded with a sleep.

For the aged Shakespeare, life was an illusion: we are all players.

Superficially Cervantes' *Don Quixote* contrasts the fiction of chivalrous knights with their idealized ladies, and the actual world of roguery, greed, illusion and hypocrisy in all social classes. But it is also a rich satire of actual vs. fictional. The fiction in which Don Quixote believes (his "madness") is set within another fiction — the mirror within the mirror (an ancestor of Pirandello, Fowles and Eco). In Cervantes, Carrasco begins by playing: he disguises himself as a knight-errant and imitates Don Quixote's own "logic." But after

Carrasco is left defeated and bruised on the battlefield by his friend, he says that the difference between the sane and insane is that, "he that of necessity is so, will remain so; and he that accidentally is so, may leave it when he will." [103] There are two modes of life: action and play, while madness is a state of undifferentiation between the two.

Court Play

The Middle Ages created symbolic allegories, whereby one thing was understood as another ("as if"). Three traditions united: the Old Testament was an allegory for the New; rural labourers danced in skins and horns, or took the parts of Robin and Marion on May Day; and the Mystery Cycle had multiple meanings. The Renascence court expanded these ideas. The Tudors had social dramas based on the "allegory of love," the tournament and the city pageants — dramatic worlds to understand life. The young Henry VIII introduced "masking" from Italy: he and his friends went masked and uninvited at a party given by Wolsey; they danced in close bodily contact with some of the ladies ("a thing not approved of") before they left. Elizabeth I made such dramatic acts into "the game" with myriad levels of illusion: the Queen was Cynthia and her courtiers had allusive names; on an official journey, she might be met by a centaur who addressed her in couplets as Cynthia or Diana. The "as if" of allegory and myth infused the whole realm.

This courtly play was transformed into the Stuart masque, mixing charade, social dance and mythological performance. A masque with dialogue by Ben Jonson and scenery and costumes by Inigo Jones was almost a theatrical form. [330] The social world of "the game" became a performed "as if" world. Charles I's masques dramatized the political myth: the Divine Right of Kings vs. the Puritans. Charles believed in the power of the performance: playing "as if" created truth. The last great masque, *Salmacida Spolia* (1642) was meant to prevent the threatening chaos and, despite the Puritans' objection to high taxation, one performance cost the equivalent, in today's terms, of the entire British defence budget for one year! It was not, of course, effective; later Charles was executed outside the Banqueting House in Whitehall, where so many masques had been staged. Belief in a political "as if" can have serious consequences.

Induction & Reason

Renascence science focused on induction, namely, that the accumulation of facts led to a universal law. Induction was popularized when Francis Bacon applied it to life and education, where observation led to the discovery of facts and causes. This should have encouraged play and the arts, but these thinkers prided themselves on being practical with no time for fiction and frills. Calvinists and Puritans also said the arts led Christians from the concrete and from "work." Bacon was not so harsh. While he disliked the professional theatre, he supported Being "as if" in schools, as "an art which strengthens the memory, regulates the tone and effect of the voice and pronunciation, teaches a decent carriage of the countenance and gesture, gives not a little assurance, and accustoms young men to bear being looked at." [25] Comenius' teachings took more "useful" inductive methods into schools.

Neo-Classicism

The Age of Reason

Descartes denied imagination and mathematicized the world. He believed in the primacy of cognition (*Cogito ergo sum*); the dualism of body and mind; and (with Newton) that people and the cosmos operated like machines. Long term, this view suggested that mind is the active agent in play, creating meaning. But the immediate effect was that play did not fit the contemporary understanding of the world. Neither Spinoza nor Leibnitz dealt directly with the concept of play, but Spinoza said that thought is always embodied: knowledge results from action, and each person can proceed to higher levels of thought by choice. Leibnitz said that time and space were mere appearance, implying that all existence is action (to Be is to be active), and that the vitality inherent in life is fundamental to it. Lessing brought Leibnitz' philosophy to the Enlightenment.

For the British empiricists, Locke, Berkeley and Hume, knowledge was not innate but acquired. The child was a miniature adult. Mind was a blank tablet absorbing from the senses simple ideas and combining them into complex ideas. Education was the growth of mental habits and reasoning; this view worked against play but it had the seeds of change. What was taught was less important than how it was taught; and learning should be as enjoyable as play — which Locke's immediate followers forgot. But Hume saw that imagination is primarily responsible for our conviction that there was an external world; that the human mind "imagines" objects and that art creates fictions — but they must be "useful."

The Enlightenment

For most thinkers play had to be useful, serving the intellect. But two novelists differed: Defoe called fiction "lying like truth," and Laurence Sterne's *Tristram Shandy* was based on the conflict of fiction and action. In 1750 Baumgarten used the term "aesthetic" for the first time: appreciation was the appropriate "distance" from art, and the link of mimesis and illusion was one of "likeness," or "replica."

Two thinkers broke the mould. Vico refuted Cartesianism, attacked abstract reason, and returned to the great humanist traditions: sentiment, intuition, imagination and passion. "Making" was knowledge (later re-stated by Rousseau, Collingwood, etc.) and truth was metaphoric, a return to the double meanings of fiction. Diderot's *Encyclopedia* gave an imaginative biological view of the universe. He denied the "replica" and returned "imitation" to before Plato. Human play was to change masks in front of a face that consists merely of actions and reactions (similar to Socrates, Bergson and Pirandello) like Aristotle's view of the actor, who, focusing his performance on real life, creates an improvement on nature.

Kant

Immanuel Kant (1724-1804) began German Idealism. In essence he said: imagination is part of perception and is the pre-condition of experience. Imagination unites experience with reason; and play is a process by which we assume an aesthetic attitude in order to understand and manipulate the world for our own purposes. This has echoes in modern educational drama.

There are three levels of reality on a continuum: the mundane world is transformed by the aesthetic; the world of reason is transformed by the analytic; and the Ideal world (much like Plato's) is transformed by the dialectic. Transformation, thus, is a major dynamic.

There is a moral law ("the categorical imperative") which we must obey. We know what is right *a priori*, by intuition, and we do so "as if": "Act as if the maxim upon which you were to act were, through your will, to become a universal law." This law, for Kant, is the form of practical reason that brings freedom. It distinguishes Kant's position from the classic Western view of Aristotle.

Play and art are modes of the aesthetic for Kant, a feeling and synthetic act. This act relates the external world to consciousness through imagination and reason. Sensory impressions are channelled through the mental constructs of time and space to be transformed into thoughts. Our understanding is thereby *a unity* of empirical/rational, objective/subjective operations.

The aesthetic is as important to consciousness as the theoretic and the practical. It mediates between them through feeling, whereby we make a judgment; we can view this judgment as subjective or objective. The aesthetic produces two effects: it can expand consciousness, releasing it in a pure spirit of enjoyment; and it can awaken a feeling of inadequacy akin to pain.

Kant uses "play" as a powerful intellectual tool that mediates between inner and outer, necessity and freedom, and destroys the subjective/objective dichotomy (like Kierkegaard's denial of the "either/or"). Kant's use of "play" profoundly influences Heidegger and modern educational drama. *Play brings practical knowledge* and, thus, Kant returns Being "as if" to the centre of Western thought. Ideas are heuristic fictions that create meaning. Fictions are tools whereby we can understand Ideas and the objective world. Knowledge is only the play of appearances. Heuristic fictions are "good" play because they are rational, but "mere play" is irrational. Play, art and literature, as modes of the aesthetic, exist in their own right because they provide knowledge. The aesthetic feeling is pure play, while appreciation of art provides a clarity of feeling above the ordinary.

In educational terms, only through experience and the use of intelligence can the child develop greater understanding, self-discipline and moral reasoning. Kant says this could best be achieved through the free play and practical experiences advocated by Rousseau.

Romanticism

Rousseau

Rousseau (1712-1778) was "the spirit of Romanticism," although Vico had anticipated him. In *Émile* (1762), Rousseau found truth in nature vs. civilization, passion vs. intellect, the spontaneous vs. the artificial. Human spontaneous freedom encourages natural instincts: repression should not exist in school; "let Nature do the teaching." So early childhood should be almost entirely play:

> Love childhood; promote its games, its pleasures, its delightful instincts. . . you must consider the man in the man and the child in the child. . . . Nature desires children to be children before being men. If we try to pervert the order, we shall produce precocious fruits which will have neither ripeness nor taste, and will soon go bad. . . . Childhood has its own ways of seeing, of feeling, which are suitable to it; nothing is less reasonable than to substitute our own. [529]

The senses must be cultivated. The child is born good, learning evil habits from bad example and harmful discipline. Play is natural learning: "Work and play are alike to him; his plays are his occupations, and he sees no difference between the two. He throws himself into everything with charming earnestness and freedom, which shows the bent of his mind and the range of his knowledge." [529] As a person, however, Rousseau understood "play" in another way; he was extremely shy: "That part that I have taken of writing and hiding myself is precisely the one that suits me. If I was present, one would never know what I was worth." [529] Thus Rousseau is well aware of at least three levels of Being "as if": Being, or consciousness; self-presentation through the social role; and the hiding of the self through such media as writing.

The Romantics

"Nature" was the basic concept. The "natural" was valued, the unnatural was not. Nature was inherently energetic. A major theme in Blake's poetry was harnessing natural energy — not a surprising idea in the industrial revolution when scientists had become mechanics. Nature also meant freedom for "the hero" to express his feelings: passion was transformed into aesthetic feeling and then artistically expressed. This freedom characterized "the heroic personality" of Byron and Beethoven. Rousseau said: "I am not made like anyone I have seen; I dare believe I am not made like anyone in existence. If I am not better, at least I am different." [529]

Romanticism bred subjective individualism: we search for an ideal order by expressing aesthetic feelings in adult art or child's play. Wordsworth used the metaphor, "trailing clouds of glory do we come." But society restricts natural childhood: "shades of the prison-house begin to close about the growing boy."

Goethe said that dramatic play had cognitive value: it shapes inner thoughts, releases them, and develops imagination, because "in their games, children can make all things out of any: a staff becomes a musket, a splinter of wood a sword, any bunch of clothes a puppet, any crevice a chamber." [246] For Goethe dramatizations develop ideas: they bring emotions and thoughts which we ought to feel (later echoed by Bergson and Shaw). There is a duality to the life process: two forces pull us, now this way, now that. For Goethe this was death/resurrection: people lose part of themselves before assimilating the new; drama must include death/rebirth if it is to have real meaning (echoed later by Frazer, Murray, Gaster, Frye, etc.). Hegel saw ideas as dialectical: "thesis" produces "antithesis" and the result is "synthesis," a working method taken over by Marx in economic history. Nietzsche later developed his own form of the duality of forces (see pp. 46-47).

The romantic artists and writers well knew Being "as if" in a variety of ways. All the English poets wrote plays, but only Byron's were stageable in their time. Coleridge's famous definition of the primary imagination as a "repetition in the finite mind of the eternal act of creation in the infinite I AM," repeats Kant, but elsewhere (e.g., *Kubla Khan*) he is the first in the Western tradition to ask: is aesthetic fiction a shadow of divine creation and, thus, only a Satanic mimicry? Shelley's *A Defence of Poetry* starts from art as Aristotle's mimesis, but its origin is imagination: the creative power of play and art, and a potent force for moral development as the artist can "create anew the universe."

19th Century Ferment

The popular idea that 19th century England was smug and stable ignores the ferment of ideas. Indeed, Victorian authors cannot be understood without reference to their contemporaries' views. Play was seen from a range of perspectives. Despite the Basedows and the Froebels, the play of children was a concern of a minority of people's. Mechanism, industrialism and Descartes' machine metaphor infused everything: people believed in cause-and-effect, quantity above quality, sequencing and a practical use of ideas — not in the value of play. The use of ideas and "the greatest happiness of the greatest number" were the bases of British utilitarianism. Only if play was of practical use could the majority of people have advocated it. Radical educational change meant different things at different times. Dickens' readers became aware of appalling school conditions, while Thomas Hardy, in *Jude the Obscure*, showed the conflict of intellect and emotion in Jude's education. Few radicals were interested enough to address the issue of play. It was left to Oscar Wilde, in *The Portrait of Dorian Gray* at the end of the 19th century, to attack those who confused art with life.

Evolution

A major trend of the 19th century was towards determinism. Three of the greatest influences on the period — Marx, Darwin and Freud — were solidly deterministic. That is, they believed that human beings were controlled by specific forces: evolution with Darwin, economy with Marx, and the unconscious with Freud.

When Darwin published his *Origin of Species* (1859), the theory of evolution was not new. But he induced it from such an immense mass of evidence that it became the basic fact of the age. He said that higher forms of life (including human) evolved from lower forms; this is still accepted today. He also said that evolution was caused by the struggle for existence and the survival of the fittest, an idea still much in dispute. Dramatic play had to be accounted for in these terms. There were various theories that tried to do so, as we shall see.

Surplus Energy

The theory that the play of animals and humans results from the release of surplus energy was held by Schiller and Spencer. Schiller said that play was "the aimless expenditure of surplus energy," which accounted for apparent aimless activities in the animal world; young animals and children are fed and protected by their parents, and, as they are not concerned with self-preservation, all their energy is "surplus." This part of the theory is clearly suspect: zoologists show that the acts of insects, birds and animals that might appear purposeless have a clear and definite end; [582] and children with the freedom to play will do so until they drop — their energy can hardly be called "surplus." But Schiller also related surplus energy to the play of human imagination:

> The imagination, like the bodily organs, has in man its free movement and its material play, a play in which, without reference to form, it simply takes pleasure in its arbitrary power, and in the absence of all hindrance. These plays of fancy . . . belong exclusively to animal life, and only prove one thing . . . that he is delivered of all external sensuous constraint . . . without our being entitled to infer that there is in it an independent plastic form. [540]

Herbert Spencer was an evolutionist who was bitterly attacked for saying that acquired characteristics could be inherited (which modern science would support). He discusses surplus energy in six issues:

1 Species no longer struggling for survival have an excess of time and energy: nerve cells increase in sensitivity to stimulation, wish to act if they are rested, and discharge along the lines of least resistance. Play activity moves towards acts that have a large part in the organism's life: "Hence play of all kinds."

2 There is an instinctive basis for this.

3 There is a strong tendency to imitate: when organisms have no serious activity, imitation is substituted; children play at what they will do seriously in adult life.

4 Art is a form of play; their similarity is that, "neither subserve, in any direct way, the processes conducive to life." [495] But, as Ebbinghaus showed, play is not identical with art. [172]

5 The form of play depends on the level of development of the player: more structural complexity brings an increased diversity of play.

6 Play can act as compensatory satisfaction.

Spencer's importance is that he was the first modern scientist to give a full explanation of play, anticipating the work of many others.

Instinct

Heredity was basic for those evolutionists who saw play as an instinct: an impulse which is innately part of a person's personality. Karl Groos' two books showed play's wide range and its value for children, both for itself and as training for later life. Groos develops Spencer's idea of play being a training ("practice," "pre-exercise") for life. Play is pleasurable and "it seems possible that such feelings of pleasure rest on the basis common to all play, which a searching examination will discover to be experimentation." [262] Groos provides two unique concepts with direct effects on education: the purpose of childhood is to provide a period of play; and play is directly related to the growth of intelligence — "many instincts are becoming rudimentary in the higher animals because they are being supplanted by another instinct — imitative impulse, and this substitution is of direct utility, for it furthers the development of intelligence." [262] Groos did not "prove" transfer from play to adult activities and his theory was attacked by behaviourists, particularly Watson. But we can agree with Groos that play improves physical and psychological mastery of the self and the environment.

Joseph Lee applied Groos' instinct theory to education. Play develops self-concept:

> If the lesson has struck home, the result is not merely more knowledge or more intelligence, but more boy or girl — more of a person there for all purposes. If his arithmetic has truly reached him, he will play better football; if his football has been the real thing, he will do better arithmetic. That is the nature of a true educational experience — that it leaves a larger personality behind. [380]

Behaviourists saw this, too, as fallacious. But Lee rationally took his support from the theory of "pre-exercise": play, as part of the law of growth, exercises body and mind in the actions towards which their growth is directed; it follows the order whereby growth and mental powers are established; children develop more fully if they have the opportunity to play than if they do not; and it always aims beyond existing powers and so is a way of learning. It took over 50 years before this view was supported by research that behaviourists might regard as adequate. [559] Lee also said that dramatic identification is a sure way to learn information, to understand others, and to learn values:

> When you are seven years old and you have acted the role of Christopher Columbus, you never forget that it was *YOU* who discovered America! . . . The best way to be anybody — to get the feel of

him as he is from the inside — is to act out his character and
function. . . . I believe that the impersonating impulse bequeaths
imaginative insight — the power to see people as they really are,
the intuitive sympathy that sees with another's eyes. . . . if you can
get King Arthur to actually enter your soul, and fight for you in
the schoolroom and in the playground, he is as valuable an ally as
any boy need have. . . . [Dramatic imagination] is the first reaching
out of the spirit, the first shaping of aspiration. [380]

Despite the fact that Lee added nothing to Groos' position that play
is purposeful, his influence was enormous, and it still continues.

Biological & Physiological Theories

Charles Bell's *Nervous System of the Human Body* (1830) showed
that motor and sensory functions are performed by different nerve
fibres. Linked to evolution, this resulted in various biological or
physiological theories: it enabled behaviourists to present life as a
stimulus/response relationship; and it grounded psycho-physical parallelism, which became the basis for a number of play theories.

The recreation theory that play restores the physically and mentally tired originated with Lord Kames, who said, "Play is necessary
for man in order to refresh himself after labour." [434] Its immediate
forerunner was Guts Muths, the German "father of physical training,"
and its main advocate was Moritz Lazarus. It was simplistic: it had
little of growth about it and was not relevant to children, most of
whose life is play.

In the relaxation theory, G. T. W. Patrick said that play was
free, spontaneous and "pursued for its own sake." Its purpose was
relaxation: an entirely adult concept as children's play is hardly
relaxing. Yet he said there were parallels between children's play,
adult sports, and the pursuits of tribal peoples. Tribal activity with
animals was reflected in the child's play with teddy bears, while
football was a mimic battle. This is another simplistic theory, but it
continues today as popular lore.

Recapitulation is a more complex relaxation theory based on
heredity and advocated by G. Stanley Hall. Humans inherit tendencies of muscular coordination that have been of racial use. In play
"we rehearse the activities of our ancestors, back we know not how
far, and repeat their life work in summative and adumbrated ways. It
is reminiscent, albeit unconsciously, of our line of descent." [274]
Each age stage has a different set of play activities, where the
content is relatively constant, and which corresponds to ancestral
activities sequenced as in evolution. Play's purpose is to free us
from ancestral residues and hasten development towards higher
stages. Today this theory is seen as fallacious: play content evolves

not with recapitulation but with the environment; known tribal peoples do not progress uniformly; and human beings do not live over a precise order of evolution.

Although fallacious, recapitulation resulted in various experimental studies. For example, Estella Appleton modified Hall so that play precedes the ability to function and gives rise to it: the hunger for play leads to action, which leads to growth, which is a practice for life. But a purely physiological theory is virtually untenable and must take other findings into account.

Today the neuro-physiological theory of "the bi-cameral mind" is popular. [468] Stated simply, the left side of the upper brain (cortex) controls the right side of the body and deals with cognition, while the right brain controls the left body and emotions. But such large generalizations are unwise: individual differences are great, and new studies alter the picture rapidly. It is true that while dramatic actions affect both hemispheres they generally emphasize the more holistic, intuitive and spontaneous activities of the right brain; these have been underdeveloped by Western education's emphasis on linear, logical and time-dependent skills of the left.

To this lateral theory must be added the Papez-MacLean vertical theory: the upper brain (cortex) deals mostly with conscious activity, while the lower brain (the limbic system) deals with unconscious and emotional thought. [356] The complexity of thought and action is better understood by combining the vertical and horizontal, which shows a four-fold structure related to the semiotic square (discussed in Chapter 16).

The genetic constitution we inherit interacts with the environment to produce a phenotype (our specific characteristics) that allows certain potentialities to be realized as we mature. Modern studies show that, while genes transmit the tendency to play, civilization has separated play from life, and this could destroy the value of play for the species and society. Related cultural theories have been developed by Johan Huizinga, Roger Callois, M. M. Bakhtin, and others.

The Last Dramatic Fling

At the end of the 19th century the last great romantic emerged: Friedrich Nietzsche. With a broad sweep, he returned Western thought to Heraclitus' view of play. Like all romantics, he first appeals to Nature. In "a revaluation of all values," he denies the Judeo-Christian tradition but accepts the implications of evolutionary naturalism: humanity is driven by the expression of animal instincts ("the will to power") towards a master race and the Superman — a concept later used negatively by the Nazis and positively by Bernard Shaw. Each person's success in overcoming the transitoriness of existence represents the human will to live. Life and drama have an oscillation between two powers: Apollo the idealist, the creator of dreams, who imitates them in art; and Dionysos the primitive, the emotional person, who creates art in ecstasy. For true art the primary Dionysos must have the help of the secondary Apollo: emotion is shaped by reason. This is to oppose Plato (returning to Heraclitus' view of Being "as if") and most of the Western history of ideas (play is irrational). What comes first for Nietzsche is fiction: appearance, representation and non-reality. Philosophy, art, religion and science are fictions that have more value than the actual. A person is both a player and a plaything.

These differing views contributed to the ferment of 19th century intellectual instability. It was a seething cauldron with one thinker in dialogic debate with another. It was in this context that Albert Einstein published two small papers creating even more ferment.

Chapter 3
Drama & Contemporary Thought

"Combinatory play seems to be the essential feature in productive thought — before there is any connection with logical construction in words or other kinds of signs which can be communicated to others"

— *Albert Einstein*

In the 20th century, Being "as if" returns to its central position in Western ideas. From Kant onwards, the importance of the co-existence of the actual and the fictional has increased until it is now a major issue among thinkers of many kinds.

Science & Technology

The Play of Science

In 1903 Einstein stated the theory of relativity as the equivalence of mass and energy, $E = mc^2$ — dramatically demonstrated by the enormous power released in an atomic explosion. It altered both science and the way humanity looked at itself. It had a great impact upon play theory.

Niels Bohr said, "We are both spectators and actors in the great drama of existence." [329] There is "play" between space and time: the rules of one "frame" are relative to another. Thinking in linear time is relative to spatial thought. The triumph of the postulate over the axiom (logical fiction vs. fixed law) leads to the use of conceptual models and metaphors in science: Einstein illustrates his theories by "picturing" two trains passing at high speed, etc. The player is a metaphor of existence: what he acts is his symbol system.

Truth is relative to an observer's perspective. We cannot accurately specify both the velocity and position (time and space) of an object simultaneously: two observers gain different meanings from one action yet both are valid if appropriate criteria are used. The universe oscillates between chance/anti-chance so play potentially results in chaos or creative meaning. Predictability is uncertain so we use probability (statistics), estimation (math), hypotheses and "informed guessing," which, Popper says, grounds all knowledge. Dramatic action is hypothesis in action: all players make hypotheses in taking roles, which they test empirically in the playing.

Henri Bergson, the French philosopher and biologist, sees play as the biological force in natural and cosmic growth. Only change is real (like Heraclitus): reality is a flux and all is relative. Play is "an impulse driving it to take ever greater and greater risks towards its goal of an ever higher and higher efficiency." [48] Intellect (reason that "fixes" life like a frame in a film) differs from intuition (instinct conscious of itself), while spontaneous action is empathetic. Being "as if" continuously creates reality, while mind *is* change, or Becoming: the only reality is the continuous transformation of the player. We only imagine an ego because we notice change. Contemporary biology retains this positive attitude: the phenomena of life are seen "whole" and systematically in a biodynamic equilibrium. The fact that there is "play" within genetic diversity is only one startling revelation of modern biology.

Information & Media

Claude Shannon, a sound engineer, said that information helps to determine human mental patterns through codes (e.g., DNA): there is an analogy between energy and information. But play, on the contrary, resists determinism. Play presents possibilities for choice and action: to be successful it must retain maximum freedom; it is not a code but a "labyrinth of meaning." [173]

Marshall McLuhan says each age is shaped by a major technology, which gives the crucial metaphors and the limits of thought (e.g., the wheel of Mesopotamia), and that media are extensions of the body (e.g., a pen is an extension of the hand, etc.). For McLuhan play is the key metaphor/medium today. The player plays at "put on," an extension of the self in role: "Real play, like the whodunit, throws the stress on process rather than product, giving the audience the chance of being a maker rather than a mere consumer." [421] Being "as if" involves the mutual inter-play of the senses, resulting in process, participation, and the "re-play" that brings cognitive intelligence. In play, the medium is the message.

Scientists since Turing (d. 1954) have tried to replicate human intelligence. In 1970 there were 65,000 computers in the USA; by 1983 there were over five million, and they breed daily. They help us work faster, but they do not "think." The human danger, for Ellul, is that ends become means and vice versa: then things are valued only if they achieve something else, or "know-how" is given ultimate value. [181]

Maps & Territories

The idea that the "territory" is "living through" experience in the "here and now" (as in life and dramatic acts), while the "map" is a relative perspective upon it, is that of Alfred Korzybski, a friend of Einstein. He founded General Semantics, where thinking and language intend to synthesize modern science with everyday concerns. This is nonlinear, post-logical, "non-Aristotelian," dynamic, processual and rational. When Korzybski says, "The map is not the territory," he implies:

1 Dramatic play *is not* what it represents.
2 Enactment does *not* represent *all* of existence.
3 Dramatic play is *self-reflexive* in that it contains "a play within a play," and both are representations of existence.

Director & Dramatists

Many theatre professionals have contributed to contemporary thought. In Stanislavsky's "Method," the actor focuses on Being "as if," asking of the character, "What would I do *if* I were. . . ." This powerful stimulus to imagination and action stirs the actor's emotions. It reveals the "subtext": the unspoken meaning behind the words. Like Slade, Stanislavsky's criteria are sincerity and absorption but for different ends: the development of the player (Slade); the effect on the audience (Stanislavsky). Stanislavsky follows Aristotle: we are concerned not with what actually occurs but what *could* happen in a theatrical world. Oscar Wilde said that life imitates art. For Artaud, art is not the imitation of life, but life is "the imitation of a transcendant principle with which art puts us back into communication."

Einstein expresses relativity as a physicist, Bergson as a biologist, Korzybski as a linguist, and Luigi Pirandello as an artist: life is indefinable, and any attempt to do so is an illusion. Personality is double: "the face" is human suffering (Bergson's "instinct"), while "the mask" (Bergson's "intellect") is the role imposed by society. The relation of the two is "the intellectual passion" of which Pirandello writes:

> Conflict between life-in-movement and form is the inexorable condition not only of the mental but also of the physical order. The life which in order to exist has become fixed in our corporeal form little by little kills that form. The tears of a nature thus fixed lament the irreparable continuous aging of our bodies. [487]

He asks: Who am I? Who am I for other people? Each play gives a different answer and his *oeuvre* is a classic of artistic relativism. As for years he looked after his insane wife, a constant question for him is, What is sanity?

In *Six Characters In Search of an Author*, each type of "mask" ranges from sincere to false; and each of us human beings varies in the intensity with which we wear them. The performer (with his "masks") acts the role of a character (with other "masks"), recognizes that the other has the same double "masks," and registers that all have dynamic relations between them. The audience, each with his own "masks" and a "mask" as an audience member, completes a relativist view of meaning. As an instructor at a women's teachers' college, Pirandello was aware of educational issues: if we innately grasp the myriad levels of illusion, we can squarely face the human condition — where a social "mask" "fixes" us like a moth pinned to a board so we feel "suspended in midair," outside the flux of change. The raw actuality of existence is Becoming — to *be* is to act as one *is*. Pirandello's influence has been enormous: on Sartre, Grotowski, etc. Beckett's people, like Pirandello's, are "caught up" in the act of the play, yet they (like us) cannot "stop playing" but must go on to the end.

Bertolt Brecht advocates rationalism vs. instinct, social relations vs. emotional expression and "alienation" vs. Aristotle/Stanislavsky/Slade. The actor dichotomizes his playing between a role and a narration: he tells a story but illustrates only part of it "as if"; thus he persuades the audience to a specific course of action (with Brecht, the cause of Marxism). John Seely shows that, in natural play, sincerity and absorption are the criteria for pre-adolescents, but at adolescence they change to Brecht's "expressive model."

American Pragmatism

What consequences does play have on our lives? The American pragmatic philosophers ask such a question by focusing on the function of contextual, relative, concrete, genetic, continuous and whole ideas. The player's actions are the nub of existence. C. S. Peirce says we conceive of possibility in play; its meaning lies in what the player does. Play for William James provides us with knowledge — not *within* it, but as a *result* of it. John Dewey had the greatest effect on education. He mixes pragmatism, idealism (his doctoral thesis was on Hegel) and "social behaviourism" — the research method he developed with G. H. Mead. Play is a social concept, mind and self are social emergents, and inquiry is its essence. Dewey's "learning by doing" is purposive problem solving, one element of which is Being "as if." Personal considerations affect all knowing but more than Dewey realized. Learning is *dramatic* doing: imagining and doing are united by the "as if." Knowing is relative to fictional doing: a fact is known if it works in our created fiction and is felt by the player. The child knows Christopher Columbus or number by re-playing them. Reality is what we know when we play. This is not to disagree with Dewey but to extend his view.

Creative Dramatics

Winifred Ward's "creative dramatics" was influenced by Hughes Mearns, who linked Dewey's social "experience" to creativity through artistic products: the purpose of play was to lead to artistic form. The dichotomy — theatre art and social order — still underpins creative dramatics. In Ward's view, children's spontaneous drama should be led from the teacher's knowledge of theatrical form; and, in dramatizing stories, the teacher should choose "good" literature to establish "good" mental and social attitudes, which, in Ward's view, were those of the white middle class. Ward was careful not to introduce artistic form too early, but in linking with children's theatre, she makes the assumption that Being "as if" would lead to order through artistic form and social control.

Others continue to emphasize artistic form. "The desire to dramatize is a basic human instinct," says Agnes Haaga, but "it is first and foremost an art form." [268] "Theatre," comments Rita Criste, "should assist children to interpret past, present and future life." [151] Geraldine Brain Siks subtitled her first book, "An Art for Children." Ann Viola says, "Personal development of players is the goal, rather than the satisfaction of a child audience," but she leads them to theatre, "because children learn much about play construction as they work on their own plays, guided by an adult who understands formal drama." [598]

Others return to Dewey's social order. Isabel Burger turned from creative dramatics in schools to using it with senior adults. Nellie McCaslin insists that dramatic activities are an essential component of the school curriculum; but she is less Deweyan and more influenced by social psychology and the work of H. S. Sullivan, so the nub of her work lies in the creativity of play: "imagination is the beginning" and Being "as if" is of value in itself (as with Slade) because it is a cohesive social force, "True play, though free, creates order — indeed, *is* order." Further from Dewey, Virginia Glasgow Koste sees play as the source of mature creative processes which may be identical with them. Being "as if" *is* transformation: paradoxical, spontaneous, holistic, energetic, nonlinear, meta-rational, non-categoric — it arouses curiosity, internalizing observation through empathy and invention.

The true break with Dewey, however, comes with Viola Spolin, who taught improvisational games to professionals. Her influence on educational drama has been profound. She focuses on the inner workings of the dramatic medium — the "as if" act, the inner pragmatics of play action — and not on its instrumental, extrinsic or aesthetic value. The "as if" experience is initiated by will and results in "penetration into the environment, total organic involvement with it" in the moment of personal freedom (the "here and now") when we face reality and act so that we re-structure the Self. Spolin's work inherently assumes an ultimate ontological and epistemological status for play. Where other pragmatists primarily ask *How*? of Being "as if" ("how do we do it?"), Spolin's first question is, *What*? ("what happens?").

Aesthetic Education is a mixture of aesthetic philosophy and Dewey's pragmatism that starts from art itself, particularly the objective criticism of visual art. Dewey says that all experience is aesthetic, a balance between dynamic process and embodied form. Others, however, such as Bernard Rosenblatt, emphasize objective form:

> Most of the work discusses the role of drama in personal development, particularly in socio-psychological terms and does not show explicitly how participation or observation relates to appreciation or understanding of the art form or aesthetic development. Appreciation and concentration require the development of "theatrical sensibility," which in turn is dependent on the ability to perceive and respond to a work of art. [527]

Where Rosenblatt combines theatrical response and cognitive order, Gil Lazier accepts the dichotomy of aesthetic education and dramatic action. Experienced in quantitative research, he sees Being "as if" as "beyond reason" and "unquantifiable" with an appeal to Oriental thought: the phenomenon of play is irrational and must be forced to be rational.

British Practical Drama

Superficially British and American educational drama look similar but there is a basic difference. Many Americans, such as Dewey and other idealists, start from the top down, from the "might be" to what "is." But British drama teachers inherit (from Locke to Mill) a bottom-up empiricism. Not "a philosophy," it is an emergent "philosophizing" that fits G. E. Moore's practical thinking (he held up his left hand and declared "the external world exists") to provide a mixture of practice/theory that indicates future action. It starts from the bottom up: from what *emerges* in practice. The "bottom-up" was clear from the beginning with Edmond Holmes' seminal *What Is and What Might Be* (1911). Children learn through dramatic play and Holmes searches for ideas and theories that will encourage it: work and play are synonymous and children "are all born actors . . . acting is a vital part of the school life of every class." This is the intellectual soil in which The Play Way grew and in which British educational drama continues.

This "bottom-up" approach has encouraged teachers of many persuasions; idealist, romantic, determinist, existential and others. Here we will deal with these differences in terms of the development of ideas rather than as one group.

Idealism & Romanticism

Idealism

In Benedetto Croce's neo-idealism, art is the first activity of the universal creative mind. Nothing exists but mind and its intuitive play: "What gives coherence and unity to the intuition is feeling; the intuition is really such because it represents a feeling, and it can only appear from and upon that. Not the idea, but the feeling, is what confers upon art the airy lightness of the symbol." [152] In extending neo-idealism to education, Giovanni Gentile said a teacher tries to take the pupil's point of view — a dramatic act.

In Ernst Cassirer's Platonic idealism, play and art are appearances, ways to grasp the universe of "symbolic forms": formal structures that, as symbols, lie behind life. Similarly for Suzanne K. Langer, art works are "forms of feeling": "virtual" objects, whose abstract content is "semblance," they express *not* feelings but *ideas of feeling*. Feeling is not expressed in the art work, which does not reveal our inner life to us but shapes our imagination of external reality. Like most extreme idealists, however, she has little interest in play. [127]

Robert W. Witkin's *The Intelligence of Feeling* combines Langer's aesthetics with Piaget's psychology in a sociology of knowledge to examine the arts in 36 British schools. The inner world (sensations and feelings, the source of motivation) is projected into the environment in media, resulting in a person's actions with both physical and symbolic objects, plus a change in the environment. Fictions exemplify the intelligence of feeling: "The expressive act consists of the projection of sensate impulse through an expressive medium, the outcome of which is a feeling form." [635] Using Piaget's criteria of abstract thought (+, -, x, ÷), Witkin describes four aesthetic mental structures: the contrasts, semblances, harmonies and discords of pre-adolescence, which become polarities, identities, syntheses and dialectics in adolescence. [136]

Romanticism

The traditions of romanticism continue. Herbert Read advocated a return to Renascence-style education, saying, "The real function of art is to express feeling and transmit understanding. . . . the aim of education is therefore the creation of artists . . . of people efficient in various modes of expression." [506] In his view, play is freedom of expression, but, as it provides the irrational with a form in which it can be sublimated, it promotes order.

Peter Slade's is a full-scale romantic approach based on dramatic instinct, but with an ideal belief in the innate goodness of children: "child drama" is natural dramatic play. It is "an art form in its own right" with intrinsic value: a productive way for personal and social development as well as a natural therapy (catharsis) promoting psychological health as it "offers continual opportunity to spit out evil in a legal framework." [557] Many of Slade's ideas remain basic to the field: developmental stages in drama and a maturational sequence of play shapes; the distinction between personal play (the whole self is used) and projected play (inner imaginings are projected out onto objects); the teaching method, where the teacher gives the *What* but the children provide the *How*; the teacher only teaches skills when they are (assumed to be) asked for; and the teleology whereby child drama develops human potential — the child draws on latent resources, which the teacher encourages in a nurturing, not a critical, climate.

Brian Way, as romantic as Slade, is, however, not an idealist. Stressing the practical, the concrete and intuition, Way is anti-intellectual and distrusts abstraction. He is committed to the development of the whole person, far less to the development of drama per se: "Education is concerned with individuals; drama is concerned with the individuality of individuals, with the uniqueness of each human essence." [615] Everyone is fundamentally creative: artistic play provides media for creativity if it is seen from the view of the doer (subjective) and from that person's readiness and experience (maturation). Being "as if" encourages original and deeply personal aspirations, elements essential for human happiness and well-being. Way and other romantics tend to be practitioners who stress means, while idealists tend to be intellectuals who focus on ends.

Determinism

Determinists say that our decision making capability in play is limited (see Chapter 2). Marx's determinism has seen many changes, including those by Lenin, who as a naive realist said play was for recreation or "serious matters like work"; Lenin also changed the dialectic into "a leap" for revolution. With Stalin, Mao, Ho Chi Minh and others, play was reduced to games, but some Marxist teachers in the West have used it for political ends. Dramatic play promotes a radical societal critique, but should this be used by teachers to promote a specific political view? Is not dramatic action already so powerful that these teachers endanger democracy? We can ask this of Marxist and Leninist drama practitioners such as Augusto Boal in Europe and Albert Hunt in Britain and Australia. Hunt, with Leninist principles and Brechtian techniques, used adult students to create a socio-political Happening that simulated the Russian Revolution in the centre of Bradford, Yorkshire. Such an approach is to be expected if Being is assumed to be socio-economically determined.

Determinism indirectly influenced Gavin Bolton. He has an emergent stance, like most British educational drama practitioners, but differs by stressing socialization — political and intellectual. He uses many frames in a "playful" relativity: he can think phenomenologically with a societal bias, or approach educational drama through the tacit like Polanyi, or through theatrical form; he relies on objectivity (but denies Dewey's form of it), while striving for the so-called "standards" of British élitist education. He uses Lenin's "leap" in his polemical disagreements (with Way's romanticism and Malcolm Ross' idealism), and, like Heathcote, he challenges students to make judgments, plan, anticipate outcomes, hypothesize and look for further implications in specific contexts. He asks the player to "bracket off" practical life (like Brecht or phenomenology) in order to assume a role on a continuum from "the dramatic playing mode" (spontaneous improvisation) to "the performance mode" (theatre). Like Brecht, Bolton tries to intellectualize emotion: dramatic action is "a protection" against emotion — Bolton is reticent about drama therapy. Play and game have the same structure: they build on patterns embedded in our social interactions. Thus Being "as if" is an abstraction that crystallizes meaning and is socially useful in providing a common understanding through the exercise of mental powers. Then Being "as if" opposes chaos (emotion) and brings social order.

Play & Being

Being is consciousness: who we *are*. Becoming is the *potentiality* of Being: our consciousness of "what happens next." Who we *are* lies at the core of dramatic action, but there are many views of what this means. For Samuel Alexander, play is the relation between the person and the object, as it is for A. N. Whitehead, who also sees it as the ontological principle of life. Modern Catholics follow Aquinas as expanded by Jacques Maritain: creative play, derived from God, allows us to freely will and choose our proper function and goal. For Edmond Husserl "I experience the world not as my own private world, but as an inter-subjective world" [311], which results in self-consciousness, and behind "the mask and the face" lies "the unobserved observer," activated by empathy.

Existential Being

Things are different for Martin Heidegger and his pupils. "Being" has many meanings, but Heidegger is more concerned with its use: man does not define play, but play defines man. The human focus is the play of self-presentation (like Socrates and Derrida) where man "risks himself" like a swimmer in the middle of a stream. Our authenticity is in choice: we decide what we are to become. Later, Heidegger (like Heraclitus and Nietzsche) sees Being as a cosmic game derived from play; time and space play in, and with, man, while God plays with man and the world.

Eugen Fink reverses Plato: for Fink play is more "real" than actuality; as a mode of knowing it is closer to Being than it is to phenomena and has a metonymic (rather than a metaphoric) relation to Being. Play provides an "enhanced" reality, a mimesis of the actual, like the ancient ritual-myths. It creates *"Weltsymbol"*: "symbolic whole," or "world symbol."

For Hans-Georg Gadamer, play is not subjective or objective but exists in and of itself, *medially*: it is a medium as much for Gadamer as it is for McLuhan. Play "absorbs the player into itself." [238] Fictions are "representations for someone": not necessarily an actual audience, but potentially so. Play exists for the player, but art exists for the audience, "even if there is no one there who listens or watches."

Dialogic Being

The central metaphor of Martin Buber is the "dialogue" of *I and Thou*. The play of two persons as they "read" (negotiate with) one another is literally and metaphorically dialogic. It is "to see things from another's point of view": the dialogic/dramatic perspective. He distinguishes this from I-and-It: treating another person as an object is monologue. He discovered this as a student when attending the Vienna theatre, where he pondered the meaning of player/player and player/audience. The theatre is an exemplar of life: it completes the human drama by making it whole.

Importantly, the human drama and theatre are *not* dialectical but dialogic. For Buber and Jacques Derrida this is because they recognize difference and do not seek simple agreement or unanimity. For A. J. Greimas it is because human negotiation is based on the fiduciary contract: a mutual trust in each other and in what they do. For M. M.

Bakhtin it is because all human inter-action in literature is based on negotiation between voices (speech and not language per se). From Buber's perspective, the aims for education are the fostering of mutual respect/sympathy for others and of each person's freedom. In the play of human relations, "sharing in an undertaking" and "entering into mutuality," we find self-direction, freedom, love and companionship.

Being & Analogue

Existentialists see the "play" between life and death. Where life *is* theatre for Buber, for Jean-Paul Sartre each is an analogue of the other. As a pupil of Heidegger, he focuses on consciousness vs. the environment, subjective freedom vs. the objective thing. Nothing exists beyond concrete phenomena. As consciousness is "no thing," he can say that man is condemned to be free: an idea that affected a whole generation.

Sartre links imagination, transformation and dramatic action into a whole. Perceiving and imagining differ: I am passively conscious of a percept but actively so of an image, which is created by consciousness. What I imagine transforms the object I perceive; if I do not see one leg of a chair, when I recall the chair it has four legs; imagining "magically transforms" objects so that I can work with them. Recall differs from imagining; what I recall exists *past*; when I image, "There I grasp *nothing*, that is, I posit *nothingness*." Emotions center on objects: "Hatred is hatred of someone, love is love of someone." Imagination achieves *the affective-cognitive synthesis*: as we cannot manage emotion directly, we create an image with which we can deal. Imagining is cognitive: "a species of knowledge" but "not an intellectual knowledge." All forms of Being "as if" are externalized analogues of imaginary life: play fictions of what we imagine; the stage, life, the actor, an imaginary person, etc. Stanislavsky saw the actor identified with his role, while Brecht disagrees; but Sartre says: "it is not the character who becomes real in the actor, it is the actor who *becomes unreal* in his character." Thus, "We are nothing without playing at Being." [129]

Being & Education

Various drama educators focus on play as Being and Becoming with the "as if" as its major characteristic. Each separates abstraction from life and accepts contradiction and paradox. What *is* has more importance than what *ought*. And each considers that the human condition is all.

The most radical of modern educators, A. S. Neill, took Rousseau's influence to its logical conclusion in his school, Summerhill. "Do as you like" is to caricature his work, which, in the first half of the 20th century, was out of its time and misunderstood. His was a genuinely "alternative" school often attended by the most difficult children, and he was a vehement romantic existentialist. Nature was his theme, the freedom and dignity of each child his watchwords. His greatest influence was on the relation of teachers and learners: an I-and-Thou negotiation with improvisation at its centre — to build self-concept, motivation to learn and independent thought while avoiding stereotypical attitudes.

Bishop James Burton (E. J. Burton) is an educator and theologian influenced by monism (Whitehead), existentialism (Sartre), humanism (H. J. Blackham) and the linking of Eastern thought with Christianity. This leads him to "theistic agnosticism"; trust in the unknown experience leads us to open new significance. We apprehend life and our place within it through Being "as if." We *are* metaphors; analogues that liken one thing to another by constant cross-referencing. Abstractions are less than experience, which must be seen first in itself, then in its context. Knowledge "emerges from play actions"; the human condition is potential. We grow into "reality" to "real-ize" it through the dramatic process: "Drama is a process of total experience assessment and analysis, leading to further hypothesis and synthesis . . . a large-scale laboratory of life examination and study." [95] The aim is purposive human life within community; a school must derive its purpose from the pupils themselves. In play we develop wholeness within ourselves, the community, the environment, the cosmos and Life.

Being "as if" in play and theatre are, for Burton, two analogues of human experience. Imagination works from the known to the possible by enactment; it progressively reveals what is as yet inexactly comprehended. Play expresses experience, works out life relationships in action; it "does not exist apart from life." Drama's rhythm repeats (symbolizes) the universal processes to be an effective dynamic of community. Learning is also an emergent. All education must start from a learner's Being "as if." Burton is committed to a specifically human view of students: "If they feel that *they* matter and the things you are doing *matter* to you — actually and really — you will probably be a most successful teacher for whom dramatic work may be both *means* and *ends*." [95] In schools, Burton aims for the continuity of activities at all ages; the teacher focuses attention on a dramatic problem in a suitable life situation and can use many types of instructional method to that end.

Also committed to the human condition is Dorothy Heathcote. A highly innovative practitioner, she is not anti-intellectual like Brian Way, but for her theory is less important than practice. Her view of Being "as if" is unique and seemingly paradoxical. Actors accept a play world as fictional (Brecht vs. Stanislavsky) but believe in the play situation (Stanislavsky vs. Brecht) as they live "at life rate" in fictional time and place. They begin from the Self (role is less important) and as personal as is consistent with the fiction. Identification with the character (Stanislavsky vs. Brecht) releases energy, deepens feeling and enables the player to elaborate experience essential for maturation.

She treats players with honesty and respect, helps their involvement, feeling and commitment to the drama, and leads them to insight about it in a highly significant moment. By questioning she makes them face the moment of awe as themselves *in extremis*: how do you feel? how do you respond? She makes the analogy actual: drama reveals that all persons face similar existential issues. Play brings out what players already know, but do not know that they know, by choosing the *What, How, When* and *Where*. By constantly asking for group decisions and commitment, she takes ultimate risks because the outcome is unpredictable. Teachers do this uniquely because they have their own "thresholds of tolerance." Heathcote uses the "teacher in role" mode to provide focus, negotiate power with the class, challenge them within the action, heighten their emotion and deepen their experience; she comes out of role to create distancing and promote reflection. She stresses the internal structure of teaching, not its form, the players' inner intention and not their communicative skills, the inner symbolic meaning of the encounter and not theatre. For Heathcote we are Becoming within the limits of our situation; we are "Being involved in knowing." That is, drama releases our inner potentialities so that we learn.

A very different human view is that of Keith Johnstone, who, along with Stanislavsky and Spolin, is one of the major improvisational innovators of the 20th century. Distrusting rational processes and with an affinity for the absurd, Johnstone himself is a paradox: an anti-intellectual intellectual. He views the education he received as evil; in contrast, he asks teachers to release the spontaneous and unconscious forces within students. The creative impulse, the associative intuition, are what make us human; if we censor them we destroy imagination and talent. His work is based on a comic, even hilarious, cooperation between players, a respect for mutual humanity; then they bring their joint spontaneity from the unconscious into a fictional world that is ambiguous and paradoxical. For Johnstone, Being "as if" is the irrational within absurdity, like his Theatresports.

The Play of Structures

Structuralism

Thinking about structures has been part of the Western intellectual tradition since classical times. Its immediate ancestors are Marx and Freud. Popular in Europe in this century (particularly France), it has only recently affected the ideas of English speakers. Structuralists assume an "inter-play" between the structures of mind, media and society. Thus Lévi-Strauss "decodes" the universal mental structure shown in social expressions to discover the objective structures of fictions. For Edmund Leach, fictions acquire meanings from their context. We communicate them as a result of genetic decoding: we create the world in fiction before we can find our way about in it. The purpose of Being "as if" is to "reorder the world." It is the teachers' job "to persuade their pupils that they can, *if they choose*, see the world quite differently from the way in which they at present see it." [377] This is determinist and is quite close to the views of Bolton.

However, Roland Barthes says that "structuralism is essentially *an activity in imitation*, which is also why there is, strictly speaking, no *technical* difference between structuralism as an intellectual activity on the one hand and literature in particular, art in general on the other; both derive from a *mimesis*." [37] Fiction is "neither real nor rational, but *functional*."

Play is characterized by time and persons, who are understood in terms of Buber's I and Thou. Being "as if" is based on the contrast of the person and the non-person, but the *I* is not homogenous: for the protagonist, the *I* is not the same as the *I* which is understood by *Thou*. Play is generated and paralleled by two types of linguist voice: the active — the player is outside the object; and the middle — the subject affects himself in acting. The first is used if a priest sacrifices a victim on my behalf, but the second is used if I make my own sacrifice. Barthes also comments on theatre: it does not express reality but signifies it (Brecht vs Stanislavsky); it is essentially an artifact — "I advance pointing to my mask." [37]

Post-Structuralism

This goes beyond structuralism to a criticism based on play itself. For Jacques Derrida, play is prior to re-play, self-presentation is prior to re-presentation. Speech and dramatic acts are nearer to consciousness than other media: "Speaking is life but writing is death." [162]

Derrida creates a modern logic based on play. Past logic was based on opposition: "A is opposed to B." But this is a negative: A is the negative of B; evil is the negative of good. In Derrida's logic, "B is both added to A and replaces A"; i.e., B "supplements" A, where (in French) "supplément" means both an addition and a substitution. Thus Derrida denies the duality of oppositions and the triangular dialectic. There is a link between Derrida's idea and Greimas' semiotic square (see pp. 183-86).

Derrida's work helps the drama teacher to make appropriate assessments of students' dramatic actions. The following distinctions must be made; the student's consciousness / the student's meaning / the character's consciousness / the character's meaning. The difficulty for the teacher is that all these distinct elements appear in the action *at the same time*. Also, they occur *in the present tense*. When teachers look back at the work of a student, they do so in the past tense. Assessments of work that is *dramatic*, properly so called, can *only* be in the present tense and in the "now" of the dramatic play.

Education

These structural and post-structural ideas are quite new to educational drama and have not yet been fully assimilated. But dramatic structures are found in the deep patterns of mind, media and society. For John McLeod, dramatic fictions have a common tacit structure: it is this which generates specific dramatic forms. We infer a dramatic structure from its outward appearance. If we make a structural change we have to change the medium. A player's previously unreflected experience is shaped by dramatic play in ways complementary (parallel) to reason, but McLeod understands them to be as ambiguous and contradictory as they are for Derrida. When we use a dramatic symbol it has a direct, apparent and motivated relation to its referent. Play and arts actions are not replicas of a structure: rather, there is an analogic relationship between a structure and its transformation.

Several Canadians contribute to structural thinking about dramatic acts. For David W. Booth, play and educational drama have similar structures but result in different forms; he illustrates this with instances from "talk" and "language." Lawrence O'Farrell indicates the ritual structures in play and aesthetic fictions, while Peter L. McLaren puts forward a valuable, if complex, theory of ritual structures that underlie schooling: he shows that students during a school day process dramatically through various ritual "states," or structures. Yet dramatic acts do not re-present deep structures as replicas. Within spontaneous drama there is a large tacit dimension: a level that is unconscious and intuitive — that cannot be expressed in words without distorting the event. The existence of this dimension makes it difficult to grasp the underlying structures except insofar as Bernard Beckerman shows that dramatic process and form have a double structure: a continuous flux with momentary attempts to create rational gestalts.

Uniquely, Gisèle Barret has developed "expression dramatique," an eclectic study that combines phenomenology, existentialism, holism and post-structuralism in practical dramatic acts. She can well claim that Being "as if" breaks down barriers. She focuses on the person in a multi-disciplinary method to unite educational practice/theory. She shows that spontaneous drama has "a double structure" originating in the attempts to solve the paradox of I and Thou. Like Derrida and Greimas, she rejects opposition as a principle of imaginative and dramatic life and, by working in a non-competitive, non-hierarchical, non-judgmental manner, she leads practitioners to similarities.

Contemporary thinkers in educational drama, in other words, base their work on Being "as if." But they differ quite radically in how they do so. Like other thinkers in contemporary Western thought, they reflect the fragmentation of modern life. They have a plurality of views based on one common factor (the dramatic). As a result, the debate among them rages furiously. And it is well that it does so because, in this dramatic way, educational drama is continuously progressive.

Part Two

Play, Drama & Psychology

Chapter 4
Dramatic Play & Depth Psychology

"Why does a child play with dolls?" "What is the meaning of playing at spacemen?"

To such questions psychoanalysts will reply that children are expressing their unconscious. They will go on to say that *How* and *What* the child plays are reflections of unconscious drives, which, although common to everyone, vary with the development of the individual. Sigmund Freud created psychoanalysis, a way to reveal a person's unconscious thoughts. Admiring Darwin, he conceived the unconscious as evolutionary and biological with a dynamic drawn from instinct. It was a concept that, in the late 19th century, revolutionized people's way of looking at themselves.

Schools of Depth Psychology

"Psychoanalysis," strictly speaking, refers to Freud's theories and the therapeutic methods based on them. Those who broke from him to found other systems used different names: e.g., Individual Psychology by Adler, and Analytic Psychology by Jung.

Despite obvious differences, these psychologists have four features in common. First, they all stress the importance of the unconscious in our mental life: as repressed emotions for Freud, as unverbalized attitudes for Adler, and as unrealized potentialities for Jung. Second, the processes and motives of the disordered are of the same kind as those of the "normal"; the difference is one of degree. Third, infancy is important as the formative period for the developing personality. For Freud, our early unconscious reactions to our parents have lasting effects on our motives; the unresolved conflicts of childhood cause trouble in later life. For Adler, a person's life style (the normal way of feeling, acting and dealing with difficulties) is derived from habitual attempts to secure adequacy in childhood. For Jung, although childhood experiences are not as important as present events, they determine which of the individual's potentialities are realized and which remain dormant. Fourth, no mental happenings are accidental: irrational happenings are meaningful. Dreams, hypnotic recollections and word associations are important for the understanding of mental life, while some aspects of normal behaviour are significant. Thus child analysts have evolved techniques for understanding children's unconscious through dramatic play. Dramatic play takes on great significance, not only for children's present adjustment to themselves, others and the environment, but also for their future adult living (see Chapter 6).

The Basic Theories of Freud

Freud's shadow reaches to the present day. Even those who reject his views must account for them — particularly the nature of the unconscious.

He began by postulating two instincts. First, self-preservation (ego) leads people to seek pleasure and avoid pain — the *Pleasure Principle*, or the urge to seek self satisfaction or gratification. It is opposed by the *Reality Principle*, which sees the consequences of seeking mere pleasure. But the *Repetition Compulsion* goes beyond both principles: a past traumatic experience may have to be re-enacted (in dreams, play or life) in order to assimilate it. Second, the preservation of the species (sexual instinct) is based on libido (sexual energy). If this is unsatisfied it can lead to substitute gratifications dominated by the pleasure principle (e.g., day-dreaming) or, if libido is withdrawn from one area, it must inevitably produce its effects somewhere else.

Freud puts forward three maturational stages in infancy: oral, anal and genital. In the *oral stage* the mouth is the primary organ for pleasure and the child is mentally introjecting: putting things in his mouth, he incorporates what he loves; wishing to be like the other person, he identifies with them. (Thus Freud shows the primacy of identification, the first mental step towards play, followed by empathy.) At about 6 months, when first cutting teeth, the child may be frustrated if the breast is not available. He attempts gratification by aggression (biting) but, as he still identifies with the mother, the image occurs of the aggressive mother who will eat him up. The *anal stage* (the wish to expel aggressively) is divided into: anal-expulsive — the child enjoys sadistic expulsion; and anal-retentive coinciding with sphincter control about 12 months — the child only parts with his feces out of love for the nurturing person. The *genital phase* begins in the third year when, with boys, interest centers on the penis. In the fourth year occurs the Oedipus complex: Oedipus unwittingly kills his father, marries his mother and punishes himself by putting out his own eyes; Freud says that the child is sexually attracted to the mother, resents his father and then fears punishment for his wish (symbolic castration). Later abnormal results may include: passivity concealing hatred and fear of the father (later, all men in authority); over-affection and dependence on the mother (the need to be loved); or, repressing desires for the mother, a passive desire for the father may develop (homosexuality).

Girls develop the Electra complex: the clitoris is the "inferior" counterpart of the penis and "penis envy" develops. Thus she may: be hostile to the mother (who "denied" the child a penis) and so desire the father's penis; identify with the mother and desire a baby (a penis substitute) and develop normal female sexuality; or, if clinging to her penis desire, she may become dominating and aggressive, developing masculine tendencies. (This part of the theory is deeply offensive to contemporary feminists.) With boys or girls, should libido development be arrested in the oral, anal or genital phases, this is a fixation: when facing obstacles later, the libido may regress to that fixation.

Freud later modified this theory. In 1914 he defined narcissism as love for oneself: primary *narcissism* is natural to the baby but secondary (morbid) narcissism may develop later in life if the individual's love is thwarted. In 1920 he postulated the life and death instincts: the tendency to bind together, and to destroy.

His first theory of personality distinguished: the *conscious*, or present awareness; the *unconscious*, of which we are not normally aware; and the *preconscious*, which, although unconscious now, can easily be recalled — as with slips of the tongue. In 1922 he made his famous division between *the ego, the superego and the id*. The id, the primitive mass of impulses of the newborn, demands immediate satisfaction, knows no precautions to ensure survival, is unconscious, stores the entire mental energy and, governed by the pleasure principle, knows no logic. Part of the id separates out to become the ego, or self, which establishes itself by "learning to bring about appropriate modifications in the external world to its own advantage through activity." [217] Where the ego is conscious, the superego (roughly, conscience) is only partly conscious. It originates in the Oedipus complex and the fear of punishment: "parental attitudes are taken over by the personality, one part of which (superego) assumes the same attitude towards the rest as the parents did previously towards the child." [7]

The ego wards off the demands of the id and the superego by eight major *defence mechanisms*: (1) rationalizing the irrational demands of the id (covering up mistakes); (2) magical undoing — the belief that former irrational deeds can be "blown away"; (3) denial — the ego withdraws from a too painful reality; (4) introjection — the ego incorporates the loved object and identifies with him/her; (5) projection — the ego gets rid of something unpleasant which belongs to the outside world; (6) isolation — separation of the emotion from the idea of the experience (sometimes leading to "dual personality"); (7) reaction formation — too firm a repression of a forbidden drive produces opposite tendencies, presenting the ego to society in a pleasant light (as with "the excessive puritan"); (8) sublimation — the normal and successful operation that channels energy into substitute goals acceptable to society (the basis of the arts and successful work).

The child sees that forbidden acts lead to punishment or loss of the mother's love, and this relationship (based on identification) is the foundation for the child's later imitations and socio-emotional attachments. Adult anxieties are based on childhood residues in the unconscious: separation from the mother is the prototype of all later anxieties. The therapist tries to understand this and achieve sublimation: with adults by free associations and dreams, and with children through play — both of which indicate anxieties through symbolism.

Adler

Adler originated the popular concept of the "inferiority complex." We all feel inferior and children develop their own methods to compensate for this. This becomes a person's "life style," the habitual attitudes that compensate for inferiority feelings and aim at superiority variously: "It may be crystallized as the ideal either of useful achievement, of personal prestige, of the domination of others, of the defence against danger, or of sexual victories." [625] Children try to overcome their sense of inferiority by: compensation — attacking and adjusting well to the three challenges of life (society, work, sex); overcompensation — assertion in an alternative way in which the striving is too apparent (like the weakling who becomes a gangster); and the retreat into fantasy, or psychogenic illness, as a means of obtaining power.

Play and other symbols are, for Adler, reflections of inferiority or the desire for expansion; they represent the individual's present attitude. In later works, Adler stressed cultural factors, and saw "social interest" in place of the power motive. His influence is found in the work of Karen Horney and social psychology generally.

Jung

Jung describes three levels of personality — conscious, personal unconscious, and collective unconscious — using the image of a chain of islands rising from the sea. The land above the ocean is the *conscious*, the ego, the knowing, the "I." Just below the surface are "repressed infantile impulses and wishes, subliminal perceptions, and countless forgotten experiences" [202], which can be recalled by will, chance associations, dreams or, with neurosis, have to be forced out. This is the personal unconscious, which consists of memories that vary from person to person. Deep on the sea bed, where all the islands are joined, is the *collective unconscious*, containing the common beliefs and myths of humanity at two levels: the racial unconscious of symbols of the person's race; and the universal unconscious, common to all humanity, which Jung deduces from three factors — instinct, which is inherited; the unanimity of theme and symbols in myths and legends; and the delusions of the insane. The fundamental image patterns of dreams, hallucinations, mythology, magic, alchemy and religion are the same for everyone and must be inherited. Not that the specific details are the same: what is inherited is the structure of symbol formation. While Jung's scholarship and synthesizing ability are remarkable, the idea of the collective unconscious is not always accepted today.

Symbolic Thought

Freud

Symbolic thought is seen variously by different thinkers. Freud sees dream symbols as the highroad to the adult's unconscious, just as play symbols are keys the child's unconscious for the child therapist. Both types of therapist deal with wishes that cannot be accepted by the conscious in the waking state. Their manifest content in dream and play (what the dreamer perceives) conceals a deep latent content: the repressed unconscious desire, which creates the manifest content (the symbolic realization of a repressed desire).

There are five major methods of symbol creation: (1) condensation: a person may be a composite image of several people; (2) displacement: significant emotional elements are made insignificant; (3) plastic representation: e.g., the sound of a word may create the image ("a view" stimulated by the word "review"); (4) secondary elaboration: the dreamer or player tries to impose order on the images; and (5) fixed symbols, common to all humanity, are normally sexual in character and, in early life, are "comparable to stage settings" — parents are kings and queens; siblings are little animals; birth is water; death is a journey; hollow objects, containers, snails, mussels, churches and chapels are female symbols; apples, peaches and oranges are breasts; a landscape with rocks, woods and water is the female organs; a cloak, a hat, or anything long and pointed is the male organ, etc. These are "from the relics of the prehistoric period (age one to three)" [328] and those representing recent action may well be similar to those of past action: we are determined by the whole of our past. Dreams and play are ego attempts to relate the id to reality. Although symbols disguise their latent content, play symbolism is never simple: polysymbolism intertwines tendencies, conflicts and repressions that give rise to a variety of meanings. At first Freud said the symbol was a disguise. Later, under the influence of Jung, Adler and Silberer, he said it was both a language and a disguise.

Jung

Where Freud saw a symbol as a generalized expression of a particular (e.g., a pencil of the phallus), Jung reversed this: a dream of an actual mother represents the generalized concept of the Great Mother, common to everyone. Symbols are of two kinds: from the personal unconscious, particular to the individual's life; and from the collective unconscious, significant to everyone, which can be interpreted through mythological analogies. Jung described a series of major symbols: the Persona, or mask we assume in social relations; the Shadow, or forbidden urges, which is our "other self"; the Anima (for men) or Animus (for women), of opposite sex to ourselves, which is *our view* of the opposite sex; and the great Archetypes, symbols from the collective unconscious.

For Jung, collective symbolism is the real language of the human soul. It corresponds to an initial phase of human thought when people were less concerned with the conquest of the external world but were turned inwards and sought to express in myth the discoveries of the psyche. Here was a new explanation for myth: the same archetypes exist in one collective unconscious innate in everybody. Water, for example, is connected with everyone's "original environment"; it is essential for crops and agricultural civilization; it is a constant oneiric symbol; mythological spirits, gods and men came out of water; in baptismal rites, water represents both rebirth and purification; and in the imaginary world told by children concerning birth it plays a major part. Many modern scholars assume, with Jung, that myth is a chosen cloak for abstract thought:

> The irrational aspect of myth becomes especially clear when we remember that the ancients were not content merely to recount their myths as stories conveying information. They dramatised them, acknowledging in them a special virtue which could be activated by recital. . . .
>
> Myth is a form of poetry which transcends poetry in that it proclaims a truth; a form of reasoning which transcends reasoning in that it wants to bring about the truth it proclaims; a form of action, of ritual behaviour, which does not find its fulfilment in the act but must proclaim and elaborate a poetic form of truth. [205]

Children

The suppositions and methods of early Greek physicists are like the rational thought of today's 7-10 year old. Piaget would say that the same genetic structures account for the thought of these children and those who were just emerging from mythological and pre-logical thought; the more primitive the society, the more lasting the influence of the child's thought on the adult. But for Jung this would not be enough: children's thought, mythological symbols, oneiric representations and pre-logical science, are part of the collective unconscious common to us all.

All dramatic acts include the symbol and the sign. These Jung distinguished. The arbitrary sign, like numbers, makes possible the formation of abstract thought. But there is some resemblance between a symbol and what it signifies: e.g., a metaphor expresses a relation between an image and an object which is comprehended by thought. Thus where signs are used for abstract and rational concepts like those of math, symbols are used for emotional and felt ideas — as with poetry. In poetry, symbolism is overt and conscious. Freud distinguishes this from the unconscious symbol, where the meaning is hidden from the person creating it. Symbolic thought is two things: individual and intimate items with their roots in the unconscious; and when expressed in dramatic play, a form of secondary symbolism.

Children's symbolic thought is the subject of some disagreement among "depth" psychologists. Freud's critics say that the unconscious impulses cannot be reduced to sex and aggression but, rather, originate in a "desire for glory" or a reaction to frustration. Others reject the unconscious and repression saying that symbolism results from scotomization: people turn a blind eye to their conflicts. [571] Otto Rank says that birth is the most traumatic event in human life. Adult worries are the result of a basic birth anxiety: birth is separation from the mother and all later forms of separation revive it as either Life Fear ("fear of having to live as an isolated individual") or Death Fear (fear of losing individuality and being swallowed up in the whole). The result, says Rank, is that the maternal symbol (vessels, receptacles, etc.) is the major human expression, and this is associated with paternal symbols, like the sun. While the idea is useful for Rank's argument, it is doubtful whether maternal/paternal symbols are caused only in the way he suggests.

Freud and Rank had major disagreements but both conceive symbolism as deriving from the past. Adler, Jung, Silberer, Rivers and Perls emphasize the present. Silberer says that in the half-sleeping state thought abandons coherent and logical structure for imagined symbolism, although the first images to occur are often a continuation of the last conscious idea. He postulated two kinds of symbols: material symbols representing particular objects or events (like Freud's unconscious symbols); and functional symbols showing the working of present thought and giving the possibility of anagogic interpretation (supported by Jung but denied by Freud). Unconscious symbolism, therefore, represents both past and present. This was supported by Rivers' findings with shell-shocked soldiers in World War I and eventually by the Gestalt therapy of Fritz Perls, whose concern was entirely in the present.

British Psychoanalysis

Most British "depth" psychologists accept the main hypotheses of Freudian theory as do many child therapists (see Chapter 6). In the tradition of the famous Tavistock Clinic, they are individualists.

Suttie

Ian Suttie agrees with Rank's emphasis on the mother and stresses the importance of love (as opposed to sex, with Freud). He relates play to a primal attachment-to-mother, which results in the need for company, attention, protectiveness, and "I think that play, cooperation, competition and culture interests generally are substitutes, for the mutually caressing relationship of child and mother. *By these substitutes we put the whole social environment in the place once occupied by the mother* — maintaining with it a mental or cultural rapport in lieu of caresses, etc., formerly enjoyed with the mother." [574] Culture is derived from play, and both are substitutes for nurture.

Hadfield

For J. A. Hadfield play and dreams reproduce our unsolved experiences and attempt solutions. Like the "substitutes" of Gombrich and Suttie, they "stand in place" of our experience: by re-playing it we re-examine our problems by trial-and-error and warn of the consequences. Repetition in play and dream serves the same purpose as imagination: they form mental images to solve problems without experiencing them. This has a close relation to the philosophic position of Karl Popper.

Children at play often work out problems using concrete symbols: they imagine situations and take up attitudes (as with a "naughty doll") without knowing they are dealing with their own personal problems (that they are trying to adjust to their own naughtiness). In condemning the sins of the doll, they condemn their own sins, which settles the problem in their minds. This type of behaviour relates to the child's need to repeat a fairy-tale again and again: "It is indeed because we do *not* understand our deeper emotional problems that we have to work those out by analogy, by myth, and by parable, and that is precisely the function of dreams." [271] Symbols are both a disguise (like Freud) and an analogy (like Jung) for an idea or an emotion. There may be fixed symbols (e.g., a snake for the phallus) or they may mean something specific to the individual.

Hadfield agrees with Jung that symbolism is a primitive language which has a physiological basis. The later developed part of the brain (cortex) goes to sleep first. This leaves mental activity to be

carried on in the lower (thalamic) area, which is primarily the seat
of emotions; it expresses itself in concrete symbols rather than
words, works by sensations rather than ideas, and follows an associa-
tional rather than a linear order of events. Play follows the same
strictures, while symbolic thought is largely illogical, works by
analogy, and is animistic. In tribal life, and in modern play and
dreams, all material things are living: there is no change and no
determinism; everything is caused by living agents. Thoughts and
feelings are personified, as they are in fairy-tales or the films of
Walt Disney: thus our feelings of revenge may be projected as a
witch. This leads Hadfield to see "dream as a drama":

> We come therefore to realize that the dream is a drama in which
> all the actors represented in the dream are parts of oneself. Our
> personalities have many attributes; we have our kindly side, our
> arrogant side, our ingratiating side, our lazy side. These are often
> in conflict and therefore create problems in the personality which
> may be reproduced in dreams. Because of the tendency of the
> human to animism, all these aspects of the personality are personal-
> ized, and in the dream may be represented as persons, whether of
> our acquaintance or an imaginary person of that same character, all
> having an argument or discussion — as they might in a play.
>
> [In a dream] all the people are *dramatis personae*, re-
> presenting, as they do on the stage, certain ideas or types of mind,
> not the people themselves. In a play a man of self-sufficient
> character stands for self-sufficiency in the abstract, a priggish man
> for priggishness, a prostitute for the sensual part of ourselves, a
> parish priest for consideration for others. These are all characteris-
> tics we ourselves possess and the dream presents a drama in which
> all these characteristics in us are represented by people fighting it
> out, debating the question, playing out the problem in dramatic
> form and therefore tending towards a solution. The value of a
> theatre is that we see ourselves as we see others; in a dream we
> see our selves as our subconscious sees us. In treating patients, the
> technique of psychodrama, in which patients play out certain roles,
> is used for much the same purpose. [271]

In terms very similar to Spencer and Groos, Hadfield sees both
play and dream as having a biological function: they sort out unsolved problems of the day instinctually, using surplus energy and
showing forms of racial play in peep-bo and hide-and-seek. Like
Groos, he says that play is related to the growth of intelligence:
"*Imaginative play* . . . owing to identification . . . serves another
interesting purpose, namely *the development of ideas*. Play is often
symbolic. . . ." [272] But its essential quality is that it expresses the
unconscious in a secondary symbolism to re-play unsolved experiences and attempt solutions.

In sum: Freud's idea of the unconscious has had a great influence, whether we agree with him or not. One of the most important ways in which his idea has had an effect is that it provides a way to explain the events in dramatic play. But there are various forms that this explanation can take, as we shall see in the next chapter, when we examine the work of several therapists.

Chapter 5
Drama Therapy

Drama therapists today do not usually belong to one "school." The majority are eclectic: they use specific strategies that are most suitable for the client. They may use techniques from psychoanalytic, individual or analytic psychology (see Chapter 4) or a variety of other alternatives which we will examine in this chapter.

Psychodrama

Jacob Moreno objected to Freud's use of the patients' talk, and created psychodrama, in which patients acted out their problems. He also initiated sociodrama, psychometry and group therapy. Moreno worked with the patient's spontaneous and improvised acting. Aristotle saw drama as an imitation of life, but Moreno sees drama as an *extension* of life: the "recapitulation of unsolved problems within a freer, broader and more flexible setting." [439] Catharsis is achieved in four ways: somatic, in bodily release; mental — the patient (who creates it and also lives it out), and the audience (who co-experience it); through the individual; and through the group. Therapeutic theatre is "the spontaneous and simultaneous realization of a poetic, dramatic work, in its process of development from its *status nascendi* on, from step to step. And according to this analysis catharsis takes place: not only in the audience — secondary desired effect — and not in the *dramatis personae* of an imaginary production, but primarily in the spontaneous actors in the drama who produce the *personae* by liberating themselves from them at the same time." [439] Moreno holds a socio-interactional theory of personality: the self is a total of social and private roles which the person plays in his interaction with others ("the social atom"). The ability to "read" roles and respond appropriately are vital skills for any human enterprise.

For Moreno, creativity has five characteristics: spontaneity, a feeling of surprise, acting, mimesis, and an "unreality which is bent upon changing the reality within which it rises." [439] Spontaneity is the ability to meet adequately each new situation: to be creative in moment-to-moment adjustments, to be flexible and aware of alternatives, and to respond resourcefully. The stereotyped person plays roles conventionally and only makes momentarily acceptable adjustments. The impulsive person misreads and misevaluates: his role response is irrelevant or irrational.

"Warming-up" is inherent in spontaneity, in all expressions of humanity "as it strives towards an act." Moreno starts from physicality:

The subject may move around or begin to breathe heavily, make grimaces, clench his fists, move his lips, shout or cry — that is, he will use physical starters in order to get started, trusting that the neuro-muscular or other physical activities will eventually clinch and release more highly organized forms of expression such as role-taking and creative inspiration, bringing him to the maximum degree of warming-up to a spontaneous act in the meeting of a novel situation. [439]

We are all improvisers, even the newborn: "He has to act quickly on the spur of the moment — that moment when a new breathing apparatus is put into function, or that moment when he must, for the first time, suck fluids from the breast or bottle." (439) Spontaneous acting is:

that quality which gives newness and vivacity to feelings, actions, and verbal utterances which are nothing but repetitions of what an individual has experienced a thousand times before — that is, they do not contain anything new, original, or creative. The life of a man may be, thus, in his expressions and social manifestations entirely uneventful but may be considered by his contemporaries and friends as unique because of the flavour he is able to add to the most inconspicuous daily acts. . . .

The same phenomenon can be observed in the productions of the legitimate actor. He takes a role, learns and rehearses it until it has become a complete conserve, a stereotype at his command, so that when he reproduces the role on the stage, no utterance or gesture is left to chance. But the great actor, like the idealized man . . . is able to inflate and warm up this conserve to an exalted expression by means of this "s" factor, that is, to add a newness, vivacity and dramatic quality to the faithful literal rendering of the playwright's script, which makes his performance appear undiluted even after repeating the same performance a thousand times — thus, drama conserves can be linked to the self giving them the character of true self expression and to the actor's illusion of a great creator. [439]

Role taking is part of our identity. Infants give and receive roles: needing help to eat, sleep and move about, they see helpers as extensions of their body (Moreno's "auxiliary egos"). The relation "of infant and mother is the nourishing matrix of the first independent role taking of the infant," [439] which is the model for all the child's later role exchanges.

The patient improvises not like a Stanislavsky actor but as in creative drama: spontaneously and for one performance. First is warm-up:

Psychodramatic Tests require that the subject be warmed-up to a *feeling level* in which he will release highly personal affect

material. Since the emphasis is deliberately on the *act and feeling* of
the subject, the director is able to glimpse functional levels of
intelligence and to detect behavioural deficiency in crisis situations.
[269] The body of the player must be as free as possible, it must
respond sensitively to every motive of mind and imagination. It must
have the power to perform as large a number of motions as possible,
and perform them easily and rapidly. These motions must, indeed, be
spontaneous so that the player may not fail in a crisis. It may well
happen that an idea may occur to a player unaccompanied by any hint
of a suitable gesture, and if he is not resourceful the whole act may
go to pieces. To eliminate this danger, (a) as large a supply of
possible movements must be stored up in the body as the player can
acquire, so that these may be called forth by the ideas as they occur,
(b) creating of responses ("creatorflex") must be learned. [439]

The therapist (Director) controls the psychodramatic event, assisted by
trained performers who act as auxiliary egos to the actor. The Director
chooses the subject of the improvisation related to the patient's
anxieties, and then trains the auxiliary egos in their expected roles: they
must remain alive to the unique response of the subject(s).

The Projective or Expressive Action Test of patients in sequence is
"a set of experimentally constructed test situations which provide a
norm for interpreting the differential response of subjects as a *planned
operational procedure.*" [160] It stresses spontaneous expression, role
concept, and explores the person's relationship to fantasy and reality by
encouraging him to externalize highly personalized fragments of his
inner world. A series of carefully planned situations is presented,
designed to release specific parts of the personality. Test situations are:

1   *Imaginary Person Situation (no auxiliary ego used)*
    Action: improvisation with any imaginary person (time,
        place, etc.) as wished.
    Aim: (a) what does social relationship mean to the
        subject? (b) how does he communicate?

2   *Imaginary Object & Real Auxiliary Ego Situation (1
        auxiliary ego)*
    Action: improvisation with imaginary object (name
        given).
    Aim: (a) does subject monopolize, share or surrender
        object? (b) are there differences in acting with a
        real/imaginary object?

3   *Triple Imaginary Objects Situation (no auxiliary ego
        used)*
    Action: improvisation with 3 imaginary objects (names
        given).
    Aim: (a) which objects are chosen, emphasised, rejected?
        (b) does he have a need to integrate them? (c) is his
        interest in them functional or aesthetic?

4   *Period Stimulation Test (several auxiliary egos)*
Action: improvisation to given situation/time/place with
several real persons (e.g., artist in studio; several
persons enter).
Aim: (a) how expansive is subject in role? (b) what
are his spontaneous adaptations to surprise
elements?

5   *Hidden Theme Situation (2 auxiliary egos)*
Action: subject enters an existing situation being acted
by 2 others and relates to them by improvisation.
Aim: (a) what is his perception of the theme situation?
(b) how well does he create his role in relation to
these?

6   *The Mute Situation (1 auxiliary ego)*
Action: improvised mime to a given situation with
another person.
Aim: what physical resources does he use for
communication and expression?

7   *Role Reversal Situation (1 auxiliary ego)*
Action: improvisation with one other in given
roles/situations; later, roles reversed and original
improvisation copied.
Aim: (a) is he aware of expression of both roles
(content/manner)? (b) how sensitive is he to others
in social contexts?

8   *The Triple Situation (auxiliary egos as required)*
Action: improvisation in 3 consecutive situations with
no break.
Aim: (a) what is his spontaneous adaptability to such
shifts? (b) what residues of role expression carry
over from one situation to another?

9   *Descriptive Situation (no auxiliary egos used)*
Action: improvised description of any locality and
action, but as though within it.
Aim: to elicit a perceptive protocol.

Analyses are then made according to the following criteria:

A   *Imaginal Content.* His choice of objects, definition of his
own role and of others, his initiation and development of
ideas.

B   *Methods of Projection.* His descriptions; perception in
action.

C   *Plastic Involvement & Organisation.* His organisation of
objects and involvement with the plastic field; his
organization of themes and situations.

D   *Social Interaction.* His social interactions; his social
interaction type (imitative, sympathetic, demonstrative, or
solitary).

This objective test in the social science mode has been quite
successful.

In sociodrama the emphasis shifts to an improvising group, small
or large, and attempts to treat those who share similar problems.
What is created is a life-like situation based on a crisis in the
community: men/women, Christian/Jew, etc. Characterization is two-
dimensional — a moralizing parson, an "Uncle Tom" black, etc. —
and the abstract role represents many persons. Sociodrama asks: how,
and how well, is the person understanding himself and others, the
co-actors in the life context?

Moreno claimed importance for his methods, particularly
spontaneity, in education. For social learning students improvise
normal life events, "live them through" from the simple to complex:
"No new step is undertaken until the preceding one is satisfactorily
mastered." [439] This activity is followed by discussion.
Improvisation in formal learning varies from practising vocations to
learning a foreign language:

> The training of language through spontaneity techniques requires
> that phrases to be learned enter the mind of the pupil when he is
> in the process of acting, that is, in a spontaneous state. In
> consequence, when the pupil at a later time is again in a process of
> acting, for instance, in social situations, these phrases will recur
> simultaneously. Since the use of them began in the course of a
> spontaneous activity, he is able to use them again in the manner of
> spontaneous expression. [439]

Transfer from dramatic play is a thorny issue but research shows that
Moreno can be correct (see Chapter 8).

"Warm-up" has been integrated by educational drama and dance.
Moreno's emphasis on bodily creativity gains strength as Western
society becomes more sedentary. I have used a simplified Projective
Action Test with slow learners with some success. Sociodramatic
methods are useful in recreational or adult education settings,
specifically in multicultural communities; e.g., Penina Mlama, of the
University of Dar es Salaam, has used a variant to revitalize ritual
life amongst urban youth in Tanzania.

Other Therapies

A drama therapist uses drama in therapy from a variety of
perspectives. Some of these are indicated below. In existential
therapy, Ludwig Binswanger, R. D. Laing, Rollo May and others,

deny the unconscious. [367, 409, 410] They say that in the therapeutic situation two concrete individualities interact, and not a patient and a blank screen. Each is a responsible human being: responsible for his or her own life and for the life of others; and facing the reality that we all die, he and the "other" both possess existential freedom. At its extreme, this view was epitomized when Sartre declared, "I am responsible for the war in Vietnam!" The rigour of facing human existence has attracted a number of drama educators, specifically Burton and Heathcote, and can be traced in some drama therapists.

In the biological approach, medical therapy had a bad press in midcentury, largely due to a series of well-publicized mistakes, not the least of which occurred with ECT (electro-convulsive therapy, "shock treatment") and radical experiments with drugs. Recently, refinement of ECT, and the rapid improvement of new drugs, has made organic approaches more effective, sometimes startling so. For example, the pioneer drama therapist Gertrud Schattner, working at the psychiatric inpatients' ward at Bellevue Hospital, New York, found that treatment could not begin until many patients had received medication, [147] particularly those who, suffering from clinical depression, are often unable to react to any stimulus and commit suicide. By using such drugs as lithium and others from a vast range of newer drugs, therapists now can often commence therapy and operate effectively and efficiently.

The Laboratory Approach to therapy is fundamentally a strategy, or way of working. It is based on *the experiences of the learners themselves* generated in various social encounters. The aim is to influence attitudes and develop competencies in, and learn about, human interactions. The experience of the learners is directed towards "learning how to learn." Many (but not all) of its techniques derive from Moreno. There are many variants of the approach, from sensitivity training to T-Groups and Transactional Analysis. [51]

The most significant is Gestalt Therapy. F. S. ("Fritz") Perls, a former Freudian and psychodramatist, had a strong influence in the 1950's and 60's. With Moreno he emphasises self-presentation in the "here and now." But Perls uses less of theatre and more of a dramatic phenomenology by stressing sensation, perception, thinking and awareness in the present tense. His work links directly with Buber's I and Thou: personal names are always used in interactions, where the patient must talk *to* not *at* the listener. Perls rejects three ways to study behaviour: the scientific, which talks *about* behaviour with little involvement; the religious and philosophical, which discusses how behaviour *should be*; and the existential, which focuses on what *is* but still looks for causes. In contrast, Perls works with a patient's experience in the *hic et nunc*: "What are you aware of now?" "What is happening now?" "What do you feel at this moment?" are his constant questions. If a patient refers to an event, Perls invokes Being "as if": the patient must dramatize it "as if" he is within it. Or if the patient identifies a physical symptom ("I'm so afraid, my eyes keep looking away from you!"), Perls uses the Being "as if" ("Can you *be* your eyes?") so that the patient dramatizes ("I am Mary's eyes. I keep jumping and darting about. . . ."). With Perls' techniques, Gestalt is a genuinely dramatic therapy.

Eric Berne's Transactional Analysis starts from the concept that at each moment a person within an interaction (transaction) plays the role of a child, an adult, or a parent, often with quick changes: i.e., the stimulus (or response) will be as a child, adult or parent *towards* the other person, who is also a child, adult or parent. Each gives a status to the other and receives one in return. Used by Berne as a therapy, it is far more useful as a dramatic method to analyze day-to-day role playing. It has direct links with Keith Johnstone's improvisational games of status: "putting others up" and "putting others down."

As befits our relative world, there are other laboratory therapies. This fact allows patients to choose what suits them best. Abraham Maslow and Carl Rogers represent two extremes of non-directive therapy: the therapist provides a free atmosphere with little direction — Rogers less, Maslow more. Both try to clarify what the patient is thinking and feeling.

Consciousness Raising aims to put people progressively in touch with themselves, others, and nature. There are said to be about 8,000 ways to "awaken in North America" and only the more reputable will be discussed here.

Psychosynthesis, begun by Roberto Assagioli, is a multi-dimensional growth therapy: the true self is the focus of awareness around which other sub-selves (parent, worker, etc.) revolve; if one becomes dominant, balance must be restored by various techniques including self-analysis, guided fantasy and the arts.

Guided fantasy is a technique used by various therapies: it is a form of inner dramatization, sometimes initiated by a leader reading a story and at other times self-directed; clients report an increase in inner strength and insight.

Among bodily techniques, biofeedback uses machines to tell the subject when he has gained control over the involuntary systems of the body; the feedback gives the right exercise to reduce tension.

The body's energy system must be kept freely flowing for the Bioenergetics of Alexander Lowen, based on the work of Wilhelm Reich. This theory mixes a variety of bodily exercises with several forms of therapy. "Rolfing," formulated by Ida Rolf, is a deep muscle manipulation focusing on emotions as well as the body.

Moshe Feldenkrais has 30,000 delicate body exercises to increase mental awareness, increase physical dexterity and change aspects of consciousness. Drama and dance therapists regularly use bodily therapies.

Trends in Drama Therapy

Drama therapists today focus on dramatic action: on Being "as if." They work within two contexts: (1) in clinical situations they use drama for diagnosis, treatment and cure, either as a psychotherapist or as an assistant in an adjunct capacity; or (2) in non-clinical situations such as schools or recreation, or with groups having dysfunctions, they work for positive mental and physical health.

Most therapists are eclectic. Not belonging to any one "school," they focus on the need of the client or group, pragmatically using any strategy that will be useful. Most of their techniques are spontaneously dramatic and they can come from disparate sources: Slade or Way, Ward or Siks, Spolin or Johnstone, Heathcote or Brook, Moreno or Perls. Some use theatre as therapy — for example, Ramon Gordon, founder-director of Cell Block Theatre for ex-prisoners, Al Fann's black theatre and Jonathan Fox of Playback Theatre, all in New York. [147] Others, such as Louis Miller in the kibbutzim of Israel, use variants of sociodrama. [147] They will even use other media, such as music, visual art, dance, puppetry, etc., if that is the client's need. What unifies these therapists is the concept that dramatic action is a positive force for learning, growth and healing.

In Britain the drama therapy movement started when Peter Slade in the 1930's began "lay therapy." He pioneered "child drama" as a cathartic method for the disadvantaged and dysfunctional but met resistance: doctors said drama therapists were "not qualified" and teachers said schools were not for therapy. Today his work is reaping rich rewards through the British Society of Dramatherapists and the efforts of therapists like Marian Lindkvist and Sue Jennings. [147]

Similarly in North America, psychodrama continued from the 1920's. However, it was only after World War II that Gertrud Schattner began her eclectic drama therapy. She is a major Viennese actress transplanted to New York, where she uses her dramatic talents to help others. As the founding President of the National Association of Drama Therapists, she, like Slade, sees her work coming to fruition in the work of others. Adam Blattner in Louisville, Kentucky, Rénee Emunah at Antioch University in San

Francisco, Eleanor Irwin at the Pittsburg Child Guidance Clinic, David Read Johnson at Yale, Robert J. Landy at New York University, and Bernie Warren at Concordia University, Montreal, are some of a new generation who work each in his or her unique way. Research grows daily and experiments with drama in therapy are many and diverse.

Chapter 6
Drama & Child Psychotherapy

Drama therapists require a background in styles of therapy (as in Chapters 4 and 5), but those who deal with children also need to understand child psychotherapy.

The Legacy of Freud

We have seen that Freud said we can learn of a child's unconscious character from his or her dramatic play, and that the foundation for the child's drama lies in the relationship of mother and child. In 1908 he made a seminal statement that continues to echo through the 20th century:

> We ought to look in the child for the first traces of imaginative activity. The child's best loved and most absorbing occupation is play. Perhaps we may say that every child at play behaves like an imaginative writer, in that he creates a world of his own or, more truly, he arranges the things of his world and orders it in a new way that pleases him better. It would be incorrect to say that he does not take his world seriously; on the contrary, he takes his play very seriously and expends a great deal of emotion on it. The opposite of play is not serious occupation, but reality. Notwithstanding the large affective cathexis of his play world, the child distinguishes it perfectly from reality: only he likes to borrow the objects and circumstances that he imagines from the tangible and real world. It is only this linking of it to reality that distinguishes a child's "play" from "daydreaming." [231]

This view, with its echoes of Kant, is new to Freud: *consciousness begins with the creation of "the play world."* It is a functional alternative to actuality, and the basis of the artistic and natural languages of the child. His symbols, taken from life, show reality as he understands it: "By dealing with things that are small and inanimate, he can master situations that to him are overwhelming." [231] Yet play is determined for Freud: it re-plays material already experienced as a form of secondary symbolism with which the child orders reality.

How is this done? Freud gives two different answers: *catharsis* and *the repetition compulsion*. In his early work Freud emphasises the catharsis that allows the child to "act out" disturbing situations: "free play in and of itself has decided cathartic value, over and above the therapeutic implications ascribed to it by the therapist." [640] But things have changed since Freud's early work when

> the child was encouraged to express his difficulties in the interests of a rather aimless catharsis. It is now realised that the essentially therapeutic element in play is that through it the child learns to

control in fantasy, impulses which are as yet difficult for him to control in reality. It is often his preferred mode of coming to terms with some aspect of reality which presents insuperable difficulties for a direct approach. [40]

That is, *specific* catharsis has been replaced by *general* catharsis. Freud himself discarded the former as a tool for lasting therapeutic change. Yet specific catharsis has some relevance. It implies enactment in effigy (sticking pins in a doll) so the content of play is important: it can show the therapist or teacher *some* facts about the symbolic thought of the child. In educational drama, only Slade and Koste fully accept catharsis.

In 1922 Freud replaced catharsis with the repetition compulsion as the major force in play:

> We see that children repeat in play everything that has made a great impression on them in actual life, that they thereby abreact the strength of the impression and so to speak make themselves masters of the situation . . . . the child repeats even the unpleasant experiences because through his own activity he gains a far more thorough mastery of the strong impression than was possible by mere passive experience. Even fresh repetition seems to strengthen this mastery for which the child strives. [218]

The repetition compulsion calls for re-play, "to assimilate the experience more completely through renewing and thereby gaining mastery over it." [603] When a dentist pries into his mouth, the child is passive, but in his play the child pretends to be the dentist and repeats the vigorous procedure on a small sister or brother, who is then as helpless as he was with the dentist. It is a way to assimilate difficult experience.

The Elements of Play Therapy

The therapist tries, by "reading" the secondary symbolism of play, to understand its symbolic language and infer the unconscious problems that beset the player. Therapists vary in applications and practices but they have a certain amount of common ground.

First, most would agree with Lowenfeld that they deal with those activities of children that are "spontaneous and self-generating, that are ends in themselves, and that are unrelated to 'lessons' or to the normal physiological needs of the child." [398] Spontaneous play helps the child to assimilate reality, even if the experience is traumatic:

> To the psychic organism just establishing its existence, for which everything is still novel — some things attractively pleasant, many things painful and menacing — excessive stimulation (trauma as it

might be called in a certain sense) is plainly a normal experience, while in the life of the adult it surely constitutes the exception. This, probably, is one of the reasons why the abreaction of traumatic experiences by games plays so important a role precisely in childhood. [603]

Second, play activities are seen as external expressions of the child's thoughts, drives and motivations that have private meanings: "What a subject does in a projective situation may be directly expressing his private world and characteristic personality processes." [204] These are affected by the age, previous experience, intelligence, physical and social maturity, and other abilities of the child, as well as the nature of the toy material. But essentially play is a surface manifestation of the unconscious. As Erikson says succinctly, play is the microcosm by which children deal with the macrocosm of the environment.

Third, Being "as if" is an inherent part of the play event. For all practical purposes, dramatic play is indistinguishable from play itself, as "a child cannot drive a car, fly an aeroplane, or go into outer space. Reversal of roles in the parent-child or teacher-pupil relationship can be achieved by the child only in a play situation. Overt expressions of hostility, of aggression, and of the desire to punish are not tolerated by the adult world, but are possible for the child in play." [640] The drama in play relates children to one another which means "sharing of a fantasy life. Through play children tell one another these fantasy truths. Through the sharing of these intimate truths, they become realities and they fall into their proper perspective, and the children become real people to one another." [28] It also allows the child to explore and come to terms with the world: "Sometimes he transforms the whole playroom into his house, street, or school, and he often re-enacts adult roles he has observed; his mother, teacher, the milkman, mailman, etc. Developmentally speaking, this play serves as a means for the child to explore and understand the social world." [285] Drama is, for example, inherent in what some call "constructional play," in which "the child not only imitates an adult world as in the representational activity; he becomes identified with the grown-up person who produces his own objects." [285] Jackson and Todd state that the rudiments of dramatic play begin to appear at about 10 months. Then

the function of imaginative or dramatic play is very complex for it may be an expression of a variety of needs. When we see a child playing at being a coachman and whipping his "horse" unmercifully, or at being a car driver and running people over in the street, we might be tempted to take a superficial view that he is merely "imitating" what he has seen or heard. We might also jump to the hasty conclusion that he is a cruel or "sadistic" child, who enjoys inflicting pain in imagination. Both these views may be partially true. Yet it may also be true that the child is seeking to satisfy a craving for power, which he has little chance of exercising in real life. He may be "doing unto others" what he has had "done unto himself," passing on to the imaginary horse or the imaginary person, the pain, the fear, the crushing sense of impotence which others had inflicted upon him. He may, by working himself up into a state of angry excitement or highly pleasurable sense of mastery, seek the experience, and learn the control of emotions which he is obliged to repress, in his everyday relationships. He may even be imagining himself as the chastised horse or the crushed pedestrian, thus allaying, through punishment, his guilt in connection with his own "naughtiness" or badness, and at the same time finding reassurance in the discovery that, after all, punishment does not annihilate the culprit — something he had unconsciously feared. . . . by "playing through" his emotional attitudes towards himself, the child puts himself in the place of the persons in his environment, tests the strengths and quality of his emotions, as well as his control over them, and builds up his personality in the process, emerging finally as a more complete and better integrated individual. [315]

Schools of Child Therapy

There are five kinds of child psychotherapy that cluster about particular analysts:

Virginia Mae Axline and other non-directive therapists consider that we all have within ourselves the ability to solve our own problems; and that this natural growth makes mature behaviour more satisfying than immature behaviour. This naturalism leads to a unique therapeutic method, different from the others all of which actively intervene to help the individual. Axline, in contrast, accepts children as they are and attempts to encourage self-expression by natural catharsis.

Margaret Lowenfeld uses specific materials, particularly trays of sand, so that in a realistic context the child builds imaginary worlds. In her "world games," the child shows his own emotional state with no interference from the adult. "World games" are extended by Bender and Shilder: "Spontaneous play in children is essentially a means of investigation and experimentation in the laws of nature and human relationships. . . . The emotional problems and the formal problems cannot be completely separated. The child's experimentation with form and configuration is an expression of his tendency to come to a better handling of objects by action. By trial and error the child comes to an insight into the structure of objects." [43] The child plays with form, configuration and construction. From this kind of play Lowenfeld builds up a picture of the child's symbolic thought but does not provide a theoretic interpretation.

Freud's daughter, Anna, stressed the relationship of the ego and the superego in children. She differed from Melanie Klein: Anna Freud analysed slightly older children, took into account information from parents, and thought that analysis of the very youngest child was not possible. In 1928 she said that helping the child to accept the growing demands of the superego calls for education rather than analysis, and that direct interpretations should be used sparingly. By 1936 she stressed the conscious: information about the child in the "now" can only be provided by play; the ego's unconscious defence mechanisms transform the basic drives. In addition to those defence mechanisms of Freudian theory, she gave five others: (1) denial in fantasy — a painful fact is denied and turned into its opposite; (2) denial in word and act — reassurance to protect the ego from the knowledge of its own helplessness; (3) restriction of the ego — as when a teenage girl, frustrated socially in mixing with the opposite sex, restricts her interests in order to excel intellectually: (4) identification with the aggressor — assumption of the opponent's qualities through introjection (e.g., playing "dentist" after having an extraction); (5) altruism — satisfying one's own desires in the lives of others (like Cyrano).

Erik H. Erikson combines spatial configurations with psychoanalytic interpretations using four criteria: (1) affective — the child's emotional attraction to/withdrawal from a person/object; (2) ideational — spoken and acted-out themes; (3) spatial — configuration in 3 dimensions; (4) verbal — expression, in voice/vocal manner/pitch/rhythm. Erikson also draws on other material (past impressions and data from parents) before making an analysis. In his later work he stresses biography. As a function of the ego, play tries to marry body and social processes with the self, which feels free from, and superior to, any confinement of space, time and social reality, or conscience. Thus, says Erikson, "man only feels human when he plays. [The child] has, as Freud put it, *turned passivity into activity*; he plays at doing something that was in reality done to him." [185] Erikson uses three kinds of play material: that which has (1) a common meaning to all the children in a com-munity; (2) a special meaning to some; and (3) a unique meaning to the individual. The same play form may have meaning in all kinds of situations. Play creates social meaning, "by creating model situations." [185] Erikson sees play as a dramatic experience and one directly related to both the modern scientist's use of models, and Burton's concept of "a large-scale laboratory of life examination and study."

The English School was a highly influential group which emerged in England in the 1920's and 30's, including educator Susan Isaacs and psychotherapists Melanie Klein, Joan Riviere, Géza Róheim, T. E.

Money-Kyrle, Ernest Jones (Freud's biographer), and later D. W. Winnicott. Klein originated a technique to analyse the play of the youngest children which, together with the elaborations of other child therapists, provides an overall picture of the development of consciousness in the first months of life. We shall see that this picture is intertwined with dramatic action.

The Growth of Consciousness

Klein said the beginnings of identification, the superego and symbol formation are in the child's first months (i.e., much earlier than for Freud and Anna Freud). The ego, exposed to inner instincts and external reality, does two things; (1) it imagines an ideal breast; and (2) the ego splits, projecting the death instinct outwards towards the actual breast, which becomes the focus for the fear of persecution. Thus arise two imaginings; the ideal breast and the persecutory breast — the "good breast" and the "bad breast." The baby oscillates between these two feelings, which merge with the actual experience of love/feeding, and pain/deprivation. (Non-analysts who object to Kleinian terminology should remember that she is trying to describe feelings which are tacit.)

The infant reaches the "paranoid-schizoid position": the chief symbolic anxiety is that the bad breast will "get inside" and overwhelm him. Imagining a bad breast can lead a hungry child to stop feeding. A hungry child imagining a good breast may, if fed, merge his feelings of his own goodness and the good breast, and so feel strong; but if not fed, he feels the bad breast is stronger than both his own love and the good breast. Then projective identification occurs: ego parts split off and are projected into the object (breast); this is then controlled by, and identified with, the projected parts. But projective identification "has its valuable aspects. To begin with, it is the earliest form of empathy, and it is on projective as well as introjective identification that is based the capacity to 'put oneself in another person's shoes'" — the basic structure for dramatization. Other projective identification forms the earliest symbols: "By projecting parts of itself into the object and identifying parts of the object with parts of the self, the ego forms its most primitive symbols." [549] Here is the first sign of Being "as if." The child's feelings about external objects are attributed by him to the objects themselves, and so there are good objects and bad objects. With a slight change in the situation, the child can love and hate the same object in rapid succession: he "lives in a world of gods and devils."

From about 6 months, as Winnicott shows, the baby gives even more meaning to objects. He plays with "the mediate object": a soft toy or piece of cloth ("a cuddle"), of which the classic instance is Linus' security blanket. It is mediate because the baby puts it in and out of his mouth, relating his inner to the outer. It is highly personal to him and is constantly with him; it can get dirty and smell; but should his mother wash it there is a great outcry. Later he drops it and his mother picks it up to return it. Finally he can give it to his mother and she gives it back: inner and outer are united in an act of love. About this time occurs "the mirror stage" of Jacques Lacan: he begins to recognize himself in a mirror as a separate entity.

At about 10 months occurs a highly significant event: his ideas of objects have grown from the good/bad breast, through "the mediate object," and now he can see himself as both subject and object. This is what I have called elsewhere "the primal act." [135] The baby performs his first full act of Being "as if": he pretends to be his mother or himself in a whole symbolic act — a moment of joy and laughter. Klein says his ego feels stronger, the power of bad objects is felt to be weaker, and he reaches the "depressive position," where "the infant recognises a whole object and relates himself to this object. This is a crucial moment in the infant's development, and one which is clearly recognised by laymen. Every one who surrounds him will perceive a change and recognise it as an enormous step in his development — they will notice and comment on the fact that the infant now recognises his mother." [549] The baby has become a child. By recognising his mother, he also realizes his own dependence. Believing he might destroy her, he is depressed: he "mourns for the good object, destroyed and lost." But he begins to understand actual vs. fictional: when his mother reappears after an absence he tests his feelings; "peek-bo" shows the degree of his adjustment.

This leads to a vital symbolic step: in the primal act the child tacitly realises that, by acting "as if" he is his mother, he himself is a *representation* of her. To Klein the superego alters: it focuses on the loved parents and to spare them he partly inhibits his instincts to displaces them on *substitutes* — a basis of creativity and sublimation:

> The giving up of an instinctual aim, or object, is a repetition and at the same time a reliving of the giving up of the breast. It can be successful, like this first situation, if the object to be given up can be assimilated in the ego, by the process of loss and internal restoration. I suggest that such an assimilation object becomes a symbol within the ego. Every aspect of the object, every situation that has to be given up in the process of growing, gives rise to symbol formation. [549]

This is the symbolic basis for mature thought: any loss in later life reawakens the anxiety of the good internal object.

A little later, when the infant can distinguish both mother and father, oral fantasies are supreme, and they "go together with fantasies of sucking, squeezing, biting, tearing, cutting, emptying and exhausting, devouring and incorporating the object; the urethral/anal aims concern burning, flooding, drowning, expelling and exploding, or sitting upon or dominating the object." [354] These are the materials the infant uses when worried about his parents' relationship to each other. Klein traces the origin of the phallic woman fantasy (the terrifying figure who will tear, rend and destroy —the witch in fairy tales) to this time. Imaginings form symbols from whole objects like the mother. Some are identified with the ego, but some remain as separate internal objects in the superego. Thus personality structure consists of the more permanent imaginings the ego has about itself.

Between the ages of 2 and 7, the child learns more obviously through dramatic play. Activities arise from unconscious imaginings in practical contexts that need knowledge of the environment. Pursued for their own sake as problems of understanding and learning, they lead to discoveries of external fact, verbal judgment, or reason:

> The child re-creates selectively those elements in past situations which can embody his emotional or intellectual need of the present, and adapt the details, moment by moment, to the present play situation. The ability to evoke the *past* in imaginative play seems to be closely connected with the growth of the power to evoke *the future* in constructive hypothesis, and to develop the consequences of "ifs." The child's make-believe play is thus significant not only for the adaptive and creative intentions . . . but also for the sense of reality, the scientific attitude and the growth of hypothetical reasoning. [354]

Susan Isaacs illustrates how dramatic play improves growth: in manipulation, imaginative art and discovery, reasoning and thought; in the cooperative expression of imagining which leads a child from anxieties to real satisfactions in social play and general learning. But to the observer the various aspects are almost indistinguishable, because "there is a continuity in the child's relationship with things as there is in his relationship with people. Just as our personal relationships contain echoes from our relations with our parents, so our adult interests in the world of things are impregnated by our infantile interests. . . . We have to see all learning as primarily motivated by unconscious fantasy." [354] And by "fantasy" she means "imagination." There is a direct relationship between these activities and educational drama and movement.

From 8 to 11 years social pressure attempts to repress imagination and tender feelings. Being "as if" remains, but the child's acts must have concrete results. School echoes the original feeding situation (the child is "taking from" and "giving to" someone), and learning is "a means of reparation." [158] Lili Peller says:

> A hobby-horse was, before the motor-car's arrival, the main toy of little boys, providing masculine pride besides its play value and adult

approved zonal gratification. The boy's play with his hobby-horse belonged to narcissistic play (the paraphrasing or aggrandising of body parts or functions), and today's hobbies belong in the same group. The body play of infants is a private affair in all aspects, while the adult's hobby is solitary in its libidinal core, but socialised in its ego aspects. Fellow hobbyists share and enhance their pleasure through many channels, like journals, exhibitions, conventions. In any case, even for the secluded collector, his interest is communicable whether he chooses to do so or not. . . .

The keeping of pets may be a more remote reflection of oedipal play, the tie between two beings, of whom one is inarticulate, helpless and direct in his body wants and body gratifications, while the other appears omnipotent. . . . [481]

Acting-out & Ego Development

Freud discovered the phenomenon of acting-out, an important aspect of consciousness. Some patients could not discuss their problem but actually *did it*: they acted-out the original situation. This also happens with some children, who, intolerant of delay, are impulsive. With psychotics it can be a regression to infantile acting-out. Acting-out is a stage of ego development, part of the sequence that establishes identity. This definition was first suggested by Ferenczi, who saw a natural progression: hallucination, magic gesture, speech symbol and object formation. This sequence Anna Freud saw as denial in fantasy, in act, in work. Mark Kanzer unifies both theories: acting-out = magic gesture + denial in act; and sublimation = speech symbolism + denial in fantasy. Dramatic play relates the unconscious to the intellect in the sequence of ego growth: (1) acting-out; (2) dream; (3) imagining; and (4) play leading to sublimation. But Ekstein and Friedman find that dramatic play leads to mature thought through a not invariable sequence of ego development: (1) in acting-out the infant's actions give immediate gratification, while ego organisation is symbiotic; (2) in simple play action, the ego struggles against symbiosis; (3) imagining gives up the need for action because the gratifying object is internalised; and (4) dramatic play is a preconscious trial solution achieved by roles — the child "unconsciously repeats ahead of time the future rather than the past." [178]

Chapter 7
Drama & Child Development

Dramatic acts change with maturation, a key idea in education. Activities suitable for students at one age are not necessarily so at another. To describe this phenomenon, educational psychologists use the framework of developmental stages, an evolutionary idea in continuous use during the 20th century. Until mid-century the most famous scheme was that of Susan Isaacs, which was intellectual, affective and social; more recently it has been popularly linked to the cognitive ideas of Jean Piaget. As I have dealt with this issue elsewhere, [133] this chapter will summarize the issues, repeating few of the citations.

Developmental Theories

Developmental stages are used to describe different domains of mental activity; e.g., cognitive, affective, etc. Too many teachers assume the stages are discrete entities instead of constituting a unified whole. Also the age stages are not precise but an approximate guide. The most useful terms for our purposes are:

A   *Cognitive*: We create a model of the world and fit new knowledge to it; the child perceives the world differently from the adult. Jean Piaget focuses on abstract reason: induction, deduction, etc., in stages. Ages of stages vary culturally but in invariable sequence.

B   *Affective*: The most well known theory of emotional stages today is that of Erik H. Erikson.

C   *Moral*: Moral reasons hinge on logical reasoning and the stages of Lawrence Kohlberg are commonly used.

D   *Empathic*: Empathy is feeling for others. Martin L. Hoffman's stages are an effective model.

Drama as the Developmental Unifier

The focus of maturation is "the costumed player": *the whole person imagining and acting*. Thus the 4 year old, just scolded by her mother, can later scold her doll in play with her reasoning about it (cognitive), her emotions (affect), her sense of choice (aesthetic), her feelings for others (empathic), her moral sense (moral), etc. The dramatic perspective (the simultaneity of Being "as if") unites all these views. The main Dramatic Age Stages are:

The Identification Stage (0-10 months)
See Chapter 6.

The Impersonatory Stage (10 months-7 years)

1 *"The Primal Act" (approx. 10 months)*
In "the primal act" *the child's acting self represents what he thinks*: his Being "as if" is a metaphor, the generic base of all subsequent actions. Then he is his mother in toto: mind, body, voice and Being. See Chapter 6.

2 *Symbolic Play (1-2 years)*
He repeats the primal act — then he does so with different objects. Now he complicates it, breaking dramatic acts into parts, and in two ways:

> A He can make it into either "personal play" or "projected play": he can keep it whole and Be "as if" he is the object, as before; or he can project it out onto a substitute object; e.g., a crown for a king (metonymy), an early form of symbolic play which is then the focus of the "as if." [557]

> B He focuses on *Being* "as if" the object (as before), or *Sounding* "as if" the object, or *Moving* "as if" the object. Also he can make Sounding or Moving personal or projected — the beginning of his expansion of media in various ways.

Thus the child expresses his imaginings in very complex ways; and he *must* do so, although slowly gratification can be delayed a little. The fictional/ actual are not distinct. He slowly comprehends the values of spoken language, less important to him than Being and Moving. Imaginings work by analogy, animism, omnipotence of thought, the irrational and the illogical. He tries out the future and acts out the past. He dances, makes exits and entrances, and loves chasing. All is "me" or "mine," yet he can have exchanges with others.

3 *Sequential Play (2-3 years)*
Representation grows. He points or reaches to refer to things(object permanence). He separates himself as symbolizer/player from others. Metaphorical thinking grows. He has a time lapse between observing an act and imitating it. He develops and expands narrative, changes roles and joins toys in a dramatic world. He develops flexible movement in speed, rhythm, up/down, front/back. He makes strategies (offers/bargains) but results must be quick. He completes sequences of action: makes running commentaries on his play to begin rudimentary sentences. He attaches words to the relations structured in his experience: to name objects;

and to express actions or desires. He acts parents' routines, uses basic time concepts ("in a minute"), plays "hide and seek" and "tag."

4   *Exploratory Play (3-4 years)*
With exploration and the ubiquitous, "Why?" the child expands roles: his model is often the parent of the same sex in exaggeration or caricature; "I" is a Vaunt of identification; he has synonyms for the self ("boy"), and asks of the mirror, "Will he be there when I go away?" He acts groups of people, dresses up, uses pretence emotions and joins in narratives. Sentences grow, early grammar begins in exaggerated stories. He explores length, weight, number, size, sharing, taking turns, puzzles, rules and creates music in rhythm and time, makes pretence environments ("homes"), plays matching games, "follow my leader," and runs from "monsters." Imaginary companions may appear by 3 years to disappear between 6 and about 10.

5   *Expansive Play (4-5 years)*
He expands his horizons, experience, dramatic acts, roles and, with a wider range of models, he is conscious of others' roles if only in two dimensions: a mother is a mother but not always a wife. He uses highly imaginative roles, different voices, and distinguishes the symbol from actuality. He has friends and enemies, and seeks the approval of his peers. He joins group pretence play and uses puppets. He begins to develop conscience, avoid aggression, anticipate the future and rely on his own judgment. He invents narrative, expands sentences and develops grammar. He creates rituals of possession and sequence. He plays games of order like "Ring around a Rosy."

6   *Flexible Play (5-7 years)*
He can imitate his own play, dramatise a range of experience, and understand complex social situations. With role flexibility from many models, he performs social roles in caricature. He reacts well to others in role and to characters in stories. He improvises conversation, movement, objects, characters, costumes and situations, but he cannot fully distinguish fantasy and reality. He uses more relations between things, e.g., bigger/smaller; movement sequences (big/small/grow); realistic themes with episodic plots and less symbolic play; and improved perception, recognising details and integrating them into a whole. He begins to plan action. At 4 movement dominated speech; now the inner/outer relation is increasingly verbal. By 7 he uses group play with hierarchies, large circles, and rules (e.g.,"proper" ways to play for boys/girls/babies). He begins to empathize and communicate with his peers. Dominant themes are: concern for the

wholeness of his body ("surgeon" play can be emotional); being chased, attacked or bitten; mothers, witches or resurrection; competence and confidence when facing adversity; and playing/acting out.

The Group Drama Stage (7-12 years)

Dramatic traits are stable. The major change is to group drama: a genuine social activity where children share ideas/actions in fairness. At 6 they had formed big rings; these break into smaller circles until, about 10, they use a horse-shoe shape backed by a curtain or wall. [557] Cumulative plots occur. Highly creative dance, team games played to win, and games of dominance ("King of the Castle") emerge. Strong social attachments begin in small groups. From large/small groups, pair and solo improvisations, leaders emerge. Improvisation improves speech flow and writing. Between 7 and 9 words must be concrete to be of use: the child plays them out physically. After 9, this is not the case. He plans to structure action: form, long/short endings, realistic/fantastic styles, occasional need to show work to peers, etc. His concrete thought distinguishes between media, classifies character by type (2 dimensions), and he sees role change within action (transformation). Until 9 dressing up continues. With his emergent awareness of self and of who is like him or not, he makes a conscious choice of friends. Esteem and morality relate to his identification with parents but school drama experience improves them. Good opportunity for role taking improves cognitive and moral development through empathy. Modelling and learning social actions improves inference, including of emotional states of other players and roles. Human intercommunication improves with increasing improvisation. Themes often reflect industry (home and family, clothing, recreation and school) or imaginative exaggeration. Myths and legends are loved.

The Role Stage (12-18 years)

1   Role "Appearance" (12-15 years)
    Adolescents face many physical and identity changes: self-image fluctuates, social status is liminal and uncertain ("I am just an in-between"), and one's growth is different from others' (each is unique). Their improvisation tests hypotheses practically, by trial-and-error, and reveals self doubt: "If I play my role as A, then my actions become Y; but if I play it as B, then they become Z. So who is the *real* me?" This hypothesis implies causality ("If I play my role as C, does it cause *this* effect?"). It isolates and tests various factors ("If we do it *this* way, then . . ." or, "If you play a policeman as a villain, then . . ."), which

requires the ability to think abstractly. They use logic for a conclusion, "then the play will be like this . . . ." They imagine an ideal, use it in dramatic play, and alternate Being "as if" with the actual, while combining and contrasting social masks. Facets of symbols are tested against reality. Emotional judgments can err. They explore social possibilities and moral decisions. They write scenarii, perhaps in "secret" codes. The adolescent changes in focus, consciousness of near/far, and movement/dance direction; increased clarity in gesture and body shape emerges. There is a curious start to a theatre sense: they alternate between "showing" and "personal and private." They experiment with form from large to small groups, pairs to solos. In the acting area where they improvise, the horse-shoe shape is developed and end shapes are explored.

2   *Role "Truth" (15-18 years)*
Not everyone reaches this stage. Students have a new understanding of the purpose of roles. They no longer ask, "Is there a real me?" but realize that they consist of a multiplicity of masks: that personality is a plurality of facets. Dramatic acts are now seen as forms of communication and there are performances to others ("theatre"). As a future-orientation, this understanding correlates with two mental changes: the development of reasoning with the ability to delay a response; and the ability to see a role as only one of many valid views. They now plan carefully before and during the action. Thus educational drama now consists of practice in life improvisation, spontaneous creative drama, and explorations in theatre. The increased development of formal operations (Piaget) creates greater possibilities: students may develop an ideal self; and practical explorations of script can increase their understanding of both the ideal and multi-dimensional aspects of personality.

Contemporary Research

One of the most revealing contemporary researchers on the psychological developments in dramatic activity is Otto Weininger. He is careful to distinguish between imagination and dramatic play. Imagination is thinking about problems — what one might do in a particular role or situation — which is the thinking function of dramatic play: imagination is the "what if" while dramatic play is the "as if."

Weininger finds the origins of "as if" actions at about 6 or 8 months when the baby attempts to "feed" the mother, and that dramatic play proper is visible in the actions of children as young as one year (as with "the primal act") when a child uses an object for something other than the thing it is. [620] Dramatic action becomes the basis of symbolism and thus it: represents a higher level of play than sensory motor or functional forms of play; reflects a change in representational thought which allows the child to substitute one thing for another; relates to the ability to abstract thought through language; and develops coincidentally with periods of major cognitive, linguistic, and social advance for "normal" children. [619] Children learn in dramatic play to transpose rules from one situation to another, to communicate and cooperate reciprocally, and to perceive and express the subtle clues necessary for the flexible and often rapid development of the play interaction.

Weininger has conducted a wide range of studies with "normal" and dysfunctional children. Some of his findings include: dramatic play becomes the basis for the child's further imaginative thinking, e.g., subsequent to dramatic play, art work appears to be part of the "as if" process; with 6 and 7 year old multi-handicapped children, and working with story-telling and dramatic play, there was a decrease in hyper-activity, and increased ability in language use, communication, cooperation, concentration, and interest in what they were doing; with seriously disturbed children between the ages of 3 and 4, the same type of approach led to increased cooperative play, attentiveness, language use and communication; and with emotionally disturbed 3 to 4 year olds on a longitudinal project, similar results were obtained together with improvements in spatial capacity, fine motor movements, short and long term memory, and more purposeful and meaningful behaviour. In surveying his own and other people's work, Weininger shows that contemporary psychologists have conducted a great many research studies directly related to "as if" actions. [619]

Various related and contemporary research studies are reported in the *Youth Theatre Journal* (formerly, *Children's Theatre Review*). For example: Karen K. Schaper reports a positive relationship between dramatic play and improved role-taking (*CTR*, 31, 1 [Jan. 1982]: 16-18); Marci Woodruff shows, from the work of Erikson, that theatre for children improves social development (*CTR*, 31, 2 [April 1982]: 22-25); and Carol Anne M. Kardash and Lin Wright demonstrate considerable improvement among children using creative drama in reading, oral and written communication, person-perception, and drama skills (*ETC*, 1, 3 [Winter 1987]: 11-189). Perhaps the most intriguing of these reported studies is that by Joyce A. Wilkinson on children's involvement in dramatic activity related to self-monitoring and hemisphericity. This included the creation of the *Development Drama Scale (DDS)*: a diagnostic tool whereby participants in creative drama can identify their drama aptitude/potential, degree of self-monitoring and right brain processing; and drama teachers can measure the involvement of students in dramatic activity (*CTR*, 32, 2 [April 1983]: 15-19). The *DDS* is a considerable achievement because it uses measurement to assess qualitative factors in a qualitative way — the sort of research tool needed for studies in educational drama.

Chapter 8
Motivation & Transfer

The majority of arguments for the effectiveness of learning through educational drama hinge on motivation, transfer, or both. As I have examined these issues elsewhere, [135] I will merely summarize them here without repetition of many references.

Motivation

Dramatic play, it is said, greatly motivates people to learn. By definition, play is what they *want* to do and this brings a deep need to learn. There are two related issues that do not fully account for this need: drama teachers are highly committed to the activity and their enthusiasm can "rub off" on the players; and the climate of the drama classroom, where student choice is paramount, gives some relief from other more formal classes. The issue is more complex than these reasons.

Motivational Theories

Can theories of motivation help us? Each theory of motivation starts from a specific model of human beings. The four major theories today are behaviourism, psychoanalysis, competence and holism.

For behaviourists and Freudians, people are inert machines that need fuel to motivate them. Behaviourists say this is reward and punishment; at best, non-reward is punishment and relief from pain is a reward. But punishment does not necessarily rob an act of its fascination for children or adults; studies show that novelty and incongruity, in moderation, improve motivation. O. H. Mowrer is driven to use a Freudian concept: that reinforcement and identification *together* are good motivators — "reward from another organism, or 'parent person.'" For Freud, identification is the key in two ways: *developmental* — fearful of losing the mother's love the child introjects her qualities, which become the link, or mediator, between the child's wants and their satisfaction (secondary reward value); and *defensive* — fearful of punishment, the child identifies with the father in the Oedipus complex and impersonates him; the child transforms himself from the person threatened to the person who makes the threat. These explanations do not fully account for the phenomenon.

For Robert W. White the human drive for competence is the basic motivation. Covering almost everything, it means many things to many people. It has the virtue of simplicity: people act to produce an effect which, aided by early encouragement and independence, helps motivation to learn. But it does not answer: Why is Being "as if" a strong motivator?

Holistic theory attempts an answer. For Abraham Maslow motivation aims to complete human potential: "self-actualization." The whole person is motivated (one motivation is unusual) from two kinds of needs: basic needs — physiological, safety, love, etc.; and meta-needs to which all human beings should aspire — wholeness, perfection, completion, etc. Maslow stresses education that develops potential and Brian Way agrees: spontaneous drama develops more of people than of drama and, with children, we should "begin from where you are." Thus emerge self-discipline and freedom of choice; internal control and respect for others (the basis of a value system); and a trust in the creations of others, unselfish cooperation and generosity. Specific studies show improvisation improves self-actualisation, spontaneity and self-confidence.

Organism & Imagination

None of the former theories quite matches our experience. For this we need a model that obeys the parameters of life, particularly of the human organism. Biology shows that organisms are unified wholes with tensions among their parts. Like atoms, people inherently have fields of force and energy, motives they share, and other factors that are unique according to their specific structures. Motivation appears to stem from cell tissue, particularly of the brain and nervous system, as "a need to know" (human intention).

Mental activity is of figure-and-ground: one thing/idea is seen in terms of another, and vice versa. Our inner reality is an oscillation between the environment and the sense we make of it: the metaphoric tension of the actual vs. the fictional. This tension generates motivation, but to what end? Each of us puts most value on those experiences which relate most closely to our own structural tensions (dynamics). An organism acts by mediating with the environment: the internal act (imagining) becomes the direct external act (dramatic). In the direct act motivation propels the organism spontaneously, and it is this spontaneity that allows us to make an adequate response to a new situation, or a new response to an old situation. Activity is inherent in the life of the organism, but the degree of activity varies according to certain well-defined conditions — of which motivation is generally revealed by increased activity.

The tensions within us (the dynamics between structures) not only create an energy flow but are also made even more energetic by imagining and dramatic actions. Imagining re-creates energy and is the source of human motivation. Being "as if" is a leap into the unknown, into the milieu of possibility, re-energizing the organism. Niels Bohr showed that the ultimate nature of matter can be seen as waves and particles in oscillation. Atomic physics, electricity, the biology of the cell, DNA, and the bi-hemisphericity of the brain, each demonstrates that oscillation between two or more tensions emits energy. Imagining requires meta-needs to be satisfied: without the ability to imagine, these needs could not be envisaged. But imaginative tension is not synonymous with dialectics or the clash of oppositions: it involves both negative and positive attraction. As William Blake said:

> Negations are not opposites;
> Contraries mutually exist.

Imagination relates to synergy. Charles Hampden-Turner put it as "the mutual enhancement between two or more helixes [which achieves] an optimal organisation of strengths that will lead the double helix to 'spiral upwards.'" [275]

Educational Implications

Students' motivation is actively engaged by spontaneous drama and consists of the acts that directly express imagining. Inner energy is naturally directed to the feeling-world of the "I am" experience and Being "as if" — and it is out of these that rational processes emerge. The teacher's stance should be that of a dramatist: this stance becomes the students' model which, by awakening their feelings, attitudes and values, leads them to dramatize their own experience and increase their motivation. Motivation is fostered by educational drama: the dramatic Vaunt expresses the students' "I am" experience; the acceptance of uniqueness encourages their intrinsic motivation; sharing a common meaning in improvisation breeds social motivation because mutual co-discovery is co-existence; and imaginative transformation of materials brings the re-creation of a world structure which deeply affects their inner Being.

But how can we account for individual differences of motivation? This is very complex but, in general, these fluctuations seem to be bound up with the dynamics of a person's mental structures. In both life and dramatic actions, the level of aspiration rises after success and drops after failure, at least in Western cultures. Students almost always aim at a higher goal than that which they have just successfully achieved. There are, however, many variables according to culture and dysfunctions.

Transfer

Teachers claim that dramatic play helps children to learn language, history, and the like. But, in fact, do such transfers occur? Does dramatic play affect short-term and long-term learning equally? The 19th century assumption that learning in one task was transferred to another (e.g., learning Latin helps the learning of French) was effectively destroyed early this century when behaviourist studies found no evidence of it. Contemporary research, led by Henry Ellis, is less interested in *whether* transfer occurs than in *why* it occurs, but there is now ample evidence that performance on one task can have three effects on performance of a second task:

> *Positive Transfer*: one aids the other
> *Negative Transfer*: one inhibits the other
> *Zero Transfer*: one has no effect on the other

Transfer is pervasive. It is found not only in cognitive tasks or motor skills but also in feelings and attitudes. We will now briefly examine those research findings that are relevant to educational drama.

Non-specific Transfer

Here there is no one-to-one relation between dramatic acts and other tasks. Non-specific transfer concerns general characteristics and three results from educational drama: "learning to learn," "warm-ups" and transformation.

It is a commonplace that people can more easily learn new tasks if they have practised similar tasks beforehand: early trials are necessary to establish a learning habit. This is "learning to learn" and occurs in many instances: e.g., from verbal learning to problem solving. Good teachers know that early dramatic play vastly improves general learning at later ages; that early practice of insights in play improves later intuition; and that early deprivation of play is irreversible. [559] In other words, the more educational drama is used the more effective it can be. We have already examined some characteristics of "warm-up" (see Chapter 5) but it also assists short-term transfer: immediate personal adjustments from one task to another. The transformation of thoughts into actions through Being "as if" will be faster and more efficient if it is through the students' free choice rather than if it is by mechanical or imposed methods. Thus, in summarizing their research, Brian Sutton-Smith and Gil Lazier say that "it could be that proponents of creative dramatics falsely proceed from the part to the whole rather than the reverse. The child's excited, if caricatured, representations may be the more proper starting point." [576]

Specific Transfer

What specific elements of tasks can be transferred in educational drama?

Findings in task similarity help us here. The more similar the two tasks, the greater the positive transfer: improvising a job interview will have greater transfer to a real interview than to (say) crossing the road; subject-content in drama can transfer to subject-content in life situations. But drama-content also transfers: thus, verbal fluency in improvising a job interview can transfer to verbal fluency in other situations as well as in interviews. Yet this issue is not simple: similarity is a complex variable and dramatic action is a complex medium. There are three principles of task similarity:

1   Where stimuli are varied and the response kept identical, positive transfer increases with increasing stimulus similarity. This is common in creative drama and creative dramatics (if not in Heathcote's" living through" version); e.g., preparation in elements of both drama and dance is given before a dance-drama.

2   If the responses in the transfer task are different from those in the first task, then the greater the similarity of stimuli, the less the transfer. If improvisation is used in social studies about life in a foreign land and the outcome is writing a diary, it is *not* effective to use diary writing in the previous or subsequent lessons.

3   If we keep the stimuli identical in the initial and transfer tasks, and vary response similarity, positive transfer will increase with increasing response similarity. Thus if the subject matter to be learned (in literature, say, or history) has to do with people's lives, we might well begin with improvisation that develops characterization or occupational mime.

These three principles apply to much work in today's drama classrooms. When a time interval elapses between two tasks, transfer of learning can vary. Where transfer relies on memory (e.g., rote learning), there is a faster decrease than when it relies on feelings, attitudes and insight. The latter is normal in educational drama and so general learning is relatively permanent. But it can be less effective than rote learning in the short-run.

Drama and Transfer

Drama transfers effectively for long-term learning because it provides high motivation and low anxiety; it is meaningful to the student when the student has freedom of choice; it has immediate application as a synthesizing activity; it assists students in learning to learn; it stimulates insight; it provides warm-up; and it can provide certain specific transfers. There are some generalized principles when teaching for transfer: the similarity of tasks must be maximized; there should be adequate experience with the original task; a variety of examples should be provided when teaching concepts and principles; important features of the task should be identified; and general principles must be understood before expecting much transfer. While spontaneous drama can provide specific transfer it is most useful in providing a general climate for learning, high motivation, meaningfulness, and learning to learn.

Chapter 9
The Unconscious, Art & Theatre

Psychologists have long been concerned with the relationship between the unconscious and creativity in the theatre. It is no accident that many Freudian terms derive from the Greek theatre. In this chapter we will first examine the unconscious in art and, thereafter, theatre art.

Art & Play

Freud & the Unconscious

Freud saw conflict as inherent in both the neurotic and the artist. Although both withdraw from an unsatisfying reality into an imagined world, the artist can find a way back from it. There is a relation between unconscious conflict and imaginative behaviour. A poet's fantasies "are also the first preliminary stage in the mind of the symptoms of illness of which our patients complain. . . . Many imaginative productions have travelled far from the original naive day-dreams, but I cannot suppress the surmise that even the most extreme variations could be brought into relationship with the model by an uninterrupted series of transitions." [231] Where the normal individual might respond to tension by establishing a neurosis, the creative artist uses it. "As the instinctual pressure rises and a neurotic solution appears imminent, the unconscious defence against it leads to the creation of an art product. The psychic effect is the discharge of pent-up emotion until a tolerable level is reached." [164]

To support this famous, if highly questionable, link between the artist and emotional dysfunction, Freud quotes from a letter by Schiller: "You worthy critics, or whatever you may call yourselves, are ashamed or afraid of the momentary and passing madness which is found in all real creators, the longer or shorter duration of which distinguishes the thinking artist from the dreamer." [76]

Freud also saw the relation of creativity and humour: "The denial of the claims of reality and the triumph of the pleasure principle, cause humour to approximate to the regressive or reactionary processes which engage our attention so largely in psychopathology." [229] Laughter and creativity are also linked by Koestler, Bakhtin and others.

Freud further said that creation is based on childhood experiences: "You will not forget that the stress laid on the writer's memories of his childhood, which perhaps seems so strange, is ultimately derived from the hypothesis that imaginative creation, like daydream-

ing, is a continuation and substitute for the play of childhood." [231]
Thus adult art is not merely an elaboration of "freely rising" fantasies
and humorous regressions, but it also derives from play activities and is
a substitute for them.

Alternate Views

There are other important views of the relation of art to the unconscious. Like J. A. Hadfield, Daniel Schneider says the artist is like the
analyst: art consists of dreams which the artist converts into beauty.
Thus *"all art form is essentially the form of a dream* . . . made by
exactly the same forces and then *turned inside out,* orientated toward
external world-reality rather than to dreamworld reality [and] artistic
technique is a *conscious mastery of the inherent power of the unconscious in its work of dream formation."* [541] Drama is like drawing a
spectator into a magic circle and showing his conflicts to induce a
dreamlike cathartic effect, which refreshes him — it is the acting-out of
an analytic interpretation. But Sophocles did not interpret the Oedipus
complex, he dramatized it.

Ernst Kris says the preconscious is the basis of art: "[Ego regres-
sion] occurs not only when the ego is weak [but] also during many
types of creative processes. [The] idea was rooted in Freud's explanation of wit according to which a preconscious thought is 'entrusted for
a moment to unconscious elaboration' and it seemed to account for a
variety of creative or other inventive processes." [361] Creativity is a
preconscious "act of regression in the service of the ego." Art is
midway between the unconscious and reality. Using striking photo-
graphs of the art of the insane, Kris ties artistic to mental style; e.g.,
the schizophrenic avoids empty spaces; produces rigid shapes, symbols
and stereotypes; and projects his own face onto his figures in an effort
to see and control himself. Catharsis works for Kris (as for drama
therapists) at a general level if not specifically.

But if controlled regressions take place, says Martin Wangh, then a
pivotal condition must exist: "the recreational situation in the theatre is
a safe one which permits the spectator to have an aesthetic experience
— but let there be an unruly crowd, and all possibility of pleasure
derived from the state of controlled regression has gone." [606] The
artist must be secure in a pivotal situation whence he engages in the
creative act.

L. S. Kubie goes further than Kris: the unconscious has no role in
creativity, it can even be harmful. Preconscious processes have "the
highest degree of freedom in allegory and in figurative imagination
which is attainable by any psychological process. The contribution of
preconscious processes to creativity depends upon their freedom in
gathering, assembling, comparing and reshuffling of ideas." [363]

Symbolism is creative and imagery is flexible only when the preconscious works against the ego and the id: "The uniqueness of creativity,
i.e., its capacity to find and put together something new, depends on
the extent to which preconscious functions can operate freely between
these two ubiquitous concurrent and oppressive prison wardens." [363]

Functions

What are the unconscious functions of play and art? For Freud art
is "a continuation and substitute for the play of children": the artist
uses imaginings as a child does in play and allows full play to personal
wishes but uses art to return to actuality. The child re-creates imaginings in a new kind of reality (what Heidegger calls "the aesthetic
world"). If play and dreams solve problems, and identification in
symbolic play matures ideas, as Hadfield says, the same applies to art.
Lilli Peller sees art as the adult counterpart of Oedipal play, while for
Kanzer dramatic play leads instinct to the sublimation of artistic creation. For Fenichel, "The psychological function of play is to get rid of
[tensions] by the active repetition or anticipation of them in a self-
chosen dosage and at a self-chosen time." [189] The arts relieve
tensions and gratify wishes in a sublimated way.

Why are there different forms of creation? Why does one artist
create *Hamlet* and another *Pygmalion*? The psychoanalyst says the
progress of play/art is universal but differs with the individual's infantile experiences. For example, poetry expresses particular early events.
"Poetry is nothing but an oral outlet, an outlet through words and
phrases to express a genuine emotion. Poetry is a sensuous or mystic
outlet through words, or, as it were, through a chewing and sucking of
nice words and phrases." [75] To produce a work of art implies an
audience. To some analysts exhibitionism is an unconscious function in
artistic creation; for others "voyeurism is unconsciously warded off by
substituting exhibitionism." [47]

Following Spencer and Groos, Kris shows three stages from play to
art:

1 mastery of the body and of the plaything: instead of doing
   what he or she wishes, the child plays at doing it (pretends
   to do it);

2 the dramatization of imaginings to maintain psychic equilibrium: the fiction is thinly separated from the actual; "the
   play world" co-exists with the certainty that "it is only play";
   "Here lie the roots of aesthetic illusion"; [362] and

3 functional pleasure from a sense of mastery: the child accepts
   the fictions of others as well as his own.

Kris also indicates the relation of play to magic. In early life, words and images provide power over what they depict, and so are magical. The "omnipotence of thought" of the infant may or may not be communicated to others. But art is created for communication: gestures must be seen and words must be heard to communicate, but pictures can be seen later — by overcoming time, they are magical. Those paintings of the prehistoric cave dwellers are magical in two ways: they collapse the past into the present ("here and now") and are "sympathetic magic." Artists are magical: they create the world anew and controls it through their work.

The Artist in the Theatre

The Actor

In the analytic view, we all need to exhibit ourselves. This need derives from an unconscious desire of infants to show the body, or body parts (specifically, the genitals), to others. Later the boy does so as a reassurance against fear of punishment, while the girl displaces the desire toward the body in general and, socially encouraged, this promotes the idea of female beauty. The unconscious desire may also become the adult perversion of exhibitionism.

The exhibitionism of actors is not perverted but comes from a failure to develop a normal body image. In "the primal act" the baby distinguishes the self/nonself but this the actor may not have completely done. Natural "billing and cooing" is a vital part of mother-child unity, but: "If the activity continues beyond the realistic affective needs of the infant, it encourages continuance of the symbolic union of the infant with the mother, and delays development of differentiation between self and nonself." [621] Case studies of *some* performers show that this type of development shaped their choice of careers; another factor was a parent with unfulfilled wishes to become an actor, who continued his or her dream through the child. Philip Weissman makes a valuable distinction between types of actors. "The actor who is limited to the play-action level of his art is usually an inferior, exhibitionist artist and may be emotionally disturbed. The play-acting actor controls and regulates his acting technique and therefore is likely to be a competent professional. Depending on his talent and training, he may give a highly creative performance." [621]

Human acting includes a variety of psychological processes:

1 The ability to create another character (related to body image).

2 The skill to express this to an audience.

3   An adjustment to narcissism. In primary narcissism, the infant feels omnipotent; later he feels adults are omnipotent and seeks to be reunited with powerful persons — an attempt to use the spectator through "specific ways of handling their anxieties by influencing an audience." [190] This is a magical way to influence an audience.

4   Display is a form of unconscious reassurance. To psycho-analysts, the man shows his penis as a weapon to frighten away demons; a woman shows her genitals as a threat of castration for the same purpose.

The origin of theatre was, in this sense, exhibitionist: a display, or "show," to influence spirits, gods and/or spectators. Exhibitionism has always played a large part in the unconscious of performers. Their unconscious aim is to make the audience feel the same emotion they are displaying, for "in a good theatrical performance (as in ancient worship) actor and audience feel, 'We do it together.' The audience, knowing it is 'only a play,' loses its fear of the deed, and the actor (likewise the author), secure in the same knowledge, loses his feeling of guilt through the approval of the brothers (audience) which releases him, the hero, of his loneliness." [190] Actors are in a key state of balance. Unconsciously they wish to seduce, charm, intimidate or destroy the audience. Yet they cannot: they would turn the audience against them. Aristotle's pity and fear must be evoked: "The fear of God who was imitated by the acting priests was certainly one of the main aims of the primeval theatre. [Also the] combination of seduction and intimidation is the essential content of all totem festivals, initiation rites, and theatrical performances." [190] Actors constantly test the possibilities of the self — test identifications. They display their physical self but conceal their actual self in the character; yet, as no good actor can create an emotion they have not experienced to some extent, in a sense they are playing themselves. We all imagine what we would like to be, but the actor has a high number of imaginary selves. By acting a part, actors displace tensions onto imaginary persons and sublimate "unmastered" anxieties by identifying with them. In a very real sense, acting is an extension of dramatic play: both are ways whereby we test reality, get rid of our anxieties, and master the environment. It is little wonder that drama therapy and dramatic learning are so powerful.

The Dramatist

The dramatist deals in the art of conflict and action like the actor, says Weissman, but without the latter's specificity. Some dramatists tend towards acting-out but this is not the source of their creative talent. A dramatist must be dissociated enough to transform unconscious tensions into creative enactments, a function of the ego. Delayed re-enactment is essential to a dramatist's creativity. The dramatist creates action, most precisely, through verbal representations of actions. Thus

> what is significant is that the dramatist must contain his personal tendencies toward action — be they impulsive, direct, delayed, or acting out — and must redirect this tendency into his creations. A playwright of political, religious, romantic, or psychological drama cannot be a ruler, a priest, a lover, or a psychiatrist. Hence, whatever his personal traits, habits, and drives may be, in his artistic life the direct expression of his personal actions must be transmuted into his dramatic actions. [621]

The playwright resolves the world as it matters to him and designs his characters as he imagines them to be. This relation of conscious/ unconscious is specific: e.g., Bernard Shaw created the *ménage à trois* of Eliza, Higgins and Pickering in *Pygmalion* from his own childhood. The dramatist tries to portray his own special views and feelings, but "he is *unconsciously* driven by revived, forgotten, unresolved, traumatic, and unpleasant childhood experiences to recreate new solutions that aspire to restore an integrated equilibrium to the disturbing effects of these long lingering incidents and fantasies." [621] Since the Greeks the dramatist has been mainly concerned with the tensions of the family situations, and the Oedipal theme has been at the core of plays by writers for centuries: Sophocles, Shakespeare, Sartre, O'Neill, Pirandello, etc. So "the dramatist's script is much like a manifest dream. The produced play can be compared to the latent content and secondary elaboration of the dream." [621] Actor and dramatist have different unconscious relations with the audience: the actor anthropomorphizes them into a single person ("warm" or "cold"), while the dramatist writes for society as a whole.

The Artistic Director

Part of the Oedipal situation is the wish to become the parent. With the director "the identification is transformed and expressed in the sublimated wish to be an artistic parent to his artistic children, the performers." [621] Gordon Craig's identification with his mother, Ellen Terry, was specific: from his youthful wish to resolve her financial problems, he identified himself with the paternalist figure of Henry Irving, who actually did solve them. His ambition to establish a permanent theatre of his own displaced his wish to provide for and protect his mother's children. From his fear of the dark (when "E. T." had to leave him to go to the theatre) came the wish for a strong father. He reversed the role: he came to be "the man who could save the theatre."

The artistic director identifies with the ego-ideals of his parents. His sublimation of rivalry with the father reinforces the child's artistic endowment "and drives toward a paternally influenced directorial career in a maternally influenced artist world." [621] He "brings up" a script as if it were his own child. Like parents with children, he may treat a script in a cavalier fashion or with devotion. He identifies with its contents. But in many famous instances (e.g., the Greek tragedians, Shakespeare and Molière) he may also be the playwright: he can fail when he does not identify with his own works, as well as those of others because, once written, it is no longer part of himself. In other instances (Irving, Gielgud), the director may also be the leading player. He may fail when the necessary self-exhibitionism of the actor conflicts with his parental identification.

The Audience

What do we appreciate in a great play? Freud said that there is a mutual identification between the artist and the audience. The hero's "repressed desire is one of those that are similarly repressed in all of us, the repression of which belongs to an early stage of our individual development, while the situation of the play shatters precisely this repression. Because of these two features it is easy for us to recognize ourselves in the hero." [228] The creating artist identifies with the audience. The audience identifies with what the artist communicates. Theatre, for Freud, is concerned with "the struggle of the repressed impulse to become conscious, recognizable though it is, is so little given to a definite name that the process of reaching consciousness goes on in turn within the spectator while his attention is distracted and he is in the grip of his emotion, rather than capable of rational judgments." [228] Fenichel says that the actor and the audience need each other and, in theatre, both feel "We do it together." [189] And Kanzer can say that the audience engages in group sublimation: "The isolation, the privacy of the proceedings, the resentment and tension of being interrupted, the recurrent and ritualistic need for renewed participation — all testify to the basic drive that is being discharged." [345]

But is an audience's identification a similar process to the identification of the infant? Daniel E. Schneider thinks so:

> We *identify* ourselves with the created protagonists and react to their antagonists as though *we* were alive upon the stage. We *identify* ourselves, in our very bowels, with the protagonist: we *project* ourselves onto the setting and on the furniture, *feel* the dialogue as though it came off our own tongues, know the am-

bivalence (conflicting virtue) of love and hate, work up to the self-
same pitch of crisis and climax, and "let go" only slowly as the
resolution of the conflict permits us to recover ourselves as audience rather than as participant. *That* is theatre! . . . When we
identify, we do not "pattern ourselves after" a model; we *become*
him. . . . Not only do we identify with the character's person —
with his *Ego*; we identify with his *traditions and ideals* — his
Super Ego; in his portrayed time and place — with his history;
for an evening in the theatre, we even take over some portion of
his Id: his repressions, organised as they are with his primitive,
archaic and elemental impulses, and held back by his traditions
and ideals. [541]

Quite obviously, the audience's identification parallels that of the
young child. But if we emphasize the preconscious, like Kris, the
audience has three relationships to the art work: *recognition* — the
content is familiar and related to a memory trace; *experience* of the
role becomes part of the spectator; and *identification* with the character.

Kris contributes to the theory of comedy and its effect upon the
audience. Comedy helps to overcome the strange and the terrifying.
It presupposes control over emotion before it becomes effective; with
control, comedy combines mastery and pleasure. The comic mask
conceals something sinister and dreaded. "When we laugh at the
fool, we never forget that in his comic fancy dress, with bladder and
cap, he still carries crown and sceptre, symbols of kingship." [362]
The fool is the human being, good and bad, who inherits power
from a spirit or demon. The uncanny and the comic are similar; the
derivation of many European words mean both: e.g., *drôle* in French
and *komisch* in German. Comedy is double-edged. Kris defines the
grotesque as "sudden and surprising relief from anxiety which leads
to laughter." [362] He also links the comic to exhibitionism: the
comic is a defence, one form of which can be exhibitionist.

There is a comic ambiguity to which an audience responds. The
effect of a comic symbol upon them is imprecise; they have a range
of responses to it which are grouped in clusters. Multiple meanings
are not necessarily explicit to the artist or audience; they remain
preconscious, "in the back of the mind." An audience's criteria for
interpretation are:

1   correspondence with the content of the work; e.g., knowl-
     edge of myth is needed to understand T. S. Eliot;

2   intent, or the person's contextual knowledge of his society;
     and

3   coherence: interpretation of the part must cohere with the
     whole.

These are synthesized by the audience. Kris extends this synthesis to ambiguity in the sociology of art: the degree to which an audience interprets a performance varies in time; with low ambiguity standards are strict, but if there is high ambiguity values are in doubt. Ambiguity affects the survival of a script through history: if written in a period of high ambiguity, it can mean different things at different times and so persist. Thus the plays of Cibber are unknown today but Shakespeare's are popular.

Response & Interpretation

An audience has an inner response to a dramatic event, which the critic examines from critical criteria and the therapist examines from universal themes of the human unconscious. The greater the play, the more universal the theme. The audience identifies primarily with the protagonist and secondarily with other performance elements; the greater the identification, the more "significant" it will appear to be. Many psychoanalysts have described the universal family themes (incest, guilt, aggression) in theatre from the Athenians to the present day. In Ernest Jones' *Hamlet and Oedipus*, Hamlet is examined as if he is on the psychoanalyst's couch. Fixated in the Oedipus complex, when the guilt of Claudius is revealed to him he exclaims, "O my prophetic soul! My uncle?" His uncle has fulfilled Hamlet's own guilty and unconscious wish; to kill his father and marry his mother. He is stunned by the reawakening of his internal conflict, which accounts for his (supposed) irresolution.

A strict Freudian interpretation is Franz Alexander's view of Falstaff. *Henry IV* is the study of Hal: "The bad boy, after he has thoroughly destroyed hopes in the future, turns out against all expectations to be good." [6] Hal overcomes two problems which we all face in infancy: male destruction symbolized by Hotspur, and the simple childish hedonism of Falstaff, who "represents the deep infantile layers of the personality, the simple innocent who wishes to live and enjoy life. He has no taste for abstract values like honour or duty and no ambition. . . . The indestructible narcissism of Falstaff which cannot be shaken by anything is the strongest factor in its effect upon us." [6]

Modern critics may use psychoanalytic views but more often they are inclined to use ideas from social science. The three Athenian tragedians may be seen as varying their treatments of the Orestes-Electra myth within the changing society in which they lived; and contemporary society's differing views of the same problems can be found in O'Neill's *Mourning Becomes Electra*, Sartre's *The Flies* and Jack Richardson's *The Prodigal*.

But psychoanalysis has had a further effect: it has produced the dramatist who, as Kris puts it, "borders on pathology and conquers it in his work." [362] One thinks immediately of Strindberg, Pirandello, Genet, Orton, Tennessee Williams, Arthur Miller's dramatic interpretation of Marilyn Monroe in *After The Fall*, and the Theatre of the Absurd, where "the author's communication and own responses are more totally in the realm of the preconscious and unconscious world." [621]

The Popular Theatre

The popular theatre (the fair, circus, and sideshow) and the variety show (comedy, illusions, acrobatics, song and dance) are always with us:

> The circus is the degraded pregenital arm of the theatre, but it is theatre nevertheless. It is the child's theatre, dramatizing the child's fantasies, conscious and unconscious, his day dreams, his games, his nightmares, his anxieties, his wildest dreams. There is little concern for reality. The child is presented not only with victory over space and gravity, magic and illusion, as well as triumphs over ferocious animals; he also is presented with an opportunity to work through specific anxieties and fantasies, mainly of a pregenital nature [577]

The circus offers child-like opportunities to work through disconnected problems as one act quickly follows another. Nothing is resolved. There may be reassurance against certain terrors (e.g., the infantile problem of maintaining an upright posture like tightrope walkers, or defying death like animal trainers), but no mature personal relationships are dramatized.

Clowns display in their disfigurement various kinds of castration, exhibitionism, masochism and aggression. Indeed,

> the circus is occupied with the same problems Lewis Carroll was as well as the problems which occupy fetishists and transvestites. . . . Certain patients, especially obsessive-compulsives and deeply masochistic ones, express many of their aggressions through facial grimacing. The clown mask may be considered a fixed, stylized grimace. [577]

With the clown children recall that they have overcome certain childish limitations, but they have a fantasy of unlimited childish gratifications. Slapstick and the anal aggression of the clown are related to the medieval devil with his awful stink, who could produce thunder by expelling flatus:

> Circuses and clowns are descendants of the wandering entertainers and court fools of the medieval period. Just as does the conventional theatre, the circus traces its origin to primitive religious festivals. The circus is the degraded, pregenital theatre: it deals with childlike

problems, avoiding problems of sexual maturity and sexual differentiation. It is suited for the mentality and grasp of the child. [577]

The appeal of Groucho, Chico and Harpo is that they represent three levels of regression to childhood.

Puppetry also had its origins in old religious rituals. Ancient puppets still appear in the Himalayas, and in Amerindian ritual dramas on the Pacific Coast of Canada. The earliest puppet theatre of which we know is the shadow stage of East India c. 5000 B.C., where a comic servant continually got his rich master into trouble. The form evolved through classical times to the Renascence, the English Punch and Judy, the French Guignol, the Russian Petrushka, the German Hanswurst (Kasper), and the Turkish Karagoz. The central figure is normally an earthy "average man," brave and cowardly, clever and naive, full of hope and despair, who trusts and is trusted but rejects and is rejected. The type remains today, as in the therapeutic puppet shows at Bellevue Hospital, New York, described by Adolf G. Woltman. The puppets were designed to correspond with what were thought to be the child audience's desires and wishes, and, as a result, they had a strong identification with them.

We come full circle. The therapist sees the theatre as a reflection of the unconscious. The audience identifies with the action, and the analyst uses this identification process for therapy and to understand what is a great play.

Experimental Theatre

Experimental or "process" theatre is a Western phenomenon from the 1960's and 70's: street theatre, ghetto theatre, Happenings, etc.

Happenings & Others

Happenings deliberately use the unconscious, as Jean-Jaques Lebel says: "The free functioning of creative abilities without regard for what pleases or what sells, or for the moral judgments pronounced against certain collective aspects of these activities [created] the necessity of going beyond the aberrant subject-object relationship." [378] Michael Kirby says the Happening mixes Brecht's social purposes with the release of the unconscious. Allan Kaprow describes how he achieves this integration:

> My works are conceived on, generally, four levels. One is the direct "suchness" of every action, whether with others, or by themselves, with no more waning than the sheer immediacy of what is going on. This physical, sensible, tangible being is to me very important. The second is that they are performed fantasies not exactly like life, though derived from it. The third is that they are

an organized structure of events. And the fourth level, no less important, is their "meaning" in a symbolic or suggestive sense. [346]

Each Happening, however, is unique. There are many theatrical uses for the unconscious. The most startling is The People Show, which appears in the streets of London and elsewhere from time to time: three of the four originators came from educational drama. In recent years, one of the most exciting theatrical experiments has been Keith Johnstone's mask work, particularly his probing of trance-induced states. The actor begins to put on the mask, very slowly, while painting it and looking in a mirror. Once it is "ready" the actor finds it is "fixed": it is united with his unconscious; it is very powerful and increases the actor's creativity.

Educational Drama & Theatre

Theatre Centre, London, toured Brian Way's participational plays in Britain. Performed by actor-teachers (the first to be so trained), these actively encouraged the children to join in the event under strict controls to forward the dramatic action. Way chose themes suitable for specific age groups, which influenced developments elsewhere; e.g., a participational play from Victoria, B.C., Colin Skinner's *The Black Box*, was based on his research identifying the most significant items in the life of 5 year olds: their names and their birthdays. Thus the play told of a wicked witch who stole a young girl's name and birthday, and the effect on the unconscious of the participating 5-year-olds was electric.

Part Three

Play, Drama & Society

Chapter 10
Drama & Social Play

While environmental factors affecting dramatic play are significant, they have not been our focus. Now we must turn to the social theories that affect dramatic play.

Social Psychology

Sociologists and social psychologists see human beings as social animals. Originating with Marx and sociologists like Durkheim, this view is that people are determined by the forces of the environment, although a few sociologists and social psychiatrists think that heredity has a small part to play in the creation of character. But most social psychologists consider that each person and group has its own identity resulting from environmental forces.

Early American Approaches

For early behaviourists, learning is reacting. Without reaction nothing is learned. [579] Play brings adjustment: it "is the principal instrument of growth. It is safe to conclude that, without play, there would be no normal adult cognitive life; without play, no healthful development of affective life; without play, no full development of the power of will." [547] Growth through play is part of the social nature of the child, who reproduces the struggles and achievements of his developed social life. Play is the making of "the social man," and "we become like those with whom we play." [547] Play affects the socializing influence of art, providing a mutual sympathy that develops into the collective life of the people.

Harvey C. Lehman and Paul A. Witty are famous for their early scientific investigations into play, in which they emphasized the continuity of play and cultural effects such as "black children are more social in their play" and "gifted children read more and engage less frequently in physical play." Lehman and Witty concede such generalizations are not appropriate today.

Compensation

Early this century, E. S. Robinson combined Spencer's idea of compensation with "depth" psychology: a weak child, surrounded by stronger playmates, compensates for his lack through Being "as if." Lehman and Witty said that dramatic play is often compensation for a feeling of inferiority, finding a marked desire for children to help their parents; Curti saw this imitative desire as directly compensatory. Jane

Reaney eclectically used many theories to say that play compensates for the child's inability to directly express personal energy; and the child's increasing ability to sublimate strong emotions through dramatic play is a sign of growing civilization, or "growing up." S. R. Slavson mixes compensation and the theory of Recreation. The child in fantasy scales down everything into patterns that can be comprehended for two reasons: "because they compensate one for organic lacks"; and from "feelings of inferiority."

The theory of Elmer D. Mitchell and Bernard S. Mason was influential amongst social psychologists by mid-century: play is self-expression *and* compensation that denies instincts but provides a series of "universal wishes" resulting from experience. Such experiences include the wish for new experience, security, response, recognition, participation and the beautiful. Mitchell and Mason stress learned responses; habits and attitudes are the sources of motivation in play. Play forms depend on physiological and anatomical structure, such as physical fitness, primary physiological needs (e.g., hunger, thirst, sex), and habits and attitudes socially acquired. But "when motives cannot be realized and desires satisfied by direct overt activity the individual seeks compensatory satisfaction through imagination, either in imaginative play or in daydreaming or in fantasy." [434]

The Group

The Group & Dramatic Acts

Group psychology affects educational drama in two ways: improvisation and rehearsals occur in groups; and theatre centres on the interaction of two groups, the players and the audience.

For Freud social groups focus on the biological unity of the family: less the actual family than as it appears to the child's imagination; the two are by no means the same. The imaginary family, says Money-Kyrle, contains four parents: two good and two bad — the prototypes of divinities/devils, good/evil, etc. So "when a number of individuals find common symbols for the elements in this unconscious pattern they form a group. They have common values to defend, a common enemy, a common leader and a common standard of behaviour." [436] In contrast, other scholars study the group as a group: work groups, or groups doing a specific task. They look for causes of behaviour within the environment. Most say that a person's ability to participate in groups is influenced by the initial mother/child group and its extensions (the family). Improvisors react to their family group in ways similar to improvisation and vice versa.

W. H. Sprott defines the group as "a plurality of persons who interact with one another in a given context more than they interact with anyone else." [569] They focus on interaction and have a moral basis, but vary in how tight their standards are. Primary groups meet face-to-face but secondary groups (nation, city, trade union) achieve unity through symbolic means (e.g., language, etc.). Members are seen as a social entity: "The self, as that which can be object to itself, is essentially a social structure, and it arises from social experience." [422] Sprott says that "a permissive social environment shapes and produces one sort of personality, an authoritarian one produces another. Permission is not the removal of social influence so that the 'natural' personality can have a chance to develop; it merely replaces one kind of social influence for another." [569] Groups in educational drama provide students with a specifically structured environment which influences their thought and acts.

Group pressure towards conformity is mainly from parents, adults and peers; other influences include the class, school, and aspects of society as a whole, like the mass media. An improvisational group is transitory: when group choice is free (as it usually is), some tend to stay in the same group. Most tend to conform; to be with those like themselves, to stick to the familiar. Friends tend to become like one another; even a judgment on matters of fact (like the size or weight of objects) tends to be influenced by the group. When drama teachers say the child "is working well within the group," they mean he is trying to reduce his dissonance with others. (A word of warning: adults who do not conform are less rigid and authoritarian but more effective intellectually, mature in social relationships, confident, objective and realistic about their parents, and more permissive in their attitudes to child-rearing. [460]) Different patterns of communication are better for different purposes; e.g., if five people try to solve a problem in a group, it is best if one is at the centre to organize solutions. Spatial relations alter communication: when two people sit at a table, it is best if they sit on two sides of one corner and not opposite each other. [273]

The whole class of young children often begin with the teacher telling a story, but only teachers using the Heathcote method continue with whole class activity all the time. Most others lead to improvisation so that students progress from pairs, small groups, to the class, increasing their responsibility for organization and freedom in preparation/performance. Adolescent problems can usually be overcome if the group is bound together by friendship; any leader is approved by the members and vice versa; the group task is within the understanding and capability of the group with good opportunity for success; and the teacher has a suitably permissive attitude to encourage group initiative. The most effective group size depends on the task (with seniors it is usually about 5).

Group Dynamics

The most popular ways of studying the dynamics of groups are sociometry, field theory, group systems and group psychotherapy. First developed by Moreno, sociometry asks group members to express their preferences for each other in terms of companionship or working partnership. A group has large reservoirs of feeling: complicated patterns of attraction, repulsion and neutrality. The sociometric test asks all participants a series of specific questions (e.g., "who would you like to share a room with?") and not general ones (e.g., "whom do you like best?"). Diagrams are prepared with a triangle for a boy, a circle for a girl; arrows show how each child chooses friends. This test reveals pairs chosen by no one but each other; cliques; chains of friendship; popular stars; and unchosen isolates; and it gives the teacher data about the social structure of the classroom. The test does *not* give total information about a student: an isolate in one class can be a star in another. Sociometry is used in many events (in work processes, group therapy, etc.), and for research.

Created by Kurt Lewin, field theory studies the individual/environment (a *psychological field*) and of the group/environment (a *social field*) through groups, sub-groups, members, barriers, channels of communication, etc., which have relative positions in a field in each group. A group has a field of forces that determine group behaviour: a person in a group is exposed to inner and outer tensions. Each culture activates its own tensions so personality types depend on a culture. For example, people behave differently in "social climates"; they show more solidarity/learning/productivity in a democratic "climate" than in others. While democracy (choice of leadership/relative freedom of action) aids good creative group work, individuality and the past history of the child are still important factors, *pace* Lewin. Also each group has a purpose, an "external system" consisting of three factors: sentiment, activity and interaction. These lead to mutual sentiments which constitute "the internal system." A group can be studied through these two systems: "The higher a rank of a person within a group, the more nearly his activities conform to the norms of a group [and] a person of higher social rank than another originates interaction for the latter more often than the latter originates action for him. [294] Most importantly, dramatic groupings must always be for a purpose that is both understood and felt.

W. R. Bion describes how a group studies its own interactional processes, and how it gradually learns to recognize and deal with the latent bonds of hostility and affection that exist within it. At first used in therapy, group psychotherapy (under various names) occurs in factories, [316] hospitals, [427] teacher education, [287] tutorial groups, [516] and other contexts. People's initial reactions to relationships are guided by the past, feelings from childhood that affect adult operations: "To be favourable, learning experiences should connect easily with our aspirations and should provide us with roles which enable us to develop the kinds of relationships in terms of which our ideal self image is cast." [443] In educational drama a successful group is dependent upon specific social learnings: whether it can persuade individuals to abandon private objectives; move from a focus on the leader to intrinsic interests; understand a common task which has adequate opportunity for the members' participation; and successfully negotiate with others ("read" them). [3, 139, 301, 443]

The Audience

An audience is a necessary precondition for theatre but not for spontaneous drama (where it might be assumed). It is a collection of persons in which each responds both as an individual and as a member of the group. Psychoanalytically three things occur within each audience member: his unconscious reacts to the unconconscious level of the presentation; he relates to the subject matter, the action and the characters; and he synthesizes its content, intent and coherence. The presence of an audience is the major difference between theatre (plays, dance, opera, etc.) and other art forms. Visual arts need only one witness and, while we can attend to music in a large audience, we can also do so as a single listener. But in the playhouse an audience is a prerequisite: it joins in the creation of the art work which, without this reaction, does not exist — as any actor knows who has performed to an empty house. Theatre art has an immediacy lacking in any other art form.

An audience is a unit made up of diverse elements; it has a lower intellectual level than its individual members; it cannot follow a logical argument; it is emotionally acute; it can be gripped by the Being "as if" and simultaneously can be distanced from it; and it does not, like a crowd or a mob, make this fiction a motive for action (with the notable exception of Brecht). [73] An audience has a pressure towards conformity: we have all found the beginning of a comedy unfunny yet, slowly, we catch the laughter of others. This conformity is not necessarily permanent (we can be "carried away" by the presentation but later reflect that "perhaps it wasn't so good after all"), and it varies with the sophistication of its members: the Edwardian music-hall required more conformity than the programme playing down the street at the Royal Court Theatre under the Vedrenne-Barker management. There are variations between periods:

a late 20th century audience rarely needs the conformity required of 19th century melodrama. *East Lynne*, played seriously, is a notable exception.

Social structures and audience behaviours can alter the nature of theatre, playwriting, direction and acting. In the early 19th century, with the custom of the evening meal coming early, a London show had time for a play in five acts with scenic splendours, and other entertainments. During the century, society moved its evening meal later: plays began later and were shortened to a three act structure. As the London public transport system grew, more middle class people attended, so meal habits became even more important. The arrival of the middle class meant a more discriminating taste; acting and production became less extravagant and more sophisticated.

The physical nature of the playhouse influences the relation of audience to the performance and, thus, the dramatic form. In the English Renascence many theatrical performances were in the open air with the audience on three sides, a natural growth from the practice in the Middle Ages: tempered by the interior form used by the Interlude performers in the great halls, the result was The Globe. But with Inigo Jones, the picture frame stage with its scenic splendours inside a building created a unique audience/actor relationship. Where Burbage had been backed by Elizabethan architecture and surrounded by the audience, now the actor performed at one end of a hall against painted scenery illuminated by artificial light. Naturally the plays differed. Essentially theatre is an art form that lives in the process of formation: dramatist, players and audience create it and without any one of these the art form cannot exist.

Dramatism

Contemporary sociology and social psychology use "the dramaturgical perspective." It originated earlier in this century as "symbolic interactionism": the study of social interactions through the symbols used.

In the 1930's Kenneth Burke sketched the beginnings of a "dramatistic model" of human acts: human behaviour is about action and purpose; it is more analyzable by theories of *action* than of *knowledge* — best achieved in terms of *drama*. This social perspective has a great impact on educational drama. Dramatism views Being "as if" as the nub of both the self and society. The person is a social entity. Meanings arise from the consensus between human actors, who are symbol users; the meaning of symbols (social meaning) is only given through interaction. Thus human reality is socially constructed [422] and meaning is relative to the self.

The self, as G. H. Mead says, is created by the activity of the self and others towards it; it is a shared, interactive phenomenon. Acts establish the self, not the other way round. A person uses the basic resources of the culture and acts in many possible ways to create new meanings and re-create old. For Mead, motives are not forces that move people to act: they are inherent in the human organism (as seen in Chapter 8). They link "who we are" with "what we are doing." Society is not an enemy that does things to the individual, as some critical pedagogues think; nor does it determine us. Society only exists in human interaction which cannot be explained through causes; but we can analyze its possible consequences as being of necessary but not of sufficient quality. People act: their appearances and stagings, together with the audiences' responses, are what defines social situations. This means that the nonverbal is as significant as the verbal: *how* people communicate is as important as *what* they say and do.

Dramatism provides an important contemporary image of human beings, one with multiform applications and considerable explanatory power. It is a shift from the mechanistic, causal and determinist models of Newton, Darwin, Marx and Freud to the Einsteinian model. Unlike other models, dramatism is not drawn from science but directly from human life: a field of human actions that are transformative, in transactional process and the mode of Being "as if," and a complexity of reciprocal social relations.

Kenneth Burke

The work of Kenneth Burke is seminal to dramatism. He makes a vital distinction between action and motion: people are "symbol-using animals," who have an inherent capacity for symbolic activity and, therefore, are not explainable in simple physicalist terms. Conscious actions are not reducible to motion. "*Things* move, *men* act." We inhabit a symbolic universe as well as a physical one. This universe is a close parallel to the "play world," "aesthetic world" and "fictional world" of other thinkers.

Life *is* drama for Burke. Action is behaviour structured by symbols. This implies choice, conflict and cooperation which we communicate to one another. Society is a drama in which actions (social symbols) are the crucial events. Life and theatre are homologous: they both deal with the fundamental problems of human existence and aim at the symbolic resolution of conflict through communication. Burke conceives action in a dramatic paradigm: *Scene, Act, Agent, Agency, Purpose* (and later he adds "attitude" as incipient act). These are the criteria whereby we understand action: actions occur in a social scene, conducted by an agent with a conception ("attitude") about what is "appropriate" to the scene; the actor uses the means available to accomplish the action which is done for some purpose. This is not an ontology but a description of what occurs.

Others

Hugh Dalziel Duncan translates Burke's paradigm (life *is* drama) into sociology: stage or social situation, kind of act, social role, means of expression, and ends, goals or values. He links the conduct of sociodrama to social communication: the communication of symbols is dramatic. Like Duncan, Peter Berger tries to link dramatism to other social theorists (e.g., Simmel and Mead) but in a phenomenological way: the dramaturgy of life is linked to "fictions." Alfred Schutz' phenomenological dramatism has a strong influence on Maurice Natanson, for whom (like Sartre) the person is an actor, and the condensed aesthetic life of the playhouse is an analogue of mundane life.

Others see the relation between life and drama as self-presentation, like Socrates. For Ernest Becker, we present ourselves to each other with our own self at stake: our self-esteem can be attacked, even destroyed, in a social encounter so we present a "mask" to the world; roles give us a buffer and tell us how to act "on-stage" as a doctor, lawyer, employer or wife.

For Erving Goffman, the expressiveness of a person results in two types of signs: the expression that he *gives*, which involves verbal symbols or their substitutes; and the expression that he *gives off*, a wide range of action that others can treat as symptomatic of the actor (putting up a front) and are the result of the setting, the actor's appearance and manner. Goffman also says that the individual typically infuses his activity with signs that dramatically highlight and portray confirmatory facts. These facts might otherwise remain unapparent or obscure. So that personal actions are significant, the individual mobilizes an activity to convey or express *a personal wish during the interaction*. Some roles — prizefighters, surgeons, violinists — easily achieve their dramatic realization because their activity is wonderfully adapted to the performance of their status. Goffman shows that it is a common view that a performance presents an idealized view of the situation. Thus, when individuals present themselves before others, their performance will tend to incorporate and exemplify the officially accredited values of that society. In most stratified societies, there is an idealization of the higher strata and some aspiration on the part of the lower to move to higher ones. Upper mobility often presents proper performances; efforts to move upward, and efforts to prevent downward movement, are often expressed by sacrifices made for the maintenance of front. [247]

Goffman's work links to the "status games" of Keith Johnstone, the TA of Eric Berne, and the "social dramas" of Victor W. Turner. Other important studies include Michael Banton's analysis of social structure through roles, Dorothy Emmet's view of roles and ethics, and Elizabeth Burns' dramatism of theatre and dramatic literature.

Critical Pedagogy

Critical pedagogy is a sociological way of working: an intellectual tool, like semiotics. Critical pedagogy comes from two sources. First is the determinist and dialectical way of thinking: it inherits from Marx a focus on "the political economy of schooling"; it relies on the Freudo-Marxism of the "Frankfurt School" (pre-World War II: Benjamin, Fromm, Marcuse, etc.) and a second generation of critics, such as Jurgen Habermas. Critical pedagogues examine education from the perspective of the poor and the oppressed: schooling is a political and economic enterprise, where social empowerment is ethically prior to the learning of skills.

But critical pedagogy also derives from the modern Brazilian educator, Paulo Freire, who agrees with these ends but arrives there from a somewhat different view. He says poverty and illiteracy are tied to politics: to oppressive social structures and the inequality of power. He tries to transform these in all of his projects, including his adult literacy programs, by giving the poor the power to engage in social analysis, political activism, and understanding so that they can change the world. When Freire advocates praxis (action based on reflection) he stresses the need for a fundamental faith in dialogue and community, which links his work with Bakhtin and Buber rather than Marx and Freud. *Freire requires "dialogical communication,"* dialogue being "living one's life in relation to others" — a *dramatic* view.

Critical pedagogy epitomizes a specific problem for some modern critics. The dialectic and dialogic traditions may have similar aims but each uses different perspectives to reach them. Dialectic vs. dialogue may be viewed as: objectivity vs. human engagement, science vs. art, collectivity vs. community, etc. Thus when Henry Giroux says that schools have different values, that conventions and knowledges intersect, he does so from a dialectical perspective. But when Peter L. McLaren asks, "what would you have done differently if you were in my place, and why?" this is a dialogic and dramatic question. The tension characterizes the field and it is, as Barthes said about structuralism, a dramatic tension.

Chapter 11
Drama & Cultural Thought

Wagner said that theatre is inconceivable except as an activity of the community. Drama is a social phenomenon inextricably linked to the origins of society. The full range of dramatic activity, from play to theatre, occurs in each civilized society but it varies according to cultural development. How do theories of the cultural origins of society affect educational drama?

Psycho-Anthropology

Freud used the determinist anthropology of his time from Darwin, Frazer, Roberston Smith and others, for his own theory. The first society was "the primal horde" (a Darwinian notion): a powerful male was the absolute ruler over the young males and kept all the women for his own use; the young males revolted, killed the "father" and ate his body; their hatred for the father included affection, so there was atonement and reparation. Thus arises the totem, a sacred animal or plant which must not be killed because it symbolizes the father and (as other males were his sons and females his wives) the whole group. The only exception is the sacred re-enactment of the initial crime (a symbolic re-play), where the totem clan eats the totem father. Competition for the father's women may repeat the patricide so males must marry outside the group (exogamy); as the women were the father's wives, incest is prohibited; and as the father was introjected, his will is the law of the society. Myths of the origins of society curb peoplcs' sexual and aggressive drives so that society's function is mainly oppressive. [215] As J. A. C. Brown says:

> In a single hypothesis, he explains the origins of society, of religion and law, of totemism, of the incest taboo and exogamy, and of ritual and myths. Law curbs the sexual and aggressive drives, religion, myth and ritual commemorate the crime and assuage guilt, and society is the overall mechanism of control. In the course of time the myths relating to the ritual (the ceremonial representation of the original act) led to the drama of Sophocles and Aeschylus which still makes use of the material supplied by myths, and at a further remove the modern theatre. Surely no theory has ever explained, or attempted to explain, so much. [78]

Freud used Jung's collective unconscious to explain the occurrence of fixed symbols in dreams and myths [334], and dramatic play has the same content as myths, rituals, folk-lore and the like.

Essentially the collective unconscious is an anthropological concept. For Jung "collective representations" are a group's basic beliefs and assumptions transmitted down the generations. Archetypes are symbols of society "expressed through individuals; on the other hand, individuals must rely on the collective material for the basic content of their personalities." [497] The intuitive symbol is beyond cognition; it is a "living thing" and "pregnant with meaning." [335] Thus

> there is no reason for believing that the psyche, with its peculiar structure, is the only thing in the world that has no history beyond its individual manifestation. Even the conscious mind cannot be denied a history stretching over at least five thousand years. But the unconscious psyche is not only immensely old, it is also able to grow increasingly into an equally remote future. [335]

Organized religion ritualizes "the living process of the unconscious in the form of the drama of repentance, sacrifice and redemption." [337] Freud tries to create an "*objective* science": religion externalizes human unconscious conflicts raised to a cosmic level; [225] it is "the universal obsessional neurosis of humanity"; a loving heavenly Father promises happiness hereafter in return for giving up instinctual desires. [224] But Jung tries to create a "*human* science": the symbols of the collective unconscious are those of humanity and society; their religious function can influence people as powerfully as sexuality and aggression.

Otto Rank alters Freud. The "father" was insignificant. The primal horde centered on group marriage: the children belonged to a group of Mothers; the birth trauma led to a desire to return to the womb; and the father was killed trying to prevent the sons from achieving this. But the youngest son "remains as it were permanently attached to her: no one after him has occupied the place in the mother." [503] He is the Hero. He overthrows the matriarchy and males dominate society; women are excluded to repress the memory of the birth trauma. For Rank the Crucifixion represents punishment for killing the father, resurrection is the birth and Mary is the sublimated mother. Contemporary theory agrees that the earliest society was matriarchal and that the Indo-Europeans made it patriarchal. The growth of society has been a gradual withdrawal from the female into sublimated forms: primitive art created vessels and statuettes as maternal symbols. As these societies modified, male elements became predominant in the growing cult of the sun-father:

> The development of sun worship always goes hand in hand with a decisive turning from the mother-culture to father-culture, as is shown in the final identification of the new born king (*infant*) with the sun. This opposition to the dominance of the woman both in the social sphere (right of the father) and in the religious, continues [to] Greece where it leads by means of the entire repression of woman even from the erotic life, to the richest blossoming of the

masculine civilization and to the artistic idealization leading to it. [Art is] imitation of one's own growing and origin from the maternal vessel [and the creative artist is] a newly created whole, the strong personality with its autonomous will, which represents the highest creation of the integration of will and spirit. [503]

Personality & Culture

The idea that personality is created by culture is shared by scholars with wide varieties of view. Amongst analysts, Wilhelm Reich said "every social order creates those character forms which it needs for its preservation. In class society, the ruling class secures its position with the aid of education and the institution of the family, by making its ideologies the ruling ideologies of all members of the society." [509] The psychologist who subordinated personality to the socio-economic system was Abraham Kardiner, who said that child-rearing patterns produce "a basic personality structure" within which exists the individual's character: "the special variation in each individual to this cultural norm." [347] Thus food anxiety affects behaviour and the formation of character: the Marquesans have serious crop failures, there are proscriptions on food, and hypochondriacal characteristics occur. A basic personality type "provides the members of the society with common understandings and values and makes possible the unified emotional response of the society's members to situations in which their common values are involved." [392] But societies divide their membership into status groups and "these status-linked configurations may be termed *status personalities* [which] are superimposed upon its basic personality type and are thoroughly integrated with the latter." [392] Culture affects children's behaviour, the behaviour of others towards them, and the children's observation of, and instruction in, the normal actions of the society. The child's response to a new situation "may be developed primarily through imitation, through logical processes, or through trial and error," [392] so that the interaction of early childhood techniques and society's institutions affect the personality, art, mythology and religion.

"Neo-Freudians" reject Freud's theories of instinct and libido. Horney, Fromm and Sullivan say that social and cultural factors form human nature. For Karen Horney, child growth depends not on oral, anal and genital stages but on how the child is treated; "if others do not love and respect [the child] for what he is they should at least pay attention to him and admire him," [297] admiration being a substitute for love. "Normal" is a cultural term: "With us a person would be neurotic or psychotic who talked by the hour with his deceased grandfather, whereas such communication with ancestors is a recognized pattern in some Indian tribes." [298] Anxiety comes from a feeling that one is "small, insignificant, helpless, endangered, in a world that is out to abuse, attack, humiliate, betray, envy." [296] Horney then attempts to show three human attitudes — a moving towards, a moving against, and a moving away — which, with neurotics, become helplessness, hostility and isolation.

Erich Fromm shows "not only how passions, desires, anxieties, change and develop as a *result* of the social process, but also how man's energies thus shaped into specific forms in their turn become *productive forces, moulding the social process.*" [236] In culture we relate to society; we store past knowledge symbolically, imagine possibilities, and adapt to society. Basic character types alter as society changes. Harry S. Sullivan sees two main purposes in human activity: satisfaction and security (physical and cultural needs). The empathy between the young child (6-27 months) and the mother is fundamentally non-verbal, and the mother's approval or disapproval produces two opposite states: euphoria and anxiety (comfort vs. discomfort). From these states emerge three possible views the infant has of the self: the "good me" when praised; the "bad me" when blamed; and the "not me" in horror or shock. Anxiety occurs when biological drives cannot be satisfied through culturally approved patterns. [373] These three thinkers are nearer to Adler than Freud while Sullivan, with an emphasis on field concepts, approaches Kurt Lewin.

Anthropology, Drama & Mind

Many socially based theories of personality occurred when anthropology provided new facts to question Freud's views. Bronislaw Malinowski denied the Oedipus complex: some Polynesians were raised by the mother's brother; the boy repressed the wish to marry his sister because he was jealous of his maternal uncle. Was Freud merely studying central European trends? Freudians try to disprove Malinowski [523] and most anthropologists dismiss Freud, but some have not been unaffected by depth psychology, as we shall see below.

Cross-Cultural Studies

Others examine peoples cross-culturally, accepting some of Freud's personality concepts but rejecting his social theories. Margaret Mead studied the relation of personality to society in many places and, although her work has recently been criticized, it contains rich data. In her view male/female differences are not biological: New Guinea tribes can vary these roles and some reverse the roles as we know them. Different cultures produce diverse personalities: the Arapesh are cooperative, unaggressive, gentle to children and disapprove of self-assertion; but the Mundugumor are uncooperative, aggressive, harsh to children, and have a natural hostility to everyone of the same sex. Like Freud, Mead correlates events in early childhood and adult life. Dramatic patterns in initiations overcome childhood influences differently: to acclaim the child as an adult in his own right; or to break an identification with the mother. Child-rearing habits and the supernatural are linked: children brought up with kindness believe the spirits or gods to be kind, but those brought up harshly do not. [424] Ruth Benedict found the same personality type amongst the Zuñi as Mead found with the Arapesh; but the Zuñi were so different from Europeans that they tried to lose a race rather than win it; they had no wish to assume authority and were bad at it. She also contrasted the Dobu, who had a permanent persecution suspicion, with the Inuit, among whom war was unknown. [44]

Contemporary studies find many items in other cultures that differ from our own. [496] Perception can be affected by a person's context: a common illusion is that when two lines of equal length are placed end to end at right angles, the vertical appears longer; but in certain African tribes the results vary — those in high open country are less prone to the illusion than those in the jungle. The ecology of peoples is probably vital to the interaction of perceiver and environment. Habitat produces functional differences in vision: Arabs in the Sahara desert tend to see in horizontals, pygmies in the forest in verticals, but Europeans are in "a carpentered world": we live in a culture in which straight lines abound, and in which perhaps 90% of the acute and obtuse angles formed on our retina by the straight lines of our visual field are realistically interpreted as right angles suspended in space. If our cultural environment affects how we see, it also affects how we think and dramatize.

The Example of Bali

Gregory Bateson and Margaret Mead's study of Bali is classic. It has been followed by so many others that Bali is a good illustration of the interplay of early childhood education, adult character, and dramatic actions within a culture. A Balinese mother stimulates her child as much as possible and then "breaks off the climax." She appears to be indifferent to the child's resulting emotion, even, sometimes, borrowing other babies to increase her own child's emotion. As a result, the infant has an intense internal drama "centered about the mother's breast and a Balinese baby habitually nurses at one breast and grasps firmly at the other nipple especially when

there are any other children about." These traumatic childhood
experiences affect adult males' emotions in relation to women:

> There is a conflict which recurs in each generation in which
> parents try to force the children of brothers to marry each other; to
> stay within the family line and to worship the same ancestral gods
> while the young people themselves rebel and if possible marry
> strangers. Fathers and brothers may help a boy to carry off a girl
> who is not kin, but no male relative of a girl nor the girl herself
> can admit complicity in any such schemes. An abduction-elopement
> is staged, but the boy fears that he will not succeed and this is
> dramatized in the theatre in a frequent plot: that of the prince who
> attempts to abduct a beautiful girl but through accident gets instead
> her ugly sister: the "Beast" princess who is always dressed in the
> distinctive costume worn by mothers and mothers-in-law. [39]

This schizophrenic anxiety in adults is reflected not only in the
theatre but also in a variety of dramatic forms. In a popular court-
ship dance:

> Little skilled girls especially decked out and trained are taken from
> village to village by an accompanying orchestra and dance in the
> street; sometimes with partners who have come with them but more
> excitingly with members of the crowd. The little *djoget* coquettes
> and flirts, follows faithfully in the pattern and rhythm the leads
> given by the villager who dances with her, but always fends him
> off with her fan, always eludes him, approaches, retreats, denies in
> a fitful unrewarding sequence, tantalizing and remote. Sometimes in
> the very midst of such a scene the tune played by the orchestra
> changes to the music of the Tjalonarang (the Witch play), a cloth
> and a doll appear as if by magic, and the little dancer, still looking
> her part as the cynosure of all male eyes, suddenly becomes the
> Witch. She strikes the characteristic attitudes, waves her cloth and
> dances, balanced on one foot, tentatively threatening to step on the
> baby doll which she has just flung upon the ground — a pan-
> tomimic statement that witches feed on newborn babies. And after
> the witch scene, the *djoget* will again return to the role of the
> desirable and remotely lovely girl. The dance sums up the besetting
> fear of each Balinese male that he will, after all, no matter how
> hard he seeks to find the lovely and unknown beyond the confines
> of his familiar village, marry the Witch, marry a woman whose
> attitude toward human relations will be exactly that of his own
> mother. [39]

Elsewhere the Tjalonarang, the Bali Witch play, is performed. This
full-scale ritual drama is performed by masked dancers. The plot is
an exorcism against witches; in dramatizing the Rangda's triumphs,
the people aim to obtain her good will. The Witch is angry with the
King because he (or his son) has rejected her (or her daughter) and
so she causes disaster in the land. The masked figure of the Witch is

clearly supernatural: she has tusk-like teeth and a flaming tongue, long nails and breasts that are both hairy and pendulous. The King is represented by a dragon (the Barong) who is friendly. Barongs vary but most commonly they have swags of hair or cut strips of material on the sides; plates of cut leather on the back; a magnificent arched tail; an elaborate carved mask with leather surroundings; and two operators who, like men in the English pantomime horse, display their bare feet and striped trousers below. The most common play structure is: a ceremonial beginning with a priest, the Prince and Barong meet, a fight between the Rangda and the Barong, and the defeat of the Barong; an attack upon the Rangda by male villagers with daggers; the trance of the villagers; the magical resurrection of the villagers by the Barong; and the villagers stab themselves. The attack upon the Rangda is made by young men armed with krisses:

> But she waves her magic cloth — (the baby sling) — and after each attack they crouch down before her, magically cowed. Finally, they rush upon her in pairs, stabbing ineffectually at the Witch who has become a half-limp bundle in their tense arms. She is uninvolved and offers no resistance but one by one they fall to the ground, in deep trance, some limp, some rigid! From this trance they are aroused by the Dragon who claps his jaws over them or by his priest sprinkling holy water. Now able to move again — in a somnambulist state, they turn their daggers which were powerless against the witch against their own breasts, fixing them against a spot which is said to itch unbearably. [39]

This is similar to other "death-and-resurrection" ritual dramas but elsewhere evil is eventually defeated. In the Bali Witch Play, as in childhood, the actor is rejected, and turns in upon himself.

Myth & Unconscious Symbol

Contemporary mythological studies, including those of Joseph Campbell and Mircea Eliade, show that in oral cultures myth (story) and ritual (action) are one entity. It is not until the invention of writing that myth is seen historically and known to be "false." Mythological meaning *implies action* and is mostly tacit, or unconscious. Some anthropologists use depth psychology to reveal mythological meaning. For example, Jung influences Carl Kerenyi's work on Greek mythology, and Heinrich Zimmer's discussion of the collective unconscious in Hindu, Buddhist, Celtic and other myths, where the archetype of the Wise Old Man is the voice of the age-old past, the personification of the wisdom of the unconscious, which appears as the Chinese aged sage, "The Old One," Lao Tse of Taoism, the guru of Hinduism, etc. Thus "the figure of Merlin is descended, through the Celtic Druids, from the ancient tribal priest and medicine man, supernaturally endowed with cosmic wisdom and the power of witchcraft, the poet and divine who can conjure invisible presences with the magic of his songs. Like Orpheus, the singer and master of the mysteries and initiations of Ancient Greece, whose harmonies tamed the wild animals and moved the mute stones to arrange themselves into walls and buildings, Merlin can command the stones." [646]

In industrial and multi-cultural societies, myth carries the thought of an underlying stratum of a population; it contains esoteric wisdom of deep traditions in a form ordinary people can understand. This is not an unusual occurrence. In medieval Britain, Christianity was the manifest mythology but other layers of the Celts, Anglo-Saxons and Vikings were *chthonic*: suppressed myths and rituals latent in various part of the population. Indian and Celtic mythology are linked: they are part of "the soul's most ancient dreams" but have no explicit meaning. Myth goes straight to the listener's intuition, or creative imagination. Thus intellectual and linguistic interpretations should be treated with circumspection.

Géza Róheim takes up a classic psychoanalytic position: "We can explain any specific ritual or custom on the basis of trends that are universally human and of such specific ones that occur in a given area." [524] Societies have some things in common: (1) both sacred and accursed are taboo; we desire what we pretend to abhor; (2) the universal incest prohibition protects against this desire; (3) survivors of the horde punish themselves, by mourning, for their evil wishes against the dead — primitive kings are first exalted and then later killed; (4) all human relations are ambivalent; and (5) the primitive "omnipotence of thought" produces magic: a wish or the acting out of a situation brings the desired result. Róheim says that cultures differ in the ways in which they compromise "between the superego and the governing trauma." Thus "the strongest impression which the Australian native retains from his childhood is his love of the 'phallic' mother. Accordingly, a society develops whose group ideal is a father endowed with a vagina (i.e. a chief with the subincised penis; penis churunga covered with concentric circles symbolizing the vagina)." [524] Róheim shows that there are many common *structures* in the dramas of many peoples. The Bali Witch Play is a particular version of a death-and-resurrection structure that appears in Tibet and northern India, in ancient Sumer and Egypt, amongst the Mayans and Incas, with the Hopi and Nootka Indians, and so on.

Central to Róheim's work is that the cultural patterns of a society are directly related to the play of children. In traditional societies there are three kinds of play: motor skills; formalized games; and imitation of adults ("playing grown up") which may vary from actual attempts to copying ritual. [526] The latter still occurs with "the play potlatch" in remote villages of the Southern Kwakiutl. All three kinds hinge on identification: "The young of our species grow up by a partial identification with adults which gradually becomes a complete identification." [526] In all tribal cultures, little girls pattern themselves on their unconscious mother-figure and boys on their father-figure; and (answering Malinowski) it makes no difference whether the child is brought up by real or surrogate parents. Róheim echoes Groos and Suttie when he says that "our specific ways of adapting to reality are based on inventions and these inventions are sublimations of infantile conflict situations. Culture itself is the creation of a substitute object. . . . In this respect it is identical with the mechanism of play: a defence against separation anxiety based on the transition from the passive to the active position." [524]

At the nub of this play/culture link lies dramatization. After showing that one thing can be substituted for another in dramatic play, Róheim cites Lafcadio Hearn's comments on Japanese mimetic acts of faith: the substitution in imagination of one action for another brings about a magical result; desiring to build a temple to Buddha, but lacking the means, the Japanese deposits a pebble before his image — "it is just the same thing." Being "as if," says Róheim, "becomes a life-long, socialized and serious attitude of primitive man, and finally in its endless ramifications gives rise to our own civilization."

Thinking of the Child & Traditional Peoples

Although many scholars say that there is a relation between the thinking of the civilized child and that of traditional peoples, it is not a one-to-one, parallel relation. Rather, both have certain thought structures in common and these are reflected in their dramatic activity.

Early Thought Patterns

There is, indeed, a far-reaching parallelism between dramatic patterns in children's play and survivals from traditional life in religion, ritual, mythology and folklore. Animism, for example, is present in tribal and infantile minds; both consider that objects have emotions and experience like their own. With "omnipotence of thought" (magic) the infant can release aggression against a model just as a tribal thinker sticks pins in an effigy of his enemy, and "to some extent this happens in the therapeutic situation between the child and the therapist and in the normal situation of group play of children." [560] Then there is little difference between the intention and the act: if an action is reprehensible, the punishment is already felt.

Many customs, rituals or formulae in today's folklore were once designed to bring about results in the environment (e.g., improvement of the crops) and were based on the belief that the human mind in some way had the power to influence natural events. "One result of this unconscious over-estimation of the power of thought is a tendency to ascribe external happenings to spiritual forces and to depreciate the significance of physical factors, just as a truly religious man must logically ascribe everything to God's will and has only a limited interest in the rest of the causative chain." [326] Yet tribal people and children have their own logic for such actions: the hunter who beats a saucepan during an eclipse is attempting to frighten off the wolf who is devouring the hero.

Dramatic play, dreams and many traditional rituals result from mental projections: an imagining dramatized as actual. Dreams can be considered to be actual — one of the bases for magic. Tribal people project wizards, witches and evil spirits like infants project witch-like figures and, while both might be explained as an unconscious hostility projected into the external world, in our terms they are dramatized as hostile and purposive agents. Many result from memories of early family life and animals in particular. Children dramatize parents or siblings, who thereby take on a different life for the imaginer. Tribes see themselves as descended from animals: the ancient English from horses, the modern Nootka from wolves. Dragons, unicorns and much of heraldry arise in this way. Once dramatized, symbols have multiple meanings. Thus a cowry shell is often viewed by traditional peoples as a symbol of female pudenda, but it also is life-giving powers, or the Great Goddess, or is nothing more than a cowry shell. [326] To the child or the hunter they are concrete yet they represent the same object seen from different perspectives. Depth psychologists and anthropologists may provide further meanings but these are usually unknown to the child or the hunter. When the psychoanalyst says that these objects symbolize about half a dozen key ideas (blood relatives, body parts, birth, love and death) these meanings are "maps" and they can differ in intention: confetti thrown at a wedding actually derives from rice, but the anthropologist says it symbolizes the wish for fertility given to the bridal couple, while the analyst sees rice as the *emblem* of fertility and the *symbol* of the seed towards which all other acts and thoughts proceed. [226] Improvisers have more concrete meanings.

Similars & Opposites

Scholars in various fields identify a primary mental structure based on similarity: A is like B. Opposites are secondary and also arise from similars. For Freud this phenomenon centers on bisexuality: unconscious thoughts are positive and their opposites are seen as identical: big/little, strong/weak, etc., are interchangeable entities — which is how Melanie Klein explained the thought of the youngest children. Anthropology shows that the same condition existed in the earliest languages, where all current differentiations emerged from an initial unity of opposite ideas. Despite Lévi-Strauss and other structuralists, the basis of human thought is not binary (either/or) but unitary. Both Jung and Lévy-Bruhl say that non-logical thought of young children and tribal peoples unites things in a way that the thought of civilized people does not. When the hunter sees himself as a bird, Jung says that thought is fused together, like society, while differentiation belongs to consciousness and individuality. Being "as if" works through similarity and is nearer to the unconscious unity of thought than to the either/or.

Fairy Tales

Fairy tales also work by similars. They are didactic: their content is the dramatization of growing up. Fairy tales are only "real" in the tribal and child-like sense and are thus parallel to dreams and play. The hero is often a human being involved in magic and even his birth is strange; he may be suckled or reared by an animal, and he can develop superhuman characteristics or incredible cleverness; and he can change his form to a bird or tree, even in death. Marriage is a common plot, but the actors are dramatized projections from the unconscious: the bad stepmother, spirits of natural things (like winds and the moon), the little people, or highly dangerous figures. [55]

Fairy tales share common structures, as Vladimir Propp shows, yet each reflects the culture from which it arises: e.g., those from Germany give a high regard to children, a low value to women, and have heroes from only the high and low strata who often are soldiers.

Such tales can dramatize specific early beliefs, such as power over a person's name having power over the man, as with Rumpelstiltskin, or reflected in Genesis where God's real name cannot be said. The tales can dramatize totemism (the Bear-Son born to a bear and his human wife), cannibalism (*The Robber Bridegroom*), and magical "omnipotence" ubiquitously. J. R. R. Tolkien says: "The mind that thought of *light, heavy, grey, yellow, still, swift*, also conceived of magic that would make heavy things light and able to fly, turn grey lead into yellow gold, and the still rock into swift water. If it could do the one, it could do the other; it inevitably did both." [584]

Death

There is a fundamental early human wish to ward off dying and perpetuate life beyond the grave, as in rituals of rebirth. The unconscious cannot understand its own death but sees it as punishment: castration for Freud, a return to the womb for Rank. Endless myths and folk beliefs are based on these notions, either partially (as coitus) or wholly (as birth). The earliest death-and-resurrection rituals began with tribal shamans who, in their initiation, were "killed" in their mundane self and then resurrected in their new personality as a shaman. This theme reappeared in ancient Babylon and Egypt, and it continually recurs in dramatic play ("Bang! You're dead!").

Chapter 12
Cultural Analysis

Given that the dramatic character of societies differ, how can we study them? What criteria do we use when analyzing dramatic action in a culture? In this chapter we will examine the most useful of these criteria.

Form & Process

Drama is a human process based on imagining ("what if?") and dramatic action ("as if"). It takes a number of forms: play, improvisation, role play, ritual, and, the most hieratic, theatre. Theatre is a particular dramatic form: it is *the tip of an iceberg where the whole is the human dramatic process*. It crystallizes social issues in a specific context: the self-presentation of personages in communication with other personages and with an audience. Theatre is modelled *on* the social process and, paradoxically, it is a model *for* the social process. While an audience is not essential for play and improvisation, communication is *necessary* for theatre to exist. The form is a theatrical event where "the costumed player" performs in the "here and now," communicating with other players, in a performance which communicates to an audience. In tribal cultures, a ritual drama aims to communicate with a spirit or a god, an act closely allied to theatre and an indissoluble part of tribal life. Modern Western theatre is an attempt to communicate between I and Thou, between the dramatist and the community or, as the psychoanalyst would have it, between the unconscious of the artist and the unconscious of the audience.

But *what* is communicated? The mimetic dances of hunters or the intellectual verse of T. S. Eliot both significantly reflect the feeling-life of the community for which they were created. These cognitive and emotional meanings exist only in the context of feeling. In aesthetic terms, drama as theatre ("the art object") oscillates between the subjectivities of artists and audience. [126] Much of what is communicated is tacit. The history of theatre is the story of the human race told explicitly in events, but implicitly it tells of the interaction of mind and society.

Styles of Analysis

There are at least three styles by which contemporary scholars attempt to grasp the cultural origins of drama and theatre: (1) Ritual Analysis (ritology); (2) Performance Analysis ("performance theory");

and (3) Sociological Analysis. These are not discrete categories. Indeed, they overlap and many scholars use more than one perspective to examine a dramatic event.

Ritual Analysis

The term "ritual" has a number of popular meanings: as an act that relates the actor to the divine ("religious ritual"), or as "mere ritual" (a repetitive or habitual action), and so forth. But, in contrast, ritologists like Ronald Grimes, Victor W. Turner and Peter McLaren synthesize findings from various fields into a continuum: from simple rites to highly complex and symbolic rituals.

For ritual analysts, rituals are *human gestural acts that are processual*: a continuous flow in the "here and now" that is autotelic (i.e, it has no goals outside itself). Rituals are acted in many areas of human life for implicit and/or explicit reasons with *performative force*. Rituals are contextual; they have cultural themes and subtexts that are important for the participants whose feeling states they embody in a metaphoric way. Rituals mediate forms that have specific relations to meaning. That is, they inherently carry meaning ("the medium is the message") particularly symbolic meaning, and they create further symbolic, indexical or self-referential meanings that reinforce cultural values which are not encoded, i.e., that do not have a one-to-one meaning. Rituals provide knowledge that is tacit and embodied on the one hand, and "practical" (procedural "know how") on the other; and they are experienced by the participants as transformative and reconstructive of reality, ambiguous and dramatistic. In fact, rituals are similar to theatrical acts except that in rituals everyone is an active participant and there is no audience. The criteria that ritologists use for their analyses are three-fold, and they can be used either singly or in combination:

1   *Rites of Passage and Rites of Intensification*
Rites of Passage are acts, like initiation, where the actor passes from one societal status to another. They have three parts:

    a   *separation*: the actor is separated from an old status;

    b   *liminality*: the actor is between statuses (an "in between"), and this is usually highly dramatic; and

    c   *aggregation*: the actor reaches a new status. [589, 590, 596]

Rites of Intensification lie on a continuum, where the actor(s) are more or less intense; i.e., from possession to distancing. Rites of Passage and Intensification often cannot be distinguished: analyses of rites of passage usually include reference to their degree of intensity.

2   *Frames*
    As "frames" that bracket off aspects of social life, Goffman says rituals are a meta-communicative system, one that symbolizes alternative domains of reality with a powerful moral force.

3   *The continuum of "open" to "closed"*
    Ritologists distinguish rituals which are more spontaneous and improvised (open) and those which are predictable and fixed.

Distinctions can also be made in contemporary rituals between:

A   *an operative act* which has become formalized: a formula which marks out what is done, such as sticking a pin in an effigy, or modelling oneself on a pop star in order to impress others;

B   *a ceremony* whose elaborateness heightens the occasion and gives it aesthetic expression, such as cutting a ribbon to open a road or a building; and

C   *the sacraments*, where matter and form are equally indispensable for the efficacy of the act.

These criteria are applied to specific stages in cultural history, e.g.: tribal acts of hunting-and-gathering or herding cultures; agricultural acts in settlements and cities; and industrial acts in industrial and post-industrial cultures.

Performance Analysis

For "performance theorists," human performance is the starting point for all descriptions or analyses. Most of these theorists tend to be allied to the avant-garde theatre: Richard Schechner, for example, an enfant terrible of the alternate theatre in the 1960's, began from two concepts. First were the five basic qualities of performance: "1) *process*, something happens here and now; 2) *consequential, irremediable*, and *irrevocable* acts, exchanges, or situations; 3) *contest*, something is *at stake* for the performers and often for the spectators; 4) *initiation*, a *change in status* for participants; 5) space is used *concretely* and *organically*." [538] Second were the six interrelated elements of theatre: performer, director, text/action, time, space and audience.

These six theatrical elements are constant criteria in performance theory, if in various guises, despite quite radical differences between theorists who come from disparate experiences and have variant theories: e.g., Allan Kaprow comes from Happenings; but Peter Brook sees a playhouse as "an empty space," the imaginative neutrality of which allows the actor to move between objective and subjective experience while involving the audience collectively in "a total experience."

A   *Performers*
At the centre of Performance Analysis lies "the costumed player." His action, together with his costume (often with mask and attributes), is a living processual symbol of transformation. His performances can be viewed on a number of continua:

1   *Style* — from belief to non-belief in the transformation.
That is: magical to actual: from the tribal shamans (priests) through professional actors to social role players;

2   *How* — the way in which transformation is achieved.
That is: from Being "as if" (possession is most extreme) through the hieratic to distancing; from mimesis through mime to social action; Stanislavsky to Brecht.

B   *Text/Action*
What he performs; the dramatic action (the "text") which ranges across genres; it is written or extempore — but even in the most formal theatre some element of spontaneity exists [130]

C   *The Director*
The director varies in status from tribal dance (least important) to formal secular theatre (most important). But even in tribal performance, when the dramatic action is complex a director is required (e.g., some ritual dramas on the Pacific North West Coast).

D   *Time & Space*
The actor "lives through" fiction in the "here and now" which transforms time. The tribal ritual-myths of "origins" re-play an ancient myth (the past) in the sacred present. Modern theatre exists in the significant and perpetual present, whether it is about past or future. Both collapse time. The dramatic "here" transforms space: into sacred space (tribal) or significant space (theatre).

E   *Audience*
An audience varies: from tribal participation and "witnessing" in the Biblical sense (giving authenticity and author-

ity to a ritual event), to "responding" in contemporary
theatre. Both contribute to the form: the first more so, the
second less.

Sociological Analysis

The sociological study of theatre considers how culture patterns
and enactments inter-relate: how a community's dramatic expression
mixes with its social structure and beliefs. Victor W. Turner shows
how many tribal ritual dramas occur as the tribes face conflict.
Zevedei Barbu examines the periods when drama reached its peak in
theatrical forms (Greece in the 5th century B.C.; China between
1279 and 1368 A.D.; India in the 5th century A.D.; and 17th century
Japan, England, France and Spain), showing that these were all times
of great social tension creating "in many individuals and groups
powerful non-conformist, deviant and even anarchic tendencies." He
indicates that the 17th century Kabuki plays of Chikamatsu are
"expressions of a critical state either in the structure of society —
conflicts of loyalty, for instance — or in the relationship between the
individual and his society, between the individual's inner life and the
norms and values of society." [33]

E. J. Burton has put forward an all-inclusive sociology of
drama and theatre [94] that involves developmental stages and
period studies:

A *Developmental Stages*
The study of dramatic play involves cultural needs and patterns
(with which dramatic practice is associated) in a developmental
sequence. These are not exclusive, because we know that individual
societies do grow uniquely; however, approximately three stages
can be identified:

1 *Tribal Drama*
   Drama in a tribal community has sociological,
   psychological and religious (magical) functions
   focused on the ritual myth that satisfy specific
   needs. Evidence in previous chapters shows that
   such needs have some parallels with children's
   play and traditional games, with their associated
   speech and movement patterns.

2 *The Temple & the Beginnings of Theatre*
   Nomadic herdsmen and/or farmers began settled
   villages, and stable civilizations led to physical,
   economic and religious growths. Religion had its
   social expression in changes in the ritual myth for
   gigantic communal enactments. This led to the

establishment of the sanctuary or temple: the model
of the higher life and divinity. The stylization of
ritual became liturgy and elements of theatre
emerged.

3   *The Emergence of Theatre*
There are still surviving temple theatres (e.g., the
Kathakali in India), but in many culture areas the
theatre emerged from the temple: e.g., in Athens and
India in the 5th century B.C., in the Chou Dynasty
in China, and in medieval Europe with the growth
of the Mystery cycles. The bonds of ritual and
liturgy were loosened, performance became more
secular, and theatre emerged.

It happened variously according to the existing structure of the
culture. All cultures used the fundamental theatrical elements: acting,
identification, language, dance, dialogue, mask, music, spectacle, costume, fantasy, improvisation, stylization. Each society emphasized particular elements according to its own historical and social traditions:
e.g., from Graeco-Hebraic traditions, Western theatre emphasized "the
Word." The division of temple priests and celebrants led to the division
of actors and audience. The ritual myth persisted as the basis for plot
in two genres; in comedy as communal adjustment, and in tragedy as
ultimate experience.

Subsequent studies focus on two issues: the relation of social patterns to theatre in a specific period; and acculturation — ways that a
dominating and dominated culture interact in theatrical terms.

B   *Period studies*

4   *The Communal Dramatic Inheritance*
Each society inherits dramatic structures. In the West
today they exist mostly as folk-lore; e.g., ballads,
festivals, folk dances; variety entertainment, with
tribal origins in prowess and expertise from ancient
wedding and funeral games; carnivals and fancy-
dress parties, etc. Other social facets include the
educational and therapeutic uses of drama.

5   *Dramatic Theory*
Ideas and concepts of drama and theatre have varied
over the centuries, and between cultures. Drama and
theatre have an artistic centrality in relation to other
art forms, as Derrida and others have shown. The
sociological approach addresses many issues, some
of which are: (a) the views of the great critics (from
Aristotle to Bharata) and artists (from Goethe to
Gielgud); (b) the relation of belief to the theories of
developed culture in dramatic forms; e.g., tragic,

comic and satyric in ancient Greece; and the types
of dramatic expression in Bali from the Witch Play
to the village dance; and (c) the nature of the audience from period to period.

We shall now extrapolate from these three styles of analysis and
apply them to specific aspects of the origins of theatre.

Chapter 13
Cultural Origins of Theatre

From the styles of analysis given in Chapter 12 we will now examine the cultural origins of drama and theatre in a number of contexts.

Tribal Drama

Drama as a dance impersonating a spirit, an animal or a person, is the oldest art. From it comes the dance (dramatic movement), music (sound for acting) and art (illustrating acting). It gives purpose to other arts, religion, belief and magic. The magic of the rites helped the hunter in the chase. He half-danced, half-acted in mimesis: identifying and dancing in large movements, jumps and leaps. Using masks and skins of the animals, he created magic ("power") for a successful hunt. In the Ice Age caves at Lascaux are drawings of real men hunting real animals beside men in animal skins acting the dramas.

The earliest rites were acts of cooperation with the spirits who possessed "power" and lived in a parallel world, one more "real" than ours. The rites were "religious" but not Christian: the Church called the dancers "pagans" — adoration as we know it was absent. Living was simple survival so the rites were based on fear and the "power" to overcome it. Actors used possession to assume the fertility of the animals and plants: in a wild, frenetic dance they felt they were spirits with their "power." The more fantastic the mask, the more other dancers thought it was identified with the spirit "power"; this belief, in turn, worked on the wearer until he felt union with the "power." Possession is the extreme state of Being "as if." [206, 591] At first the whole tribe danced; then males and females separated, with the others chanting (a remote origin of the chorus). The animal priests (shamans) danced with "power" to "transform" others: initiate them, "killing" their personality and "resurrecting" them with "power." The shamans spread out from Central Asia: the Romans met them as Druids, and Western explorers met them in Africa as witch doctors, who "doctored" witches. The tribes had many personal rites, ritual feasts, and ritual dramas of "the origin myth" acted by clans.

We can see differences in Being "as if" in two descriptions of a war dance. Louis Havemeyer described a Naga war dance in Northeast India:

> It commences with a review of the warriors who later advance and retreat, parrying blows, and throwing spears as though in a real

fight. They creep along in battle array, keeping as near the ground as possible so that nothing shows but a line of shields. When they are near enough to the imaginary enemy they spring up and attack. After they have killed the opposing party they grab tufts of grass, which represent the heads, and these they sever with their battle axes. Returning home they carry the clods over their shoulders as they would the heads of real men. At the village they are met by the women who join in a triumphant song and dance. [279]

A small shift in intensity and a war dance of the Dyaks can be dramatic:

One warrior is engaged in picking a thorn out of his foot, but is ever on the alert for the lurking enemy, with his arms ready to hand. The enemy is at length suddenly discovered, and after some rapid attack and defence, a sudden lunge is made at him and he is dead on the ground. The taking of his head follows in pantomime. . . . The story then concludes with the startling discovery that the slain man is not an enemy at all but the brother of the warrior who has slain him. At this point the dance gives way to what was perhaps the least pleasing part of the performance — a man in a fit, writhing in frightful convulsions, being charmed into life and sanity by a necromantic physician. [528]

Resurrection and an emphasis on the victim give a hint of tragedy.

The Ancient Near-East

In the Near-Eastern neolithic revolution, people settled in regular communities, first as nomadic herders and later as farmers. The rivalry of the two, symbolized by Cain and Abel, echoes in the conflict of cattlemen and "sodbusters" in Western movies like *Shane*. Civilization began on the Euphrates. Regular existence and communal structures shaped ritual to a continuing pattern in life (myth).

Growth of the Ritual Myth

Early neolithic ritual dramas were simple but double. Farmers relied on the seasons: they had a great terror of a ruined harvest and a bitter winter (death), the sowing of seeds (burial), the hope of spring (life) and reaping the harvest (resurrection). This metaphoric theme (corn/life) became an annual death-and-resurrection story dramatized in ritual. It told of a year-king (or year-priest) who turned into the daemon of death, then was overcome by the new year-king. More deeds of the king enlarged the myth: a substitute year-king, or "mock king," was fêted briefly and then killed; the true year-king survived. In the final form of the ritual drama, the actual king acted "as if" he was the god: then Mesopotamians sought

Inanna or Damuzzi. The god's story (the seasonal pattern) was dramatized in several ways so a series of days ("holy days," our "holi-days") reiterated the change of the Old and New Year: death was driven out ("the scapegoat") at the winter solstice; purification followed. The vernal equinox had a spring ritual and the calendar became full of dramatic Festivals.

The myth and the ritual developed. Mimesis grew into mime as we know it, a more formalized and accurate movement which was also more secret: "The time-honoured orderly sequence itself was endowed with such magical significance that any infringement of the customary order of enactment was prohibited at the peril of life." [379] Civilized infants also think there is magic in order, demanding strict sequence in what is read or acted. In the Near East action came first, followed by chanted words; elsewhere there were different emphases. These ritual-myths appeared at Sumer c. 3,500 B.C., and then Akkad, Babylon and Assyria. Mesopotamian rituals all had the same structure. Egypt's king drama grew as the pharaoh acted the god — a wise king, Osiris, murdered by his brother Set, was revenged by his son, Horus — a death-and-resurrection plot later echoed by *Hamlet*. Similar ritual myths grew throughout the Near East (Hittites, Canaanites, etc.): fertility semi-dramas of the death of the old king and rebirth of the new, a "sacred marriage" of the god and goddess (acted by the king and a priestess), ritual combats, communal feasts, and other rites. Elements reach us in folklore: in Thracian and Macedonian folk plays and the English Mummers' Play of today. Their structure is the same: off with the Old (expulsion, the scapegoat, death) and on with the New (Year, king, vegetation, maypole); a ritual battle of old/new, summer/winter, rain/drought, with a wedding (sexuality, indecency) or a mock death/burial/resurrection.

Agricultural dance was performed in terms of "similars": mime. In ancient Egypt there were dramatic dances within the Osirian ritual drama: the dance of lamentation by both sexes represented the goddesses Isis and Nephthys in their sorrow over Osiris' death; a dance by armed men mimed the protection of the pharaoh-god; and a mixed fertility dance tried to resurrect the god and give vitality to the land. At funerals there were two official mourners (actresses) and dances by *nemou*: African dwarfs or pygmies who skipped and balanced, but also acted burlesque "kings" within a ritual dance. They exist in the wall paintings of Aurignacian man and their descendants appear as the medieval "mock King," the humpbacked clown, Dossennus, and Punch. [564] The pharaoh performed "the dance of the land": a dance of power showing his relationship to both Lower and Upper Egypt — a double concept — and that is why he had to dance it twice.

The Temple

These changes led to a need for a physical focus for spiritual life. The sanctuary, or temple, was a model of the higher life: the dramatization of the concept of divinity as the focus of each city. Some acts became "secret," known only to the priests (liturgy). The temple was "the centre of the world," an ancient concept still held by the Hopi. The season over, the temple was cleansed to prepare for the new lease of life as among the Babylonians, Egyptians, Hittites, and others in the Near East, Rome, Israel, the great American civilizations, Cambodia, Eastern Russia, East Africa, New Guinea, India, and among Christians today. [206] Replacing old boughs and twigs with new was part of the liturgy — another dramatic display of the divine life. The liturgy also implied "explanation": when the ritual became so detailed and mysterious, the action was a signifier communicating elements of deep meanings to all the people.

Ancient Greece

The Attic theatre of the 5th century B.C. grew from the temple. Rituals in city temples were already communal expressions on a grand scale but not in theatrical form. They were structured like the rest of the Near East which had many direct links with Greece and Rome. In Babylonia they celebrated Damuzzi (later Tammuz Adon) who, as Adonis, was a powerful god of Greece in the 7th century B.C. In 499 B.C. Herodotus reported two surviving Egyptian resurrection dramas and their influence on Greek rituals. Such dramas had the strong emotion of bloody deeds and violent acts: the emotional rituals of Attis spread throughout Asia Minor and caused a sensation in Rome in the 3rd century A.D.

The other major influence on Attic theatre was Dionysos. North and east of Greece, early shamanic acts had become possessed dances for various gods, one of whom was Dionysos of Thrace. Homer mentions his Maenads: wild women raging through the mountains, frantically dancing in circles, wearing flowing garments of animal-skins with horns, and carrying sacred snakes. Dionysos was dramatized as a bull or a goat which in a frenzy the Maenads tore to pieces, limb from limb, and devoured raw (*omophagia*) to spread his "power" over the land. Possession, linked to the phallus attribute, aimed at union with the god and led directly to omophagia.

These ecstatic rites of passage forced the human soul into the god by intensity. (When man can do this, says Plato in *Ion*, the streams will run with milk and honey, and life will be eternal bliss.) When Dionysos reached the Greek islands his myth grew quickly, absorbing other ritual myths as the god of fertility, spring and growth. Later he made his triumphal entry into Athens as also the god of wine and the dead. The Attic plays were performed in his honour at the Theatre of Dionysos in Athens, still standing today. Paradoxically, the plots of the plays were taken from Homer. Only in the last great tragedy (Euripides' *Bacchae*, c. 408-406 B.C.) was the subject Dionysos.

Both the ritual myths of Sumer and the tragedies of Euripides were set in a liturgical framework, and they told of the most elemental problems of life and death. But the Attic theatre changed the emphasis: the bonds of ritual were released; the temple was also an open-air theatre. With Aeschylus to Euripides there were other changes: from an acceptance of the gods to questioning them; and instead of one kind of structure, the Greeks created tragic, comic and satyric forms.

Tragedy & Comedy

According to Aristotle theatre "began with improvisations: [tragedy] from the leaders of the dithyramb, [comedy] from those who led off the phallic songs which still exist as institutions in some of our cities." [16] The dithyramb was a poetic song for Dionysos about the springtime lust for life, sung and danced through the streets, accompanied by the Phrygian flute. Originally improvised and rhapsodical, the dithyramb became more literary but was still passionate. In the 6th century B.C., Homer's works were read aloud at great public meetings as the Dionysian chorus danced in the streets with a leader (*exarchon*). The leader (now *coryphaeus*) became a commentator (*hypokrites*) and then a particular actor (character) who was answered by the chorus. This great change is assigned by tradition to the legendary Thespis of Icara (c. 535 B.C.), the first actor-dramatist, who stood on a cart or table in the middle of a circle directing his verse to a chorus around him. When the performance moved onto a stage tragedy began. On three of the six days of the Dionysian celebrations there were three tragedies (by one poet) and a comedy, written for only one performance. All was highly competitive: to win the dramatic contest was a religious honour for those who took part. The Greek change of ritual into theatrical art lay in the reduction of action and its replacement by substitute elements. [362]

There are three major theories about the origin of tragedy. The first, that year-gods, symbols of seasonal change, were transformed into tragedy (held by distinguished scholars [241, 278, 449, 451]), does not account for everything. The second says it came from the sacrificial prize (a goat, *tragos*) awarded to the first winner of the tragic contests (Thespis); or from the "song of the *tragoi*" sung by the Dionysians who killed the god/goat and ate him in a sacrificial meal: tragedy "arose out of human sacrifice; it is still a substitute for it." [5] The substitution of an animal victim may have been the initial change in Dionysian rituals; later there was the second shift of interest *from the act* of sacrifice *to its victim*, begun in tribal war dances. The third theory is that tragedy grew from shamanism [352]; for example, Dionysos had shamanic origins. Like the other theories, this theory cannot account for many aspects. All these theories, then, are likely true: tragedy emerged when all three acts met in Athens at a specific moment of time.

Attic comedy had a lower social origin: the ribald and noisy Dionysian street procession which ended in a phallic song. [119] Tragedy had one chorus, comedy two, and the satiric shouts of the onlookers were mixed into the plays. Dionysian links are found in the obscenities, the animal choruses, and the aggression in the *parabasis* (the oldest part of the play). But there is also evidence of the influence of the farces of the Dorians of Megara. Aristotle said they claimed the first comedy, naming it after one of their villages (the *comai*) and we need not doubt him. The Dorian mime existed in the Peloponnesus from the 6th century B.C. and is illustrated on period vases [457]: pairs of masked figures dance in grossly padded tight-fitting costumes to burlesque the gods in scenes of orgy and theft; a buffoonish Herakles, animal masks, and clowns such as the mimic fool, and a slapstick clown-dancer-juggler who comes down to Harlequin and Chaplin. Aristophanes inherited the two comic traditions of Athens and Doria.

Dance

Dance brings myth and ritual to life. "It is thus a living frieze of ritual action from which the myth emanates in the choral song which frequently accompanied the sacred dance. Yet all three — ritual, dance and myth — are really one; they were originally indivisible parts of a single thought-process." [564]

Greek dramatic dance aimed "to make gesture represent feeling, passion and action." All body parts were used. Choral dances were so mimetic that Gilbert Murray saw them as the origin of tragedy. The *Geranos* (Crane) Dance, said to have been performed by Theseus returning from the Cretan Labyrinth, dramatized the windings of the maze at Knossos: the strophe, from right to left (the ominous rule of the Minotaur); the antistrophe, the reverse movement (the release from the Minotaur); and the stationary, slow and grave (thanksgiving). The dancers in line mimed cranes following the clue by which Theseus solved the Labyrinth. The *Phaiakan* Dance of young men circling around a singer was like the Egyptian protective dance. At Dionysian festivals at least three dances were performed — the *Eucmeleia*, *Kordax* and *Sikinnis* (tragic, comic and satyric) — which tradition said came from the Osirian rituals. The *Hyporchema* Dance, sacred to Apollo, was sometimes danced for Dionysos and Pallas Athene, while the *Pyrric* Dance, imitative of battle, was said to have been Dorian.

Medieval Europe

Tribal Drama

When Rome fell, Europe returned to its tribal origins. Rites that were a vital part of early medieval life, the Church called "pagan." The Germanic tribes were not easily made Christian. [308] Rome opposed the pagan rites rigorously but had little success until Gregory the Great began to assimilate them as part of the Church's missionary policy (c. 600 A.D.) and only residues continue today. Their purpose was to make the crops grow by the eternal struggle; sun/moon, winter/summer, darkness/light, death/life. "The king is dead: long live the king!" The periodic sacrifice and death of the year-king was essential to the well-being of the community: e.g., in the Feast of Fools; [104] the revival by the Doctor in the English Mummers' Plays; and a mock Death (a doll, some twigs or straw) carried round the village and expelled. The villagers brought back with them the summer tree. Sometimes the "scapegoat" was an actual man: the Pfingstl in Bavaria, "Jack o' Lent" in England, etc. [105]

The people lived in an animistic world, worshipping the spirits of both trees and animals, and dressed in leaves, horns and skins. They honoured and feared the dead, asked their help in war and the seasonal struggle, and kept them in good humour by food — often beans and peas (even in Tudor times a King of the Bean and Queen of the Pea were chosen on Twelfth Night) — at a banquet when "The Table of Fortune" was left for the ghostly "Wild Hunt" from the spirit world. [306] They also had expulsory rites for the dead: shouting, ringing bells and waving swords; or sweeping them out of the house (still in some English Mummers' Plays). Ancient Babylon purged death by fire. Medieval villagers expelled the dead with bonfires or by running round fields with flaming torches. [623]

Rituals mostly occurred at "critical" times of the year. But as the Celto-Teutonic, Roman and Christian calendars were absorbed within a comparatively short time, there was confusion as to *what* rites were to be celebrated *when*; similar ones were performed several times a year. The mid-winter rituals mingled the Celtic Yule, the

Roman Kalends and Saturnalia, and the Christian Christmas. [623] Yule created magic for future prosperity: it was a festival for the dead (All Saints' and All Souls' Day) and a time for sacrifice; November was Bede's "Blot-Monath" — beasts that could not be fed over winter were sacrificially slaughtered. The Kalends eased rules of conduct and inverted social status: masters and slaves changed places, took each other's roles, feasted and played dice together; "turning the world upside down" is an old concept that erupts in modern comedy. The Church denounced the Kalends and its survival, the Feast of Fools, with its mummers in animal skins, masks, women's clothes, and the *cervulus* (the hobby-horse), perhaps a survival of either the sacrificial victim, or of ancient British horse worship.

The Twelve Days of Christmas was an intercalary (epagomenal) period: a gap in the lunar and calendar years. Anciently celebrated everywhere, it was "outside time," of suspended animation. Superstitions clung to it. Officially ending on the first Monday after Twelfth Night (Epiphany, or Plough Monday), it extended to Shrovetide, or Carnival — a relic of the Roman Saturnalia with rites of sowing and ploughing, waiving social rules like the Kalends, a mock-king presiding over the revels and dramatic acts like masquerades, broom sweeping, the burial of the fool, etc. [623] Also in the Twelve Days is the Perchta ritual myth (*perchtenlauf*), still acted in the Tyrol today: terrifying figures in masks, black sheepskins and hoods of badger skins run, leap, crack whips, blow ash in people's faces and create uproar — the Fool and his girl, the drummer, the man in woman's clothes, and the Doctor. Suddenly the Wild Perchta leaps among them, they dance ecstatically, leap higher and higher over a well and either flee to safety from the Perchta in a nearby house, or chase the man in the Perchta mask. Next day, a man of the village is missing. Isolated stone crosses show the result. [561]

Spring and summer festivals were also confused. In Rome on May Day precautions, such as spitting out black beans, were taken against the dead. In later Europe and England May Day was merry: it celebrated the rite of the sacred tree (maypole), an ancient phallic cult common everywhere. In England it was simple fertility magic with two dances: the "round" about the maypole; and the procession around the village boundaries ("beating the bounds" of the parish today). The May spirit ("soul of the tree") was "as if" a doll, puppet, twigs, or human form. "Jack-in-the-green" was acted by an English village lad in green leaves; later a town lad was blackened (like one of the mumming chimney sweeps) because magic was created by reversal of natural body colour.

Sacred games dramatized the lives of gods from secondary myths, or extensions of the god's adventures; e.g., the Nemean games celebrated the killing of the Nemean lion by Herakles, Greek games placated the ghost of the god and asked his help with physical contests, musical turns and dramatic scenes about the lives of the gods. Games promoted growth: their dramatizations strengthened the dead through human blood and force, [564] a universal idea from the Olympic to the Irish Tailltenn games. In medieval games there were mimetic dances and plays at propitious times. On May Day in Yorkshire, hard-boiled eggs were rolled down hills and Pace-Egg plays were acted, as they are today. May Day was increasingly popular with songs, dances and games round the maypole. From the 13th century a May "king" and "queen" were elected. By the 14th century they were "Robin" and "Marion." Robin was linked to three Robin Hood traditions: the historical outlaw Robin Hood (mentioned in *Piers Plowman*, c. 1377) who, from 1500, was celebrated in many popular ballads; the travelling French minstrels who sang of the shepherd Robin in love with the shepherdess Marion (Adam de la Halle of Arras wrote the late 13th century play *Jeu de Robin et Marion*); and the old English vegetation deity who had to fight for his title annually, but now with bow or quarter-stave. [502] By the 16th century this old ritual had become a series of folk plays: "the games of Robin Hood represented the last shadow of an enacted rite which narrated the life and adventures of a god or wood spirit, and ended with the sacrifice of his human representative, who was despatched with a flight of arrows [which] symbolized the rain-shower, for in all parts of the world the flint arrow-head is the emblem of rain." [564]

The old dramatic dance is today folk dance. Usually there is also a middle stage when the form remains but its belief system is forgotten (as with the *nautch* girls of India), but not in Europe. The sword dances of the Aegean dancing smiths and the Salian priests of Rome (a brotherhood dancing at stations along a route, banging their swords on their shields, with magical words spoken by a Soothsayer) became in the 15th century two dances: the sword dance had a presenter introducing each character, while the rough dialogue and ritual combat associate it with folk dramas; [9, 467] and the Morris dance was a danced mock combat, with bells on ankles and knees, faces masked or blackened, and much clashing of sticks and waving of handkerchiefs. Both exist today.

In England the sword dance mixed with the Plough Play of Plough Monday, January 6th, the old New Year's Day. Ploughmen harnessed to a plough dragged it round the village with sword dancers. In origin Anglo-Saxon (perhaps the horse sacrifice), it enforced Plough alms. The plough-car was linked to the Egyptian ship-car: the ceremonial plough was kept in the church, like the horns of the Abbots Bromley deer dancers today. The "Tommy" (Fool) had an animal's skin and tail. The "Bessy" was a man dressed as a woman. The old year (father) was killed by the new (sons). There were bawdy scenes, a hobby-horse and a dragon. [105] The plough was a fertility symbol in the sense that Shakespeare used it of Cleopatra:

> Royal wench!
> She made great Caesar lay his sword to bed:
> He ploughed her, and she cropped.

Today the English Mummers' Play is a mixture of the Plough Plays and Christian elements, likely re-structured from Richard Johnson's romance *Seven Champions of Christendom* (1595), or John Kirke's 17th century play (printed 1638; later a travelling puppet play). [105, 467, 580] The Play came from the seasonal ritual: the ritual battle is a comic joust between the "gallant Christian knight" and an evil enemy; and there is a comic Doctor with his huge pair of pliers to stage a "resurrection." All are processional: they march from house to house, or to "stations" along a street, where each role has a sing-song chant, obscure because by medieval times magic was obscure. Each character introduces himself with the Vaunt ("I am," and so "I am St. George," etc.), also common in ritual plays from Cornish Cycles to the Japanese *No*. When two players vaunt in opposition before others, *agon* and *antagonist* are before a chorus. [561] These dramatic forms occurred when games abounded. On Midsummer Day, Celts lit bonfires; at Whiteborough in Cornwall a fire with a great pole at the centre was lit, and wrestlers contended for prizes at a tumulus where giants were supposed to be buried. Statues of a dragon and a giant were dragged through the streets of Burford, Oxfordshire, in memory of the god's victory over an evil figure — much like the Indian god Vittra and the Persian god Titra. Universally secondary agricultural myths bring about ritual games and their associated dramas: fertility activities trying to placate the dead and re-invigorate the cosmos.

The Temple (Church)

The Church drama was subject to two influences. First were the ancient rituals in which the vernal equinox (March 25th) was significant. The early mysteries of Tammuz, Attis and others culminated then; and on that date the Church had been forced to associate the birth of Mithra, a sun-god, with that of Christ. The newly converted pagans confused the reasons for the festival so Easter, together with Christmas, had the most frequently danced processions. On Christmas night in 1020, as Mass was about to be celebrated at the church in

Kolbigk, Anhalt, it was invaded by wild men and women who danced with primitive fury. [308] Second were the travelling players, descendants of the irreligious professional mimes, who now performed at wayside fairs and in ritual games. The lesser clergy joined in their dances. As early as 911 these *tripudia* (dances in three-step) were performed at the monastery of St. Gall. [308] In the Feast of Fools, clergy danced in the choir dressed as women, pandars or minstrels, and wore masks. Like all such dances, they were free and mimetic; a rigorous basis upon which the Church drama could grow.

But it was from the Church itself that the true drama emerged. The Mass had the seeds of drama: it was seen as "the drama of life"; it had chanted dialogue and a theme of action; and the clergy encouraged its dramatic qualities. [277] Direct impersonation began in the 10th century at the Benedictine Abbey of St. Gall, Switzerland, with the *trope* (an extra chant) sung during the night before Easter:

Quem quaeritis in sepulchre, o Christicolae?
(The Angel asks: "who do you seek in the sepulchre, O followers of Christ?")
Jesum Nazarenum crucifixum, o coelicolae.
("Jesus of Nazareth, the crucified, O heavenly one," say the Marys.)
Non est hic: Surrexit sicut praedixerat.
Ite, nuniate quia surrexit de sepulchre.
(Angel: "He is not here. He is risen as he foretold. Go and announce that He is risen from the dead.")

This *trope* was first sung by the two halves of the choir within the Mass. Later it was moved to Matins, the prayers before daybreak, and put between the Last Response and the final *Te Deum*, where it had time and place to develop. There it coincided with the spring equinox and the old pagan festivals. A book of *tropes* from this period [308] is illuminated by figures of mimes, so it is possible that they were used by the Church to introduce impersonation. At first the *trope* had been sung. Repositioned it became a separate little scene: like a tiny opera, where three people impersonated the Marys and one the Angel before an improvised sepulchre.

About 970 St. Ethelwold, Bishop of Winchester, wrote a prompt book, with directions for the production of the *trope* [104] which was now a small drama with impersonation and action. It was gradually added to. In the 11th century, the apostles Peter and John raced through the church to the sepulchre; later Christ appeared and Mary took him for the gardener. Processions began: characters marched up one aisle and down the other. A comic character was introduced: the unguent merchant who bargained with the Holy Women; and in the

Christmas plays that grew slightly later, there was a Herod who "roared and raged." These figures may have been invented by the professionals: the merchant (*mercator*) was sometimes known as *medicus* — "Doctor," a name from the shamans, the Roman mime, the Mummers' Plays and the later *commedia dell'arte*. Vernacular replaced Latin. One incident grew to a full sequence of Biblical stories. The performances moved from the choir to the nave and then to the church exterior; already the marriage ceremony (but not the Nuptial Mass) took place in the porch. The exodus of the plays was not uniform; it ocurred when the size of the plays demanded it. Yet the popularity of the plays gave the Church second thoughts and, by the time the plays went outside (at the west door, in the churchyard, or by procession through the town), priests were forbidden to perform in those outside their own walls.

The Emergence of Theatre

The church plays grew into Mystery Cycles: plays from the Creation to the Last Judgment grouped as one whole. Although based on the Bible, there was additional matter for good measure. Their control passed into the hands of the quasi-religious trade guilds. But everyone was still a member of the Church and there was no lessening of the religious motive. It is likely that the lay clergy took a more important part than has hitherto been thought. The Cycles gained great momentum when in 1311 Corpus Christi (Thursday after Trinity) was inaugurated as a Festival where the most characteristic celebration was the procession of the guilds carrying banners denoting their craft. It is one step from a banner to a stage on wheels (pageant-wagon). Yet cost prohibited all but the large towns from staging a Cycle. Villagers had to be content with their mummings and ritual games.

In the Cycles the influence of professional players was mainly in the comic scenes, as broad and farcical as the Roman mime. [457] Comic servants, shrewish wives and rustic shepherds appeared. But humour is akin to horror. The medieval fool and devil traditions often mingled: hairy creatures with terrifying masks (much like figures of tribal rituals) were also comic, and taken to be so by the audience. There were also stock figures which were common to the Roman mime and *commedia dell'arte*: in the York *Joseph and Mary* play the row between Joseph and Mary about the Conception resembles the adultery mimes; and the mimic braggart (the *Miles Gloriosus* of Rome and *Il Capitano* of the *commedia*) is the Herod who rants and raves in a variety of languages.

The Christian Cycles combined elements of the irreligious mimes and the dances and customs of the pagans. Despite isolated dramatic heights (the rough comedy of *The Second Shepherd's Play*, the beauty of the verse in the Brome *Abraham and Isaac*, and the work of the Wakefield Master) the medievals did not allow tragedy to flower. They were corporate animals, only conscious of themselves as members of a community, a guild or a family. [236] To Euripides, divine suffering was like human suffering and "sacrificial" plays resulted. But the medievals knew their place. In a society so stratified, tragedy belonged only to Christ: divine suffering was greater than human. Medieval plays (like the Japanese *No*) reflect on sacrifice: the real struggle is over, victory is won, but care is needed to prevent evil from conquering again. And there emerged the secular Interlude: a theatrical form created for small troupes of professional players, the basis of the later Elizabethan theatre troupes.

Other Cultures

China

Space precludes all but a cursory glimpse of dramatic acts and the culture pattern elsewhere. In China about 3-2,000 B.C. semi-nomadic tribes using early mimesis settled in the Yangtse-kiang and the Hoang-ho valleys, and more formal elements began. By the Shang dynasty (1766-1122 B.C.) ritual dance dramas of the seasons grew. The Chou dynasty (1050-255 B.C.) was the height of ancient Chinese civilization and the danced agricultural performances became a temple theatre. After political chaos, ritual dramas began again in the Han dynasty (206 B.C.-A.D. 220); later, when the first Buddhist monks reached China, ritual drama was based on highly stylized dramatic dance. The dramatic elements had a particular emphasis and, by the 6th century, they combined in unique Chinese conventions. The classic Chinese theatre emerged about the 8th century, coinciding with the arrival of many people from Persia, India and the Middle East. The theatre had various forms: within the Court, with marionettes, and in many popular styles. Although the Mongol invasions disturbed dramatic growth, the Yuang dynasty encouraged development so that, by the Ming period, theatre was well established. From the 19th century Western influences affected the theatre, but in the 1960's Mao Tse-Tung virtually destroyed the old Peking Opera. Recently it has been restored to its previous greatness. [13, 17, 92, 107, 342, 545, 647, 648]

Japan

The exceptionally disturbed social history of Japan has necessarily affected the development of theatre. Dancing shamans and dramatic rice rituals exist even today, bringing fertility, placating the dead, and celebrating the death of the "Year Demon." Theatre development has only occurred in periods of stability. The *No* theatre in the 14th and 15th centuries was an upper-class theatre and today it retains its original form and dialogue. The *Kabuki* theatre of the 17th century was a popular form of the *No*, now evolved into a middle-class theatre. There are a variety of other forms, including the majestic *Bunraku* puppet theatre, and popular "variety" entertainments. [13, 70, 92, 175, 339, 349, 394, 435, 495, 604]

India

India has many cultures which have developed differently. The earliest civilization, centered on the Indus, grew much like those on the Euphrates and the Nile with its own rituals. Similar ritual dramas continue today among the Tamils to the south and in Sri Lanka. The Indo-Europeans brought Sanskrit, the caste system and the beginnings of a Hindu temple drama. Their invasion of such a vast area was piecemeal so dramatic growths were uneven: the earliest fragments of a written drama (by Asvaghosa) occur c. 100 A.D., while the spectacular *Kathakali* dance dramas, and shamanic rituals in mountain areas, are still performed. The classical Sanskrit theatre of the 4th and 5th centuries A.D., comparable with the Attic theatre, centered on the city of Ujjain. It grew out of rituals and only later was performed in a temple or royal palace. Unlike Athens, there was no physical theatre building; rather, like the Stuart Masgue, everything was arranged for a specific performance. The Aristotelian figure, Bharata, established canons for later theatre. Amongst a group of major dramatists was Kalidasa whose *Sakuntala* is comparable with the *Oresteia* as a major statement of dramatic vitality. Later, touring theatrical companies emerged, much like the European Interlude players. [12, 13, 92, 253, 256, 264, 341, 348, 352, 543, 643]

South-East Asia

Burmese drama varies between the rituals of the hill tribes, such as the Shans, to the Buddhist cities where dance dramas (more entertainments than plays) have highly stylized dancing, rich costumes and songs accompanied by large orchestras. The forms include large scale all-night entertainments based on classical and Buddhist stories; extracts from these arranged as separate clown-like performances; processional pageants based on allegories; audience participation plays of the dead; and general interest stories using spectacle, song and dance. In Thailand theatrical forms vary from danced mimesis to theatrical presentations. In Cambodia dramas are based on a chanting chorus accompanied by an orchestra, myths, gorgeous costumes and highly stylized dance. Thai, Cambodian and Laotian forms are centered on dramatic dance and shadow theatre. In remote parts of Malaya ancient fertility forms exist; professional troupes tour stories from old romances and danced interludes, farcical elements and masks, with the audience gathered round three sides. Urban groups enjoy danced musical satires of their own community. Indonesia is full of ritual dances and dramas: the *ludruk* form in Java is a ritual drama of revitalization for tribal people working in urban centres. [22, 39, 71, 80, 370, 388, 389, 401, 423, 424, 479, 528, 533]

The Americas

The indigenous Amerindian and Inuit tribes have their own traditions based on spirit beliefs that include shamanic performances, feasts and ritual dramas. These are particularly rich in the Canadian Northwest and the American Southwest. In South America many traditions were altered by contact with whites: in some areas they were changed by priests so that today traditional South American beliefs are mixed with Christian stories. In Cuba, Brazil and elsewhere, African influences predominate to produce such variations as Voodoo in Haiti. Mexico is full of ceremonial religious pageants; some based on ancient rituals but with a Christian veneer: others are truly ancient activities, like "flying" from high poles (related to the maypole), and *carpa* — small improvised comedies in the European mime tradition. Additionally the great urban centers have developed theatrical traditions in the European style but with unique features of their own. [56, 62, 137, 138, 161, 179, 279, 355, 593, 597]

Yiddish Theatre

The influence of social and political events on Yiddish Theatre is clear and informative. In 1876, Abraham Goldfadden moulded Jewish variety entertainments into an improvised plot in Roumanian wine taverns. A little later in America, Jacob Gordin wrote the first play scripts in Yiddish. From these two events, this theatrical form grew in the early 20th century, responding to the relaxation of prohibitions in Slav Europe. The Hirschbein Troupe of Odessa was created in 1908 and thereafter toured Russia with Yiddish plays. In 1916 the Vilna Troupe was formed, later to perform the premiere of *The Dybbuk* in 1920. Companies experimented with acting shapes in Poland after World War I. In its early days the Soviet government encouraged Yiddish culture: one result was the famous Habima company which later emigrated to Israel. But from the beginning of World War II Yiddish theatre was suppressed in Russia and most of Europe. After the Jewish exodus to America it increasingly flourished there. Whereas earlier Yiddish theatre was closely related to one or more Eastern European cultures, since 1945 it has become increasingly American. [371]

Key Issues

Time & Space

Time and space are key issues in the sociology of dramatic action. Human performance collapses all time into the "here and now": the continuous present tense only. Ritual myths collapse cosmic time into sacred time; theatre into significant time. The shape of the acting area and its relation to the audience varies with culture. Early tribal dramatic dance is performed in an arena shape surrounded by an audience (theatre-in-the-round) at 360°. Most agricultural ritual-myths occur in an arena shape with the audience on three sides at 180+°. Urban Western theatre evolved end stages with the audience on one side c. 1600; the development of the proscenium with the audience as voyeurs was not complete until the end of the 19th century. In the 20th century, various other complex shapes have evolved. [125] Culture affects shape, and vice versa. Thus the kaleidoscopic effect of the end of Act V of *Troilus and Cressida* could only have been created for an unlocalized stage with more than one level and various entrances: the flexibility of the culture required an equally flexible acting area. The needs of the audience and the theatre are symbiotic, as Bonamy Dobrée shows with the Restoration. The effect of an audience relates to its unity/diversity, a lower intellect than its individual members, and the cultural view of the fiction-actual, participation/distancing paradox. [459]

The Hidden Culture: Games & Rhymes

Dramatic action includes cultural acts of which players and audience may be unconscious prior to the acts. Being "as if" foregrounds them: makes the tacit explicit. Games bring multiplex meanings. Egyptian and Minoan labyrinths were transformed into Greek dance and medieval games like "Troy Towns" and mazes. "Hopscotch" began when early Christians replaced the first temple shape with the basilica. Many traditional games derive from ancient rituals: "The Mulberry Bush" — marriage dance round a sacred bush or tree; "Nuts in May" — marriage by capture and exogamy, etc. Most sports came from ritual games. The Irish shinty was a favourite of "the little people." Football comes from teams kicking the ball in one direction: the ancient ritual drama of the god imitated the sun's course. Rolling spheres in ritual became not only Pace-Egging but also cricket: once "stool ball," two sides on Easter Eve used a dairy maid's stool as a wicket with prizes of kisses and cakes. Children's popular rhymes are full of cultural residues: "Old King Cole" was an ancient British king but "Little Jack Horner" is a bowdlerization of *Robin Goodfellow* (1628). "Ride a Cock Horse" (hobby-horse) came from Anglo-Saxon rituals where nude women rode on white horses (from which came Lady Godiva). These acts have compelling force to the child in dramatic play. [24, 55, 91, 93, 105, 106, 206, 249, 250, 305, 306, 327, 465, 466, 467, 498, 502]

Part Four

Drama, Mind & Society

Chapter 14
Imitation, Identification & Roles

Having looked at drama and our inner psychology in Part 2, and the effect of society in Part 3, we are now in a position to put them together: to see them whole. In the terms of this book, we shall do so as "mind": our total consciousness, our Being and Becoming as one entity.

Imitation

Imitation is not a total action, but it is an important *part* of all dramatic actions from play to theatre. It is significant in socialization because modern civilization is increasingly relying on symbolic models for learners to imitate. Too often, however, imitation is seen as the total learning process.

Behaviourists view imitation as either conditioning or as instrumental. Few these days stop at Pavlovian conditioning. Most say that the child imitates to get the act started, and then circular reaction keeps it going. [27] Thus when children hear themselves cry, simultaneous association results and a reflex circle is begun. [293] This is iteration. But when a second person is the stimulus it is called imitation: "When others speak syllables to the child, they put into operation the ear-vocal reflexes which the child has already fixated by hearing himself talk." [10] When an adult repeats an approximation of the child's babbling, together with a demonstration to which the word refers, the child is conditioned to repeat the word — and that is imitation. But this theory overlooks far too much: it does not explain how a reflex circle, once started, ever stops. Nor does it account for novel responses. It is also linear, while most human learnings, particularly speech, are more complex than can be accounted for in such a simplistic approach.

Instrumentally N. E. Miller and J. Dollard say that all human behaviour is learned through the paradigm, Drive-Cue-Response-Reward (want/notice/do/get something). Imitation is an acquired drive that, once generated, acts like a primary drive. Children are taught special responses (the language of the group) which influence learning. The baby first learns to use words spoken by others as cues for his responses: e.g., "No!" may be followed by punishment. He learns to talk because society makes it worth while: his response as a cue produces the appropriate word (an anticipatory response). Reason shortens trial and error: a combination of two separate items of experience (putting two and two together) is characteristic of simple reasoning; but most reasoning consists of longer sequences of cue-producing responses which the child usually learns as part of his culture. In essence, for Miller and Dollard, imitation helps learning by forcing the subject to respond more quickly to the proper cue than he otherwise would. But, for O. H. Mowrer, "It might be said that Miller and Dollard were not really studying imitation at all, but simply discrimination in which the cue stimulus is provided by the behaviour of other organisms. Their rejoinder would probably be that imitation is 'simply discrimination' of the kind just described." [445]

The Two-Factor Theory

O. H. Mowrer rightly goes on to say that "according to the Miller-Dollard analysis, the only way a bird could learn to say 'Hello' imitatively would be to *say it* while noticing another bird (or person?) saying the same thing — and getting rewarded. The question is: How is the bird going to learn to make this improbable sound in the first place? A two-factor analysis of the process resolves this difficulty." [444] Mowrer states two factors: (1) Continuity — a bird becomes "glad to see" and "glad to *hear*" the trainer, so the trainer's sights and sounds take on a secondary-reward value for the bird; and (2) Reward — should the bird, in making sounds, happen to produce one like the trainer's, this will have a secondary reward value. Thus he adds the behavioural "imitation" to the psychoanalytic "identification": birds talk when a human teacher becomes a *love object* for them. But when C. W. Valentine provides evidence of many variations in a child's imitation, perhaps things are not as simple as they seem.

Identification

Imitation occurs when *specific items* of a culture are taken over but it is not necessary that there should be any emotional relation between the actor and the model. Differently, identification is the process, built on empathy, whereby the actor *internalizes the values of the model* and is motivated to imitate. That is, Being "as if" is *implicit* within identification: the actor *shares* the values of the model and acts "as if" he is the model.

Identification & Imitation

We have previously discussed developmental and defensive identification but we need to note their relationship to imitation. For behaviourists, imitation is primary: where they do acknowledge identification, it is developmental and it is only a precipitate of conditioning. Yet it allows the child to introject the qualities of the mother and, later, others. Behaviourists do not mention defensive identification. Indeed, they would have a hard time trying to explain Anna Freud's example of a girl who was afraid of the dark and ghosts (ghosts often being the intermediate link between the parents and the establishment of the ego) who suddenly hit upon a device:

> she would run across the hall, making all sorts of peculiar gestures as she went. Before long, she triumphantly told her little brother the secret of how she got over her anxiety. "There's no need to be afraid in the hall," she said, "you just have to pretend that you're the ghost who might meet you." This shows that her magic gestures represented the movements which she imagined that ghosts would make. [214]

Mowrer, for example, who is one of the few behaviourists to use identification, deals entirely with the developmental:

> As the infant learns to make conventional word sounds, the bond stage of word functioning emerges. Now he utters a specifically meaningful word which serves, literally, to re-present the mother, recall, recapture, recreate her; and in so doing the infant reduces the necessity for relying upon the autistic, self supplied satisfactions. Now, instead of merely *playing* with words, the infant makes them *work*. [445]

While we can admire Mowrer's struggle to make his synthetic point, he has missed the essential issue because of his behavioural perspective.

Identification as a Double Gestalt

We are dealing with the dynamics of *mediation*: the meaningful acts that operate *between* inner/outer, self/other, person/environment, subject/object, etc. [444] We create a dialogic relationship between the two: an active gestalt where self-consciousness understands the dynamics by alternation — first from the inner perspective, and second from the outer. Although in alternation, the two sides operate as one unified whole as follows:

*   Developmental identification is the first alternative: threatened by loss of the mother, the child introjects her qualities and then attempts to represent them *in the external world* — to others.

*   The child can "switch" to defensive identification: fearing punishment from the environment, he takes on the role of the other and tries to represent it in the internal world — to the self.

In behavioural terms, the behaviour of the mother and father (or surrogates) takes on a secondary reward value and, in a quasi-magical way, the child begins elements of Being "as if."

Re-phrased in our terms, identification is a human mental process that is:

1   *Mediate*, as activated developmentally and defensively. It is a processual gestalt: we understand one in relation to the other; even while we foreground the one, the other is assumed, and vice versa.

2   *Double*, two processes in one that alternate with one another in rapid succession. The double is the mental ground upon which many human acts occur: the genetic basis whereby human beings deal with the world.

Imitation, motivation, transfer, etc., are functions of this process from which derives, appropriately, the double nature of meaning:

*   *Personal functions*:
    Mediation is the active relation of inner/outer: the creation of meaning through the actual/fictional; and the metaphorical structures of expression within language and all media that activate symbolic meanings within culture and society, etc.

*   *Societal functions*:
    Mediation permits the environment to affect the self; the use of roles to create perspectives on meaning, the acknowledgement of differences (lack of stereotyping), compromise (basis of society), the fiduciary contract (trust), etc.

These factors are fundamental to Being "as if."

Identification & Development

Although obvious, it must be said that identification changes with maturation. In Western cultures, younger children are inclined to identify "whole" more often than older students and adults who, in social life, are inclined to increasingly identify with fragments of roles. In contrast, tribal cultures encourage strong identification with culture types based on rites of passage, e.g., pre-initiate, liminal, post-initiate.

R. R. Sears indicates three developmental steps for young children: (1) they develop a dependency drive for the mother's affectionate nurture; (2) they imitate (act "as if") they are the mother; and (3) they are so gratified by their performance that it becomes habitual. This then becomes a secondary motivational system, which functions as self-rewarding so long as the reward system is consistent. [546]

The strength of identification will vary with the kind of affectionate nurture given to children. If the nurture is continuous they will never have occasion to act "as if" they are the mother. If the nurture is punitive they will not want to. Identification in young children "produces the behaviour that is replicative of the parents' qualities, role behaviours and demands. . . . It has the effect of transmitting the values of the culture from one generation to the next, and of providing for the continuity, in a society, of persons appropriately trained for the roles of which the society is composed." [546] With maturation, the role models for identification increase from parents to peers, teachers, heroes and heroines. Although some drama therapists acknowledge transference between themselves and their patients, drama teachers are not always aware of their power as role models.

Role Theory

A disappointing part of contemporary drama work is that role play and simulation are not always as successful as they can be. Lack of success is attributed to the use of imitation over identification. The method and results may, perhaps, seem more "objective" but this is no substitute for high calibre practical work.

Role theory originated earlier in the 20th century from three sources. We have discussed two: the theatrical theory of Stanislavsky and Moreno's psychodrama. The third source was from G. H. Mead and Theodore R. Sarbin. For them and other social psychologists, people organize their actions into roles; human conduct and social learning are products of the self and role. Sarbin says "*A role* is a patterned sequence of learned *actions* or deeds performed by a person in an interaction situation"; "the self is what a person 'is,' the role is what a person 'does.'" Culture is an organization of learned behaviours which are shared and transmitted while all societies are organized around positions (roles). Those who occupy these positions use specialized actions: the roles we perform are seen as linked to the positions and not to us. Roles can be learned by intentional instruction or incidental learning.

More recently, however, "role" has become a ubiquitous term used by social psychologists to discuss almost every facet of social life. Social structure has been emphasized at the expense of human interaction. However, G. H. Mead was one of the first to emphasize the importance of play in the adoptive learning of social roles. He also said that imaginative impersonation is the keystone of social learning:

> The imaginative processes are central in play acting. They are likewise central in covert processes, such as fantasy. The silent rehearsal of roles appropriate to real or imagined positions, and of roles appropriate to the position of the other, provides a large reservoir of experience. In all cultures, a good part of the content of imaginative behaviour is institutionalized in the form of folk tales, myths, and other story forms. The imaginative process is central likewise in that form of acquiring roles which has been variously named identification, introjection, empathy, and taking-the-

role-of-the-other. Dependent on the ability of the person (child or adult) to engage in *as if* processes, identification provides numerous avenues for acquiring roles. The number and kinds of persons with whom one may identify, of course, is limited by the number and kinds of persons in the environment and by cultural practices. [422]

From the dramaturgical perspective it is best to see roles not as a set of expectancies, or norms to which people conform but rather, as Ralph Turner argues, as outcomes of human interaction: roles are created in the process of interaction. This is a significant change to views about roles: from the passive to the active voice. Erving Goffman goes further: people continually create their own roles and those of others in order to facilitate interaction; and they can separate themselves from their roles or, at least, from what the roles imply about them. People are not "just the role" in which they have been cast: the role does not play with the person but the individual "plays with the role."

This leads us to "role distance": the degree to which a person is near/far from his/her role. In theatrical terms this is Stanislavsky vs. Brecht. There are at least two key issues here:

1 *How far do people vary in their degrees of intensity within roles?* This issue has been implied in Part 3. Tribal peoples use dramatic dance to drive towards possession by a spirit in Rites of Intensification. This action is an exemplar of their attitude to roles (e.g., as daughter, wife, "Wolf," etc.), where each role is taken with great intensity and seriousness within a concept of "tribal personality." In general terms, role flexibility increases with the advent of industrial and post-industrial societies; and, within these, flexibility decreases with degrees of psychological dysfunction.

2 *How far does a particular role determine a person's actions?* As roles may be enacted with different degrees of organic involvement, some require more intensity, some less. This is illustrated in Sarbin's levels of the Organismic Dimension (see Figure 3).

Most of us use Levels I and II every day when we put on our "masks." Brechtian actors perform at Level II, Stanislavsky actors at Level III. The identification process of childhood is extended into social roles according to cultural norms: thus while it is socially acceptable to enter Level VII with Voodoo in Haiti this is not the case at Rotary Clubs in North America.

Modelling & Anti-social Behaviour

Are children who watch violent movies, read pornographic magazines, or improvise anti-social behaviour, more likely to use similar

Level	Style	Example
Level I	Role & Self differentiated	casual customer in supermarket
Level II	Actor performs the motions necessary for portrayal	employee "puts up a good front" to impress the boss
Level III	Actor "lives the role"	but maintains some contact to change tempo, intensity
Level IV	Hypnosis: more of organism responding than in play acting	catalepsies
Level V	Hysteria	hysteric seizures/anorexia/ paralysis/anesthesia
Level VI	Ecstatic states	trance, possession, etc.
Level VII	Moribund person	object of witchcraft/sorcery

Figure 3

Organismic Dimension (based on T. R. Sarbin)

roles and imitate these actions in actual life? There is a wide diversity of opinion on this issue. Behavioural social psychologists have produced many studies to show that there is positive transfer. [30, 31] Unfortunately, many such studies have been carried out in clinical conditions which do not replicate everyday life. Critics say that the design of these studies predispose the children to imitate antisocial behaviour. In contrast, others (e.g., Moreno, Slade) consider that "playing out evil in a legal framework" acts as a catharsis; that "letting off steam" in an appropriate environment prevents people from imitating anti-social behaviour in ordinary life.

There is no single answer to the problem of imitation. The practical knowledge of drama teachers informs us that extremes of

There is no single answer to the problem of imitation. The practical knowledge of drama teachers informs us that extremes of modelling always exist. Over-inhibited children may benefit cathartically from dramatic play. Strongly conditioned children may display antisocial behaviour. Reality lies somewhere mid-way between these extremes. On the one hand, parents and teachers would be advised not to over-expose children to models of anti-social behaviour. On the other hand, Lord Boyle, formerly Secretary of State for Education in Britain, and Vice-Chancellor of Leeds University, has said of educational drama:

> I have felt the importance of this subject, not only from the conventional point of view that it enables a large number of boys and girls to "discover" themselves, in a way that is true of very few other activities, but for a deeper reason. It's my impression that a growing number of . . . older teenagers in schools, living in the kind of world we have today, do concern themselves a great deal with and are naturally interested in, not just the conventional emotions but the wilder, untamed emotions. [289]

Chapter 15
The Thought Process

In our experience, thought/action is one whole, a unified process of representation. Brain may be a physiological entity but mind is much greater. Mind is all that we think and do. It is our total consciousness: the conscious and unconscious, and how these affect the world. Experientially, consciousness is always consciousness-*of*. When we are truly conscious, we are always conscious of *something*: an object, a person, or the conscious self. This is what is signified in dramatic acts.

Imagining

Thought consists of the flow of ideas: the dynamics of mind. These energetic processes carry us along in our "experience." We can make a "map" of these processes (as in Fig. 4) provided we remember that such a map is merely a convenient way to stop the flux in order to examine it. This map has two parts in one: the sequential and the continuous.

1   *The sequential.*
    The dynamics of change are shown in the paradigm, Percept-Image-Act. We each perceive differently. My percepts [P] are not necessarily the same as yours. What we see, hear, smell, taste and feel depends largely on our state of awareness and our ability to concentrate; both can be improved by dramatic activity. We *transform* a percept into an image [I] (when we see a table from an odd perspective it has only 3 legs but, when we recall it, the table has 4 legs). We transform it by comparing it with previous experience. An image is a mental unit. When images are grouped together they become imaginings (Iˣ): clusters of thought. Images connect up to imaginings in many patterns. Each pattern or cluster may or may not be linear. But it always consists of many images where tension oscillates between those that are similar/different. This cluster tension has two poles:

*   Sets: well-worn paths, common connections that tend towards "stock" links, e.g.: table-chair-sit-down-up-along, etc.

*   Associations: unusual and surprising connections that tend towards unique links, e.g.: table-chair-leg-body-moon-garage-car, etc. The links of body-moon and moon-garage are different in kind from the others which are sets.

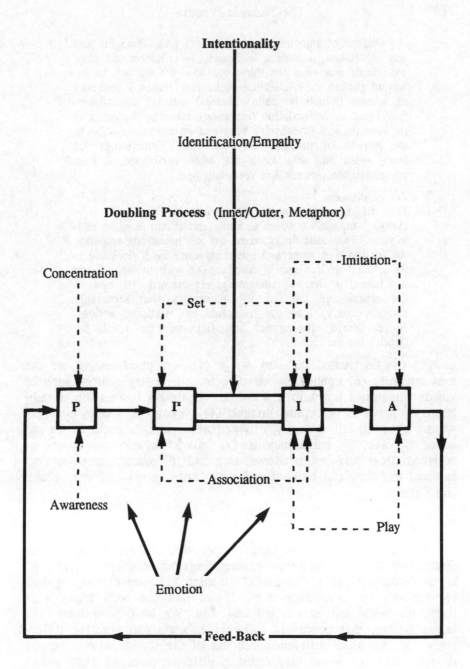

Figure 4

The Imagination Process

Groups of imaginings become acts [A]. Thoughts and acts are linked, according to Piaget, by imitation and play; we inherit not *what* we think but *how* we do so. An inherited pattern of intellectual structures creates a sequence of actions (which he calls *schemas*) through assimilation (play) and accommodation (imitation), whereby we adapt to the environment (synthesis). Play and imitation are basic to the growth of thought: ways in which imaginings are *transformed* into acts. Each act, when performed, is then perceived: the process is a spiralling one.

2   *The continuous.*
Like all organisms, the human being is intentional: it is curious, inquisitive, wants to know and it can have an end-in-view. This attitude is based on identification/ empathy: the feeling that inner and outer are one. Such doubling is the ground of thinking in Similars (as with metaphor) and is inherent in the way imaginings are created. To think of the actual and the "as if" alternately (but seemingly simultaneously) leads us to actual and fictional actions. By comparing the actual and fictional, we reach the "truth" for us.

Images can be created in many ways: (1) perceptual images are the vast majority; (2) images can develop from a neutral matrix, such as voices sometimes heard in a sea-shell; (3) dream images are usually based on previous perceptual images; (4) hypnagogic images occur as we are about to fall asleep; (5) hypnopompic images occur as we are about to wake; (6) hallucinations; (7) "silver" images can appear in polished silver surfaces, windows, etc.; and (8) eidetic images are so external that they can be confused with perceptions — as with Blake and Goethe.

Emotions

Emotions affect how we perceive, imagine and act. Emotions can distort our view of actuality, e.g.: anger against neighbors might lead us to perceive them as "enemies," imagine they are plotting against us, and act by ostracizing them. If we had not been angry with them, we might not have acted that way. We have seen also, in a larger setting, that people in different habitats can perceive differently and can make different sense out of the world: what a person in one culture perceives may result in different emotions from someone in a different culture. In this instance, emotions affect our ideas (I may be afraid of snakes and think of the Amazon jungle with horror) and our acts (I may refuse a job offer on the Amazon).

Drama practitioners disagree as to *how* dramatic action educates emotion through imagery, yet do not doubt that it *does* do so. Spontaneous drama teaches the player two things: (a) an emotion around one image cluster may be appropriate in one situation but not in another; (b) a performance can be improved by altering the distancing of the self from the role. Experts say this happens in different ways: Moreno, Slade and some therapists use catharsis; theatre educators use modelling; and creative drama teachers use "acting out" and "playing out." There appears to be more than one answer to the problem.

Imagery as Developmental

Prior to "the primal act," the baby's fundamental image cluster was bodily. At ten months old, the Self becomes the focus of the image cluster. This focus is "the primal image," a cluster of images that codifies doubling so that the babe thinks "as if" he is someone else. The cluster exists in parallel with other clusters whereby he thinks about the actual. Imagistically considered, this is to metaphorize the Self and the Other so that one kind of cluster is parallel with another; to see the Self and the Other as Similars, and their differences as poles on a continuum. Then the child masters the inner-outer relation. The two parallel image clusters allow the child to have double thoughts and so become "a costumed player." From then, the child learns through play that various image clusters can, through action, be transformed into various media. Image clusters form around each medium to become the basis for adult art. In sum, therefore, we can talk about the relation of imagining to dramatic action in the following ways:

1   To imagine the world "from someone else's point of view" is a dramatic way of thinking and acting: impersonating and discovering the similarities/differences between Self/ Others.

2   Images are not objects but are movements or processual rhythms, which *operate as structures and dynamics in inter-play.*

3   Imaginings produce metaphoric meanings: doubling occurs at an imagistic level and is metaphoric. This metaphysical act occurs in language and all media. Images link to each other by sets and associations.

4   Image structures and dynamics are not discrete:

   *   structures alternately work as dynamics and vice versa;
   *   they are metaphors one of the other;
   *   they are in a continuous gestalt and oscillation;
   *   they operate dialogically: each assumes the position of the Other; takes into itself parts of the Other and vice versa.

5   Life, human performance and images are all in movement:

they are always in change and have their own rhythms, pace and timing — whether we are awake or asleep. They are living activities: processes/energies/relationships. Most of the time we do not know that images occur: languages suppress them.

6   We experience images and imaginings in the present tense — they exist *now* and then are gone. We might recall them later. We know them in our living experience. But we do not necessarily know that we know them. Imaginings mostly exist "here and now" in a tacit experience.

Talking about it is *not* to be part of it. When we talk about images they change. If I describe my dream to you the words may not capture the dream I experienced. This problem is acute in Indo-European languages. As they are based on nominals, we might assume that our mental life is structured in the same way — as nouns, categories, or discrete parts of a mechanism — and we can operate so that the parts determine the whole. Images are not like that. When those who speak Fijian or Wakashan describe similar dreams differently, it is clear that imagery is not constituted like European languages. The more we study children, the more we realize that images are less like nouns and more like verbs. They are not like tables or chairs. They are more like running or dancing, wishing or hoping, feeling or loving. But not quite. In fact, no language can entirely capture them.

Imagining as a State of Mind

The meanings which images carry vary with *the use* we make of them. We can use them in five states of mind:

*   *Remembering* brings back images we have previously created. It is used by the other states. What it recalls are past images in the context of the present.

*   *Dreaming* connects images in metaphoric ways with no difference between past, present or future.

*   *Fantasizing* is a dissociated state, existing for itself. It consumes the energy needed by other states but it does not contribute to them. It can be the predominant state of some disturbed persons.

*   *Living* is the state we work with in the mundane world. Living uses images in a subjective way (in felt-time and felt-space) although it tries to be objective by acting rationally.

*   *Imagining* proper is what is normally called "the imagination" but, as this is an abstract noun, it can have unfortunate connotations. The idea of "the imagination" might lead us to suppose that it is an object, which it is not. Imagining, as

we have seen, is a processual dynamic. It uses images
differently from other states by directing them towards the
possible future.

These states of mind originate in the tension between consciousness
and imagistic life. They are not discrete entities: they are more like
loose groupings than categories and their differences lie in feelings
around which images cluster. Dreaming, remembering, living and
imagining relate well and contribute to each other. Fantasy does not.
Each state only exists in the present tense as it is operating. But
three are *about* time: remembering of the past, living of the present,
and imagining of the future. Dreaming and fantasizing use images
formed in the past; they are suspended in time.

Imagining (as "the imagination") is uniquely human: by projecting images into an imagined future, only human beings can "suppose," or think "as if." As a state of mind it has the following
qualities:

1 Imagining is the fundamental double operation which
  grounds all others: it is the mode whereby we relate subject and object, inner to outer, and vice versa. It takes
  environmental elements and re-creates them subjectively.
  This is "mediation."

2 By re-creating the objective subjectively, imagining gives the
  subjective/objective a unity that creates metaphoric thinking.

3 Imagining develops the actual/fictional relation: from "what
  is" to "what might be" and back again. People view the
  Other "as a person like myself" — the basis of our social
  world.

4 The logic of imagining is dialogic rather than dialectical.
  The inner/outer relation (the double gestalt) is primordial:
  we understand others, events and things through comparison.

5 The sequencing of imaginings is best understood as possibility. Only when imaginings are expressed in the external world do they become realized concretely.

Memory

Memory deals with images we have previously experienced. It is
fundamental to all education. To remember that "William the Con-
queror won the Battle of Hastings in 1066," or that "12 x 12 =
144," is an act of recall which has three phases: experience, retaining
and remembering.

1   *To Experience (to Memorize)*

   Memory hinges on experience: I hear a tune, I see an incident, etc. My senses are activated so that perception occurs and images are created. This is not simple: it needs time and a complex of activities resulting from previous learning.

2   *To Retain*

   To retain an item we commit it to memory over a long period of time: days, months, even years. (This is different from short-term retention, a factor often assessed in experimental studies.) We know little about methods of retention but the more vivid the initial experience, the better the event will be retained.

3   *To Recall*

   To recall an experience is an activity: we must *do* something. We re-play existing images. Inability to do so may be due to inadequate memorizing; failure to retain, which is uncommon; or forgetting — the inability to recall an experience immediately (we have all forgotten something, only to remember it some time later).

Memory learning links to identification. Recall hinges on how vivid the experience was. With identification recall is *felt*. But recall must not be too vivid: trauma can force it into the deep unconscious. William James said:

> Most men have a good memory for facts connected with their own pursuits. The college athlete who remains a dunce at his books will astonish you by his knowledge of men's "records" in various feats and games, and will be a walking dictionary of sporting statistics. . . . In a system, every fact is connected with every other by some thought-relation. The consequence is that every fact is retained by the combined suggestive power of all the other facts in the system, and forgetfulness is well-nigh impossible. [318]

Memorizing depends on sense experience, meaning and repetition. Images that are clustered in a system can recall the total system. Teachers whose ideas about teaching/learning cluster to a clear metaphor (e.g., "watering the flowers" of Slade, the "midwifery" of Heathcote) recall data better than those who do not. A fact must be meaningful if it is to be memorized over time. Facts in play and dramatic acts have inherent meaning for us: they are acts we really *want* to do. When we try to memorize something of no meaning to us (e.g., nonsense jumbles of words), it can be more easily recalled if we put it into familiar terms: mnemonics, or dramatization.

   Repetition greatly helps retention. To be effective, repetition must be active: the learner must use the information in some way. [310] It is more effective to recite it than to read it — and even more effective to *act* it. Learning items in relation to one another (learning by wholes) is a sign of intelligent behaviour. A good actor, memorizing a part, first reads the whole play to comprehend its basic elements (plot, structure, characterization, etc.). In a second reading he or she may understand the role related to other characters/situations, etc. At first rehearsal, he "walks through" it with script in hand, grasping the salient features of the part, relating what is said to what is done. Physicalizing what is to be learned, and relating word to action, are keys to memorization. But:

> With the whole method much more time and work is required before any results of learning are manifest . . . a learner gets the feeling of success sooner with the part method. . . . The experienced and informed learner knows that the readings in the whole method are not a waste of time. . . . While he must work longer before results are manifest, the final returns fully justify his patience and endurance. [351]

In learning a foreign language, quick results by rote may not last. But if the learner is in a living context (immersion or simulation) results are more permanent if not necessarily immediately testable.

Perceptual quality is vital to recall. People differ in image formation: in the West, visual imagery is the most common, followed by auditory, tactile, kinaesthetic, gustatory, organic and olfactory imaging. For Hughes and Hughes strong imaging, as the basis of recall, is best achieved through highly sensory experience in which the learners have an intense interest, while Bruner says that the initial experience in learning is enactive. Dramatic activity specifically fulfils such conditions. It does so by making the material to be memorized more meaningful, by aiding the process of repetition, and by providing memorization in depth through a gestalt understanding.

Metaphor

Metaphorization is important for this book for two main reasons. First, it is the way in which double ideas are framed in the mind: we think metaphorically. Second, when dramatic action is the signifier, metaphor is signified. *Play has inner metaphoric meaning for the player.*

Definitions & Meanings

Metaphor defies all definitional and even encyclopedic descriptions. It relates two concepts, one to the other. This relation can be seen as: (1) a figure of speech (limited use); or (2) a mental operation (general use). As a figure of speech, metaphor is part of rhetoric. The most basic figure, synecdoche, allows us to move from part to whole, from whole to part, from member to class and from class to member. We shall be mainly concerned with the second usage: metaphor used as "metaphorization" — a description of thought and action that implies an idea is metaphorical. The base concept here is one of likeness, of Similarity, where one thing is seen in terms of another. Relationship is fundamental. One instance of this usage is the artistic use of metaphor: that some aspect or the whole of an art work implies a metaphorical meaning; only some metaphors are linguistic.

Whereas we can agree with the Venerable Bede that metaphor is "a genus of which all other tropes are species," the term has been used for virtually all rhetorical figures and devices that carry more than one meaning. The most common dictionary definitions of metaphor are two concepts related by likeness (metaphor proper); the substitution of one thing for another; the substitution of one thing for another through extension (part for whole, species for genus, singular for plural, and vice versa), sometimes called synecdoche, and sometimes called metonymy; and the substitution of one thing for another by contiguity (cause/effect, container/contained, etc.), or metonymy proper. This ambiguity needs some discussion.

Ancient Views

Aristotle's comments on metaphor in the *Poetics* are the foundation for all subsequent thought on the matter: "Metaphor consists in giving the thing a name that belongs to something else; the transference being either from genus to species, or from species to genus, or from species to species, or on grounds of analogy." Here he is talking of "metaphorization." Characteristically he links this to mimesis: the function of metaphor is to present men "as acting" and all things "as in act" — a function of Being where every latent capacity for action is actualized. Aristotle also held that metaphor is particularly cognitive: using it involves some process of learning. In connecting metaphor to intelligence, Aristotle said that the best metaphors "show things in a state of activity" and that, thereby, metaphorical knowledge is knowledge of the real. Thus they "should be drawn from objects that are related to the object in question, but not obviously related; in rhetoric as in philosophy the adept will perceive resemblances even in things that are far apart."

For medieval Neoplatonists, people functioned as a metaphor or metonymy of the One: they dramatized the Divine metaphorically in their own acts. All living things also operated by mimesis; as metaphors or dramatizations of symbolic things. Thus arose the bestiaries, the *imagines mundi*, and similar cultural networks. In the early Middle Ages, the metaphor grew that the cosmos was dramatic, as we have seen. The congregation was illiterate so Christ's passion was re-played by the priest in the Mass as a religious and educational medium.

Modern Science

> The author and the recipient of a metaphor connive, as it were, in agreeing to a tacit "as if." There is an act of creation at the heart of metaphor which distinguishes it from simpler, more passive comparisons, and explains its essential value in the arts. . . . I define metaphor as an evocation of the inner connection among things. . . [that is] all things are related to one another through an underlying unity. [329]

This is the view of Roger S. Jones, a physicist who views physics itself as metaphor. He shows that the four foundation concepts of modern physics — space, time, matter, and number — are metaphors of consciousness. In traditional cultures, space was and is *felt* as organic, connective, nurturing and alive with meaning much like a home environment. In the contemporary world, however, individuals feel "singled out" against a background of separated things and so space means extension, distance, separation, and isolation. Among the Hopi, time is seen not as sequential but as organic, simultaneous, and repetitive. Time was spatialized in the classical physics of Newton and Galileo. Since Einstein and Heisenberg, however, time is seen as uneven, cumulative, and cyclic while causality is metaphorically linked to space/time. Matter is today understood in terms of the Principle of Indeterminacy, and it is not seen as substance which, in Newton's metaphor, can be visualized as "stuff." Rather, matter exists in space-time as a highly abstract and mathematical probability — it is not a material substance at all. Number, which used to be entirely quantitative, has become (as it was for Pythagoras) qualitative and symbolic. Metaphorically number has become nearer to the rhythm and harmony of music than to the materialist Victorian concept of uniquely identifiable things. In other words, the concepts of physics are metaphorically conceived in terms of a culture's underlying root metaphors.

Contemporary Views

Among contemporary studies of metaphor, that of Paul Ricoeur emphasizes that metaphor is related to resemblance:

> . . . for the semantic innovation through which a previously unnoticed "proximity" of two ideas is perceived despite their logical distance must in fact be related to the work of resemblance. "To metaphorize

well," said Aristotle, "implies an intuitive perception of the similarity in dissimulars." Thus, resemblance itself must be understood as a tension between identity and difference in the predicative operation set in motion by semantic innovation. This analysis of the work of resemblance suggests in turn that the notions of "productive imagination" and "iconic function" must be reinterpreted. Indeed, imagination must cease being seen as a function of the image, in the quasi-sensorial sense of the word; it consists rather in "seeing as" according to a Wittgensteinian expression — a power that is an aspect of the properly semantic operation consisting of seeing the similar in the dissimilar. [518].

More recently Lakoff and Johnson have said that metaphors are part of everyday speech; they affect the ways in which we perceive, think, and act; and truth is not an objective concept. Rather, personal perception, feeling, and encounter (all aesthetic qualities) are the real grounds for human understanding of which metaphor is the central feature. Thus they disagree with those who say that we use sloppy language when we use inorganic metaphors to describe living things. For Lakoff and Johnson, reality itself is defined by metaphor and, as metaphors vary from culture to culture, so do the realities they define. For example, from the conceptual metaphor in English, "Argument is war," we can say, "He attacked every weak point in my argument," "Your claims are indefensible," or "I demolished his argument." But:

> It is important to see that we don't just talk about arguments in terms of war. . . . We see the person we are arguing with as an opponent. We attack his positions and we defend our own. . . . It is in this sense that the "Argument is war" metaphor is one that we live by in this culture; it structures the actions we perform in arguing. . . . The concept is metaphorically structured, the activity is metaphorically structured, and, consequently, the language is metaphorically structured. [368]

Thought, action, and medium are by their nature metaphorical. This assumption has support from laboratory research: the use of mental or visual imagery within metaphor is a key element in verbal effectiveness; and the use of metaphor improves language production, comprehension, and memory. [475] "Root metaphors" are those by which we understand the cosmos and our world within it; the root metaphors of a culture can best be identified in ritual dramas or theatre.

What of Being "as if"? According to Ricoeur, *metaphor codifies the double by linking its tensions into a unity while also seeing them as separate. This action is heuristic*: it "presents itself as a strategy of discourse that, while preserving and developing the creative power of language, preserves and develops the heuristic power wielded by fiction." [518] But it provides a "split reference" based on a "fictional redescription." In other words, metaphorical thought *is* "as if" thinking. It is not a simple "as," which is Ricoeur's opinion. By originating in infantile empathy and identification, it is more akin to the "dialogue" of Buber and Bahktin than to the "dialectic" of Hegel and Marx — more a double gestalt than a triangulation of thought. In this sense, *metaphor is part of all thinking* either overtly (when one item is explicitly seen in terms of another) or implicitly (when this process is tacit). What Lakoff and Johnson call "personification" ensures that thought/action/medium are unified; and this helps ground abstract concepts in more physically based images. When expressed, this is acting "as if." Metaphors are an expressive mode that always has cognitive value; yet metaphors are not actual but fictional — serious assertions that are beyond literal truth.

Imaginatively in our felt-world, the actual (the "real") and the fictional (the metaphorical) co-exist. We operate "as if" we were in these two worlds at the same time. This action appears (falsely) to be simultaneous. In fact, mind oscillates between the two. Metaphor's great explanatory power gives it ontological meaning: "The metaphorical 'is' at once signifies both 'is not' and 'is like.' If this is really so, we are allowed to speak of metaphorical truth, but in an equally 'tensive' sense of the word 'truth.'" [518] When this meaning is located ("referenced") within a medium (e.g., language or drama/theatre) it is heuristic.

Metaphor is also important for learning in a variety of ways. There is a genuine need to construct effective classroom techniques that make use of memorable imagery. As root metaphors vary with culture, they can teach us much about our multicultural world. Imagining also relates to the promotion of creativity; contemporary schools are in real need of the power of active metaphor to stimulate innovative and expressive thought.

Metaphor & Dramatic Acts

Imaginative thought has a metaphoric relation to action. As actors, we see one in terms of the other: as we act, we think. When we are very young, as we think we must act — which is why young children can never be still. Later, we learn that thinking itself is covert action. We can see this most clearly when we rehearse a forthcoming interview "in our heads." Also, as observers, we infer from what people do that they are thinking: that they use imagery in order to act. As either actors or observers, we are engaged in doubling. The implication is clear: *the relation of our inner world to the outer world is metaphoric and we achieve this through the medium of dramatic action.*

To put this another way: We relate images metaphorically based on identification/empathy. A metaphor in language is, "The roses in her cheeks." One thing is partially identified with another, viewed in terms of another: "her cheeks" are seen in terms of "roses," and the new idea is greater than either. But metaphors exist in more than language: they are fundamental to art (e.g., Rembrandt's visual metaphors of the human face become symbolic of us all) and to science (e.g., Einstein conceived his theories in visual metaphors, like dramatizing himself between two trains passing each other). The baby's maturation builds this process. Initially the baby's body is a metaphor. Research shows that the very first linguistic constructions are bodily images: the metaphors of inside/outside, near/far, open/closed and so forth. [368] Mind operates through a continual process of doubling. When Captain Cook arrived off Nootka Sound in 1778, the first night he and his men witnessed the local Indians dancing. But the second night, when he witnessed another dance, some of the Indians were dressed in imitation of English sailors! The Indians had doubled their imagery by creating fictional sailors. Their mental metaphorization became external dramatization.

All forms of metaphorization relate two concepts. In doing so, they transform these concepts and create a new idea. In the simplest terms, there are two major metaphorical structures that concern us here: metaphor proper and metonymy. "My love is like a red, red rose" is a metaphor, which presents two different things as identical in a relationship that is temporary and arbitrary. "A crown for a king" is metonymy which is also a relationship between two things but as a whole to a part: the substitution of one thing for another through contiguity (cause/effect, container/contained, etc.). The distinction between metaphor and metonymy becomes important in Chapter 16.

Chapter 16
Drama, Thought & Structure

We have seen in Chapter 15 that there is an interplay of structures and dynamics in the mind. What is a dynamic at one moment can become a structure at the next: the ideas contained in mental activity, working by a continuous double gestalt, are excessively complex and very flexible. How well we use ideas indicates our use of intelligence. Some scholars group ideas: cognitive, affective, psychomotor and aesthetic (feelings). These cannot be exclusive: there is no thought that is entirely of one kind. All ideas have cognitive, affective, psychomotor and aesthetic parts. It is the emphasis we give each that matters.

Despite the prevailing notion of a single intelligence, Howard Gardner says intelligences are multiple: linguistic, logical-mathematical, musical, bodily-kinesthetic, spatial, and personal. [240] Are there as many intelligences as there are kinds of mental activities? Probably. Dramatic activity is intelligent. While it is primarily aesthetic in quality, it is also cognitive, affective and psycho-motor.

Cognition

In general usage, cognition is the ability to know. In experimental psychology it used more narrowly: the ability to categorize concepts.

Concepts

Concepts are ideas which group or classify experience: "representations that have some generality of application." [382] Thus we classify "robin" and "sparrow" as "birds"; but the concept of the category "birds" includes many other birds as well. "Birds" is a cognitive concept. There are other kinds of concepts, some of them difficult to put into words. There is fear of death, fear of heights, and a "generalized fear" suffered by some people with affective disorders. There are aesthetic concepts: we may feel that *this* sunset is not as beautiful as *that*. Psychomotor concepts differ between running, standing, etc. Because all these concepts are difficult to write about does not mean they can be ignored.

In theory an infinite number of concepts is possible but, in practice, they are often based on earlier classifications of experience that we have found useful in some way. Thus we acquire a repertory of concepts which tend to become more complex and more logical with increasing age.

What kinds of concepts are there? We can distinguish primary and secondary concepts:

1   internal representations of classes/categories of experience
     which can be named; and

2   those built out of other concepts, that is, out of partial
     similarities in the *responses* to sensations — e.g., "opposit-
     eness" is built out of noticed instances. [100]

Looked at in another way, Bruner, Goodnow and Austin provide us
with three types of concepts:

A   *Conjunctive*: the criterion is a specified combination of
     attributes (e.g., "red figures with borders");

B   *Relational*: the criterion is a specified relation between
     attributes (e.g., "fewer figures than borders"); and

C   *Disjunctive*: the criterion is any two or more alternative
     combinations or attributes (e.g., "either a red figure or one
     with two borders"). [83]

The ability to discriminate positive from negative instances frequently
precedes the ability to formulate the concept in words. Information
from positive instances can be assimilated and used more readily
than information from negative instances. [613] Cognitive dissonance
is "a state of affairs that occurs whenever two ideas are in marked
conflict as when one is presented with an objective fact that appears
to undercut one's cherished beliefs. Festinger shows that people are
strongly motivated to reduce such cognitive conflict — either by
changing their attitudes, seeking more information, or restructuring or
reinterpreting the information available to them." [101] The ability to
live and work with paradoxes, however, indicates a highly developed
intellectual ability.

Knowing

If cognition is the ability to know, then imaginings are the way
we link thoughts, and concepts are the way we classify and order
ideas. There are three kinds of knowing available to us. First, *explicit* knowledge is the knowing we know we know: we express
what we know in words and can talk to people about it. It is
Knowledge *About*: mainly conscious and obtained when we think or
talk about our experience. Second, *personal* knowledge is different. It
is tacit: mainly unconscious, we do not usually know when we know
it. [492] Personal knowledge is Knowledge *In*: it occurs within our
experience in the "here and now" and it is mainly tacit; it is a
combination of thinking/action/learning as we "live through" existence. Personal knowledge includes feelings, hunches, guesses and
intuitions. The tacit and explicit are complementary. The second is
built on the first. Both are cognitive but with different emphases.

And third, *practical* knowledge combines elements of explicit and personal knowledge. It is knowing procedures ("procedural knowledge") in order to pursue a task — *"know how."* Drama teachers have practical knowledge about educational drama just as players have practical knowledge about playing. Practical knowledge can be revealed as the sub-text from what people say and do — particularly from the metaphors they use. [148]

Mental Structures

How are thoughts and ideas structured? When we try to discover the nature of mental structures, we face a formidable task. Library shelves are scattered with unsuccessful attempts to do so. One of the most famous is that of Lévi-Strauss, who postulated an initial binary structure which, in transmission to an adjacent culture, became inverted. This is not only excessively simplistic, it is plainly not true. Structures are not binary. They do not operate through either/or like a computer. They are not categoric, in Aristotle's sense. Nor are they linear for, as Arthur Koestler says, they include "knight's move thinking," as in chess. [357]

Here, in contrast, we offer a developmental, or genetic, account of mental structures. It is based on the innate flexibility of mind and how this flexibility develops with maturation. Our account asks, How do such structures begin and how do they develop in the life span? The neonate forms thought structures around meaning and we continue the same functional process throughout life. We do so in a double way, from inner and outer, psychologically and sociologically: from our biological basis, and from the culture we live in. We intentionally create thought structures to find meaning.

Previous structural theories have assumed that structures and dynamics are different in kind. But is this really so? Thought structures, as they exist and as we experience them, are processes: dynamics that operate through oscillation. *Paradoxically, our dynamics and structures are reversible,* as we have seen in Chapter 15. For example, at one moment perception and imaging (A and B) operate as dynamics while imitation and play (Y and Z) operate as structures; and at the next moment they reverse their functions: Y and Z are dynamics while A and B are structures. The more our oscillations, the more we increase our intelligence.

Initial Structures

*   *The primordial mental structure is Likeness.*
     When we are born, as William James said, the world is "a blooming, buzzing confusion." Then we see life

whole. On the first day of life, we will not look if you switch on a light, or turn our head if you drop a book. At birth, everything is similar, including lights and sounds.

* *Part of Likeness is Doubling.*
    As we have seen in Chapter 15, doubling is inherent in all thinking processes.

* *This develops to the mental structure of Similar/Difference, or Whole/Part.*
    What is different is part of what is similar. Soon after birth, the baby can distinguish what is similar from what is different. Slowly the baby distinguishes one thing from another thing, and has begun a process of differentiation: a specific sound is heard amongst the noise; or a light can be seen in the darkness; and a continuity is generalized.
    Opposition is set within the context of Similarity; so analogues are prior to digital structures, and wholes are prior to binary structures. To put this another way, we first see the likeness between things; the contrasts and conflicts between things are built upon their likeness. We relate to people and things through the unity of dialogue — we understand other people as beings like ourselves — so that we are doubles of each other.

* *The next developmental step is the mental structure of Continua.*
    The ability to imagine ideas as poles, and then to see other ideas on a continuum, is to understand imagery as degrees of Difference within one whole Similarity. Continua, in other words, are extensions of the Similarity dynamic. Likeness and Difference are conceived in terms of Similarity just as the diverse poles are seen in terms of the continuum.

From our initial structures we develop others: metaphor, for example, is a growth from whole/part. One part is seen in terms of another. *When a part of a metaphor is seen separately it operates as a mental structure; when seen as a whole it operates as a dynamic.* Metaphoric thought is specifically aesthetic: it is based on feeling (it must "feel right") and, as each thought is double, we must exercise judgment when we come to work with both. From metaphor we learn to work mentally in two "worlds": the actual and the fictional, which includes those of play and art. In the actual world we work with actual objects but in the fictional world we work with representations. Metaphors in action become symbolic, an issue we shall address in Chapter 18.

Metaphor, Drama & Semiotics

Semiotics is called "the science of signs." It is not an academic field but a unique method, or tool, for inquiry. It is most well known for studies in Specific Semiotics: examinations of particular languages, sign systems (as for the deaf), etc. In contrast, General Semiotics (which we will use here) addresses the issues that cross particular systems and deals with them in a philosophic way.

General Semiotics sees dramatic thought and actions as sign systems, ones that are infinitely more complex than the simplistic input/output model of behaviourism. The principles of semiotic inquiry rely on the distinction between: (1) Signifiers, or forms (of the signs themselves); and (2) Signifieds, or expressions (what signs signify).

To put this another way, an investigator infers the player's inherent meaning (signifieds) within his dramatic act (signifier). The perspective of General Semiotics is a valid method of inquiry into such a whole provided it is rational (through "criteria in contexts") and, thereby, objective. In other words, this method and the empirical are viewed as complementary objective methods. One technique from General Semiotics that is particularly useful to us is the semiotic square.

The Semiotic Square

Algirdas Greimas has uniquely developed the semiotic square, a way of mapping ideas based on meaning (semantics). [257] His research indicates that *the major elements of a thought, or idea, are similarities, contrasts, conflicts, and complementarities.* He then maps these as the structure of a thought in fours ("quaternities") as points on a square.

Thus a semiotic square, as illustrated in *Fig. 5*, consists of four inter-related aspects of an idea: notion X1 generates notion Y1 by conflict; each then generates its contrast, X2 and Y2; the quincunx, or midpoint (Z), is the complementary of X1/Y2 and Y1/X2. It is the fourth position of the square (Y2) that is capable of the "leap" of creativity. This semiotic square is the template for all kinds of similar squares that reveal the structures of different ideas. We are specifically concerned with the ideas represented by metaphor and, thus, dramatic acts.

The semiotic square could not be more different from the input/output model of behaviourism, which is linear and exclusive. Rather, the semiotic square resembles Navaho sand-paintings or Tibetan mandalas, shamanic inscriptions or alchemic symbols: ancient maps of living quaternity structures that stress the whole rather than parts. Quaternity methods generate multiple meanings, spatial and inclusive.

When we analyze ideas through semiotic squares we are using two inter-linked Similarity/Difference structures as four inter-related poles: [257] Similarity/Difference generates Contiguity and Opposition. To put this more simply, image clusters are structured around items that are similar, items that are metonymic, items that are in opposition, and items that are different.

The whole seen as individual parts is a structure, but viewed as a unified whole it is a dynamic. When the whole operates as a structure, any one of the four parts is related to another by three dynamics: contrasts, conflicts and complementarities; e.g., *the four-fold structure (Similarity, Contiguity, Opposition, Differentiation) works by three dynamics (contrasts, conflicts, complementarities).*

But the positions on the semiotic square are only "fixed" for one idea. They change as thoughts change. With maturation, Similarity becomes increasingly complex. The dramatic doubling, by seeing A from the position of B and also seeing B from the position of A, increasingly metaphorizes our imagery. And when A becomes B it is *not exactly* the same as A. A is never quite the same as B and B is never quite the same as A. In dramatic terms, I am never quite the same as the other, and the other is never quite the same as me, no matter how good our impersonations. Ideas are never simple one-to-one relations. That is, imagery is an excessively complex mental operation whose dynamics and structures are in flux. No one semiotic square matches another. One imagery structure does not have exactly the same dynamic balance as another. Just as no thought is entirely cognitive or entirely affective, so each idea has its own emphasis between Similarity, Contiguity, Opposition and Differentiation.

Further, Opposition and Conflict both function as aspects of Similarity. That is to say, if Likeness is the fundamental structure of the human mind, then "the territorial imperative" of Robert Ardrey is simply not true. It is not the case that human beings are basically competitive, in conflict, and continually warlike. That is a particularly destructive aspect of the Aryan myth. On the contrary, because our imagery is structured around Likeness, human beings operate basically in terms of harmony, feelings for others, drama and peace. Nor should the assumptions inherent in our particular language persuade us otherwise. Thus should we be able to persuade our leaders to genuinely examine their mental processes, there may be some hope that our children and grandchildren might escape a nuclear holocaust.

The Metaphoric (Dramatic) Square

What is valuable for educational drama is that the semiotic square adapts to form the metaphoric square, which displays the structure of ideas expressed in dramatic acts. Drama externalizes a metaphoric mode of thought that, as we have seen in Chapter 15, is

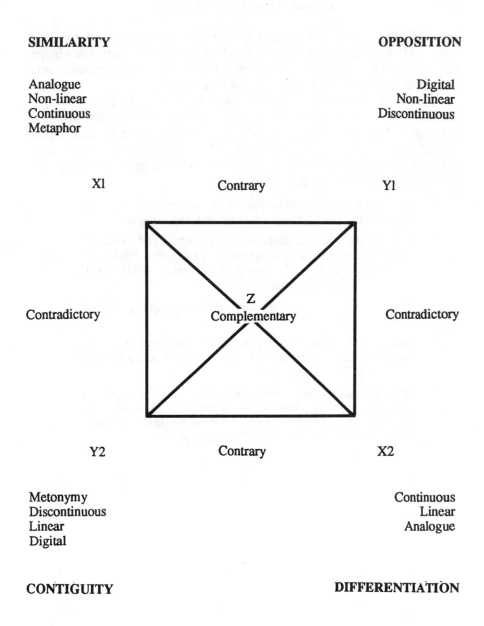

SIMILARITY

OPPOSITION

Analogue
Non-linear
Continuous
Metaphor

Digital
Non-linear
Discontinuous

X1

Contrary

Y1

Contradictory

Z
Complementary

Contradictory

Y2

Contrary

X2

Metonymy
Discontinuous
Linear
Digital

Continuous
Linear
Analogue

CONTIGUITY

DIFFERENTIATION

Figure 5

The Metaphoric Square (after Floyd Merrell)

grounded in feeling: it is related to emotion but is more discriminatory; and its cognitive elements form personal and tacit knowledge and belief. The structures of metaphoric thought and dramatic acts vary with culture, but also have some commonalities.

This metaphoric square is illustrated in Fig. 5. In this typology, Similarity and Opposition are gestalt wholes while Contiguity and Differentiation are parts of a whole, as both Greimas and Floyd Merrell have shown. [256, 257, 428, 429] Opposition is not literally required in metaphor, yet it is assumed. Thus we can say that metaphoric thought and dramatic action:

* are founded on Likeness and create Similarities, the axiological basis for meaning, learning and knowledge;

* underlie the way we apprehend and comprehend existence: what others have called scientific paradigms, [364] root metaphors, [259, 589] world hypotheses, [482] world views, [505] and forms of life; [86]

* work with metonymy so that ambiguity and paradoxes exist;

* give meaning that rests on Similarity, analogue, the non-linear and the continuous; this is to compare actual/fictional within a holistic perspective;

* are primarily aesthetic (tacit and of feeling) and provide aesthetic learning: harmonies, semblances, discords and contrasts in pre-adolescence; and syntheses, identities, dialectics and polarities in adolescence. [635]

Chapter 17
Play, Drama & Intuition

When Freud talks of "the unconscious" or Polanyi talks of "the tacit," workers in educational drama talk of "intuition." So far in this book we have discussed intuition in other people's terms. But intuition plays such a key role in all dramatic actions that we must address the issue in our own terms.

Intuition is an innate grasping by the mind. [460] It happens immediately as a direct insight and is accompanied by the feeling of being "just right." The kind of knowledge it produces is unique: it occurs without reasoning; and we say on such occasions that we "just know." It is, therefore, a kind of knowledge that relates to belief: it seems to fit to our tacit knowledge, to confirm what we already knew but did not know that we knew. When we achieve this kind of knowledge, we cannot always explain it in words: it is related to personal knowing. Indeed, when we try to make it explicit, we often find that the words we use change it in some way. Intuition is a highly significant factor in human thinking, and one that has been held in high regard throughout history.

Background to Intuition

Ancient communities held the intuitions of seers and oracles in awe and reverence. The classical Greeks and Romans generally considered that both intuitive and rational knowledge were valid: Pythagoras and the followers of Dionysos emphasized the first while Plato stressed the second. Aristotle, however, said that reason was based on intuition. Although both Augustine and Aquinas believed in non-rational revelation, Christianity's claim to ultimate truth, together with the rise of induction in the Renascence, led to a lower value for intuition. Intuition was even disregarded by the mechanism that resulted from Descartes and Newton.

It was not until Kant that intuition as a way of knowing began to be acknowledged once more. For him, intuition was a necessary part of sense perception, the basis of the mental process. Rousseau said that children should be encouraged to act on their intuitions and not be stifled by rigorous instruction — the basis for romantic thought to the present day. After Kant, Schleiermacher created an all-inclusive theory of intuition and knowledge that included four types of wisdom: self-intuition, intuition of the environment, aesthetic intuition, and philosophic speculation. Although intuition was highly regarded by 19th century writers and artists (e.g., Goethe, Schiller, Wordsworth, Coleridge, etc.), and it became the basis of the educational methodologies of Froebel, Pestalozzi and others, it was still not the predominant view. It was even dismissed by the empiricism of the Utilitarians, Bentham and Mill.

It was with the Einsteinian revolution at the beginning of this century that intuition became highly regarded once more by major thinkers. Einstein himself gave high priority to intuition. Philosophers as diverse as Bergson, Croce, Husserl, Whitehead, Heidegger, Fink and Gadamer have all been deeply concerned with intuition. It is the basis of the work of Marshall McLuhan and Buckminster Fuller.

Psychology

Psychologists have a variety of views about intuition. For Jung, intuition was the way we orient ourselves to the future. He also considered that there are four common ways to learn, based on four types of learners: feelers, thinkers, sensors, and intuitors — which is similar to the work of Kolb. Evolutionists, Freudians and others tend to use "instinct" instead of "intuition." From the Gestalt viewpoint, Wertheimer said that intuition was the spontaneous and non-rational understanding of the deep structure of a problem, which he illustrated by his interview with Einstein.

Eric Berne describes "the intuitive mood" as a state where intuitive thinking is encouraged. Berne studied intuition empirically and found that:

1　it functions as a series of perceptive processes working in an integrated fashion;

2　what is intuited is different from what the intuiter verbalizes as his intuition;

3　it works both above and below the level of consciousness in an integrated fashion, with shifting emphases according to prevailing conditions;

4　it may be more important than is often admitted in influencing judgments about reality in everyday life. [51]

In educational psychology, intuition is not often related to learning. Piaget, for example, does not concern himself with it to any great degree. Yet when he says that we "know" the world in terms of "our actions upon it rather than relations among objects," [486] intuition is implied. Jerome Bruner identified two kinds of intuition in mathematics; "informed guessing" (hypothesis), and the ability to solve a problem without formal proof. Elsewhere he writes, "Intuition implies the act of grasping the meaning or significance or structure of a problem without explicit reliance on the analytic apparatus of one's craft." [82] Among teachers of drama and the creative arts intuition is highly regarded.

Qualities of Intuition

Given this background, we need to ask: what are the qualities of intuition that specifically effect the practical knowledge of drama and creative arts teachers?

Intuition & Mind

Contemporary research shows intuition to be related to mental clustering: images and ideas are "lumped" in the right hemisphere (compared with "splitting" that occurs in the left). Intuitive "lumping" relates complex symbolic activities, and this brings about "a kind of internal dialogue between whole and parts, between image and sequence." [517]

This view parallels those of both Buber and gestaltists. Intuition grasps the whole of a circumstance because of its image-making power. It makes rapid and complex syntheses using combinations, amalgamations and generalizations of imagery. These are based on Similarity rather than Oppositions — unified mental processes rather than digital operations. In other words, intuition works in an aesthetic mode: it uses rich associative patterns and is based on feeling; at the same time it both recognizes and interprets emotional cues, while forming a basis for deduction through hypothesis. Where intuition differs from sequential cognition is that intuition perceives qualitative relationships, e.g., liking, appreciating, etc.

Intuition and imagination are closely allied. Of the many examples of intuition amongst scientists and artists, [244] that of Einstein is perhaps the most revealing. He used it in visual imagining and dramatizing for many of his discoveries: for his theory of light, he imagined what a light wave would look like to an observer riding along with it; his theory of general relativity was based on the image of a man in a falling elevator; and his curved four-dimensional space-time continuum he envisaged as a suspended rubber sheet stretched taut, but distorted wherever heavy objects (such as stars and galaxies) were placed upon it.

Intuition & Communication

Human communication is a complex process. As Hofstadter narrates, everyone is a product of a different set of circumstances and, as a result, misunderstandings abound. Yet on the other hand, a communication by an obscure poet of the 15th century can provoke a wealth of meaning in a great many people. Hofstadter's conclusions are: partial isomorphism is possible between people "whose style of thinking is similar"; and, although people differ in trivial ways, all are the same in important ones. Using examples of translations from one language to another, Hofstadter shows that global and holistic meanings can be communicated if the local, and specifically cultural, meanings are re-phrased into the second language. Some metaphors and symbols are shared by all; but some are approximations based on similar experiences. Decoding a written language cannot be matched line by line if it is to carry metaphoric and symbolic meaning. [290]

Ambiguity particularly occurs with intuitive thinking. As intuition is a personal and largely tacit activity, and operates by "lumping" of images, it does not communicate on a one-to-one basis. Nor does communication happen merely through partial isomorphism. Tacit operations are basic to the explicit; a message, to be communicated, must be translated into the personal and tacit levels of the receivers. As Hofstadter shows, [290] information from modern studies in DNA reveals that there are genetic structural patterns for the process of "dialogue" as envisaged by Buber and Bakhtin.

Intuition & Drama Teachers

This background to intuition has particular significance because drama and creative arts educators claim a predominance of intuition in their thinking. [148] Intuitions cannot be the subject of direct instruction, such as the lecture method of presentation. Rather, they are communi-cated indirectly from teacher to student at the personal and tacit level. This communication is most likely to occur through the process of "dialogue" rather than digital or dialectic processes. If, as Robert Witkin says, arts teachers are concerned with the way in which "expressive form realizes and articulates qualitative feelings" which "demands objectivity," [635] then they must engage the intuitions of their students in a genuine dialogue.

If there is only a small body of literature that refers to the practical knowledge of drama and arts teachers, there is even less about their attitude to intuition. But we need to ask: How does intuition relate to dramatic and practical knowledge? At first glance, it appears that the intuitive is an aspect of personal knowledge, that it is a tacit aspect of practical knowledge. While in general this is true, the nature of the intuitive is so complex that some issues can be confused.

Confusions about Intuition

In common-sense terms, the major confusions facing the use of intui-tion in education are two: those of drama and creative arts teachers, and those of teachers who do not use drama and the arts in their classrooms.

Teachers of Drama & the Creative Arts

Picasso said, "Art *is*." Similarly, the average teacher of drama and the creative arts in the classroom is not inclined to give much credence to empirical or rational statements about the activity. This is particularly the case with valuing. Valuing is something we *do*. What is valued, *is*. However much discussion takes place about the value of *this* painting when compared to *that*, in the final analysis the issue often comes down to intuition. This may not be the case with those teachers who emphasize arts appreciation. But those engaged in creative drama, it is said, "just know" what is of value and what is not. While scholars can claim that rational and objective arguments can be made about artistic value, [54] the average teacher does not use them. This attitude is evidenced in the conferences of the voluntary associations in drama and arts education, and documented in their records. They say drama teachers engage in intuitive rather than reasoned thinking; and it is their practice (their skills in creating with students) that makes intuition valid.

In other words, normally drama and creative arts teachers indirectly claim that it is their practical knowledge of drama and the arts that provides them with their unique perspective. Although this argument may give them some difficulty when they argue with others for educational priorities, and they may have some disagreement with authorities in the literature, the position they take rests on the validity of their practical knowledge in a particular way: intuition is a tacit component of practical knowledge. In contrast to many other teachers, those in educational drama clearly separate the dramatic activity (tacit knowledge within "living through" the experience) from talking about it (explicit knowledge of the practice). To them, the skills of creating drama are intuitive but not necessarily explicit; the concluding discussion is usually turned to other ends — social problems, language or extrinsic content. They are liable to justify the discussion in terms other than the dramatic experience: clarity of thought, say, or improving oral skills. But what is important about dramatic activities, they say implicitly, is intuition within Being "as if." As we shall see, although there is some truth in this notion, it is not the total story by any means.

Non-Arts Teachers

Yet it is also fair to state that many non-arts teachers and therapists have also been confused about intuition. Some have ignored it. Others have treated it contemptuously or denounced it as merely imprecise thinking. In so doing, "educators avoid a process that has been credited with producing some of the most important advances in the sciences and that has contributed immeasurably to the arts and humanities.

Ignoring the potential benefits of intuition also cuts off educators from one of the most exciting and least explored areas of learning in children and adults." [460] Much has been due to the difficulty in grasping the nature of intuition. After all, it is difficult to measure such things!

The Familiar

Positivists and behaviourists can argue against the existence of intuition. They say it is just a name for certain familiar events: if we have a great deal of knowledge, what is difficult for others can seem easy to us; or, if we think so rapidly that we cannot retrace our steps, we can falsely use the label, "intuition." They say teachers should focus on their students' acquisition of information and leave intuition alone!

Familiarity does not only help intuition. "Intuition is essential to the development of familiarity": [460] e.g., in problem-solving the first thing is to see that a problem exists. The initial steps of learning and creation hinge on intuitive impulses that are aesthetic (of feeling). For example, Poincaré says that there are special sensibilities in mathematical creation. [454]

The Aesthetic

Intuition is the springboard from which aesthetic activity begins.

Intuition is directly related to sense perception. We engage the senses directly. In the purely intuitive mode, checks are made between perceptions and concepts but we do not work mainly through them. Rather, we try out our perceptual information against the cognitive, yet we always return to the direct apprehension. Painters work with what they see and with their paint, trying out cognitive frames, rejecting some, accepting some, and inventing others. When they are satisfied, the work is "just right." They need no conceptual explanation of what they are doing. Their intuition is directly involved in their sensory awareness, their subjective response, and their need to discover and create meaning. Intuition, then, is a necessary first step for creation to occur. Before artists can act, they concentrate on their perception, on their understanding of the world around them. The human "need to know" commences from a receptive sensorium: *the ability to think concretely*, to have an inner response to the environment. This is empathic: it is a two-way process (a "dialogue," or a dramatic act) between the inner and outer, generated by mind. It provides understanding in a unique form: *insight.*

Intuition aims at "grasping": insight towards an uncertain end. Einstein said his intuition as a scientist was a feeling of going straight towards something concrete. He implied insight: *spontaneity is added to intuition.* Spontaneity, as Moreno said, "is the readiness to act" [451] and involves the loosening of normal constrictions, the opening of possibilities, the ability to go in the direction that "feels right." Where insight is more internal, spontaneity is directed towards action. Thus we can say that mental aesthetic activity has:

A   Two psychological operations: (1) reactions to external stimuli; and (2) reactions to internal stimuli;

B   Two focuses: (1) the internal: the intuitive to gain insight; and (2) the spontaneous: which prepares us for action.

Intuition & Education

What types of strategies in intuition should be part of the practical knowledge of the drama teacher? A previous study has examined related issues for arts teachers in Elementary schools [146] while a review of the research [460] has demonstrated the key theoretic issues. Other studies have examined related issues.

Teachers & Intuition

All teachers, and not just those in the arts, need to use intuition in their classes. As Rico and Claggett say, "The best teachers seem naturally to provide their students with images to give them a holistic framework into which the details will fit as they are delineated." [517] Good teachers use intuition when they:

1   provide students with rich experience, both actual and fictional ("doing" and "dramatic doing"); and

2   encourage such factors as metaphors, puns, paradoxes and other ambiguities which serve to unify and enrich their students' experience.

Teachers know more about their intuition if they can identify their own learning style. If they do so, they have a better chance of identifying the intuitive learning styles of their students. David Hunt has shown that learning styles vary on the dimensions concrete/abstract, active/reflective, theoretical/practical, systematic/intuitive, individual/group, self-directed/teacher-directed, personal/objective; and according to factors such as auditory, visual, temperature, tactile, time, etc. [309] In workshops with teachers, Hunt has used the Kolb Learning Style Inventory [359] which is based on the two dimensions — concrete/abstract and active/reflective — as in Figure 6.

Teachers made an intuitive self-assessment and placed themselves in one of the four quadrants. Thereafter, they conducted experiments to see if these were accurate. From exercises such as this, teachers can apply their own learning styles to classrooms. [309] Hunt developed the inventory of Kolb to discover four kinds of learners: divergers, assimilators, convergers and accommodators. Others have used it in a variety of ways. [411]. But Hunt's research has related teachers' and students' intuitions in ways that are revealing of practical knowledge.

Even drama teachers do not always recognize the intuitive workings of their students. Few teachers have thought deeply about intuition and even less discuss it with their students. Two examples will suffice. Teachers of writing need to acknowledge intuition as "the culmination of perceptions that we accumulate, internalize and synthesize into patterns." [562] Writing skills, at least at the elementary level, are based on invention, accurate observation, and visual forms — all foundational to intuition. Similarly, teachers of visual arts can use methods of "encouraging the inner eye": [517] framing, colouring, centering, shaping, clustering, the use of mandalas, etc.

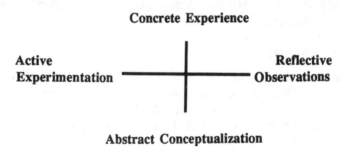

Concrete Experience

Active Experimentation   **Reflective Observations**

Abstract Conceptualization

Figure 6

Dimensions of Kolb's Learning Style Inventory

It was Robert W. Witkin who first asked drama teachers, if they were instructors *of drama*, why their discussion with students after they had improvised was not about the inner workings of drama per se. Those who use the games of Spolin and Johnstone do so, but most others direct the students' talk to extrinsic ends. Even fewer encourage students to talk about the intuitions they had while they were playing. Why not?

Several studies show that theatre directors rely on intuition for the choice and treatment of dramatic material. [240, 532] Many resist cognitive analysis in such tasks. They tend to visualize or hear the work "as if" it was being performed; this they balance with those items that emerge during rehearsals. They see themselves working intuitively, based on their experience and skills; but they also allow each individual artist/student to reach his or her own potential through intuition, interpersonal relations, and skills. This intuitive way of working also applies to school drama teachers but, paradoxically, few of them talk about intuition with their students.

One reason may be the pseudo-science that infuses teacher education. But "scientific studies have not carried us very far in the improvement of teaching. Perhaps it is time in teacher education to stress intuition, the artist's sixth sense. The aesthetics of teaching have barely been studied and may prove fruitful in further investigation." [532] Intuition must be accounted for by any "human science." Investigators have shown that intuition can be used by teachers to:

a   assess the effectiveness of materials;

b   assess and develop the quality of inter-personal relations;

c   modify materials and plans;

d   allow the emergence of individual performances within a whole;

e   work within a framework;

f   develop a sense of rhythm and flow;

g   increase imagination, enthusiasm and commitment;

h   use the whole Self as an instrument of teaching;

i   develop "educated guesses" (intuitive hypotheses). [532]

There have also been studies in music education that address intuition. [29, 369] By training teachers to recognize intuitive knowledge, Jeanne Bamberger shows that they build a store of common-sense information from personal experimentation on the physical environment. The framework of questions she used with music teachers was: How are the child's intuitive descriptions different from those formal descriptions accepted as norms in the school setting? What is the nature of the mismatch? How can the teacher help the child to integrate intuitive knowing with scholastic expectations? Bamberger's experiments had the following results on music teachers' thinking:

a   They expanded their ideas about knowing something (including what the knowers figured out for themselves).

b   They were more aware of their thinking processes and their ability to "figure things out."

c   They recognized the differences between the formal and intuitive modes of knowing.

d   They found difficulty in accepting that the two forms of knowing (at c) could be integrated (What is the relation of intuitive answers to "the right answers"? Are "the right answers" right? etc.) Bamberger discovered that the teachers' own "stories" of what happened in classrooms show that they

were well able to work out alternative strategies which elim-
inated choosing between the two forms of knowing. That is,
although they did not have the language for what they did
intuitively, they knew more than they could say.

Although Bamberger's research does not appear to have been replicated,
the results can inform our understanding of intuition in the practical
knowledge of drama teachers.

Strategies for Drama Teachers

To develop students' intuition, the following are strategies available
to the practical knowledge of each drama teacher:

1   "Having a fresh vision," even on old material, should be
    encouraged, including: accepting the strange/unfamiliar;
    understanding that students may find intuition difficult one
    day but not the next; and helping students to take risks/be
    brave enough to work in a new way.

2   Warming-up exercises help. Common in spontaneous creative
    drama, they are not normally used by teachers who work in
    other arts.

3   A warm atmosphere and a pleasant place to work encourages
    intuition. Statements from artists [244] clearly show that this
    is the case.

4   The trivial should be avoided. Students respond intuitively to
    the major issues in their lives. This can only occur when the
    teacher is a model — seeing the task through because it is
    deeply felt.

5   Obstacles must be overcome. Routines that permit intuition
    should be developed. Students should face genuine issues that
    require identification and solving of problems; and develop
    procedures that help intuition grow, but they must never
    become ends in themselves.

6   Teachers/students must engage in a genuine human inter-
    action: honest, open, and sincere. This includes ensuring that
    each student faces the issue of identifying a problem. Little
    purpose is served if the teacher identifies problems which
    students then solve.

7   Students must make the key decisions in a classroom. Intui-
    tion is about feeling/choice/judgment. E.g., in spontaneous
    improvisation, the first question Dorothy Heathcote asks of
    adolescents is, "Will the play be about past, present, or
    future?" [321] The onus is placed upon the students. These
    questions open up multiple pathways. Storytelling with very
    young children can also use their choices:

"Once upon a time there was a . . . Yes, there was
a mouse. What was its name . . . . Yes, it was
Peter. Well, one day, Peter was walking down the
road. What do you think he saw? . . . Yes, he saw
a gate. It was a big white gate with — " (adapted
from Slade [557])

Intuition comes from actions — helping to tell a story or
making decisions about a created play — and not by verbal
explanations. Having (and keeping to) clearly defined "behavioural objectives" does not necessarily allow the teacher to
operate in such a way. Intuition is best encouraged if as
many options as possible are open — for teachers as well as
students.

8 Students should directly engage their perceptions and intuitions: the ways in which they are aware of the world and
their inner operations. Teachers can encourage this by the
continual use of immediate dramatic experience; presenting
materials in a variety of media (pictorial for music, poetry in
dance, etc.); challenge and debate; new perspectives; the use
of images and metaphors; the use of different media to
express the same intuition; small group work and considering
the work of peers; etc.

9 Identifying the students' own needs, concerns and interests.
"Begin from where you are," says Brian Way. [615] Understanding can only be built upon previous understandings
("from the known to the unknown") and, when this occurs,
the students' own purposes and goals can be satisfied.

10 Allowing time. Intuition does not obey the time slots of
school bells; nor is its pace the same with everyone. Thus
"to slow down the pace is not necessarily to teach and learn
less. Delight, humour, contemplation and sharing [are] parts
of an education that takes intuition seriously." [460]

11 Focusing on the fictional. It is this, and only this, which
makes action dramatic. Clearly there is a close relationship
between intuition and imagination, empathy, and tacit knowing. All are linked in the practical knowledge of drama and
arts teachers.

Chapter 18
Drama, Theatre & Symbol

Our thoughts are metaphorical, but when we externalize them in dramatic action, they may become symbolic. Symbols are cultural. Players talk about metaphors within the action but critics talk about symbols. Symbols signify various things at the same time, and many things to different people. This multiplicity of meaning makes symbols difficult to define.

Definitions of Symbol

Signs and symbols are similar but not synonymous. All signs are symbols but not every symbol is a sign. Symbols are multi-vocal. Thus

> in the interpretation of a symbol the conditions of its presentation are such that the interpreter ordinarily has much scope for exercising his own judgment. Hence one way of distinguishing broadly between signal and symbol may be to class as symbols those presentations where there is much greater lack of fit — even perhaps intentionally — in the attribution of the fabricator and the interpreter. [198]

Umberto Eco and others talk of signs as a subclass of symbols: that symbols convey more meaning than signs. But sign and symbol are virtually the same for Cassirer, Lévi-Strauss, and Todorov.

A symbol, then, has wide significance. Not all its many meanings are understood at any one time; nor does one person obtain the same meaning as the next. It differs from allegory. Whereas a metaphor has a double meaning, both symbol and allegory have wider meanings and can be interpreted in two different ways: symbolically and literally. Allegory is sustained narration which we interpret through a key contained within it. A symbol is not necessarily part of sustained narration and can, indeed, even disturb the narrative. Symbolic representation occurs particularly in the aesthetic mode. Aesthetic and artistic symbols are not synonymous: aesthetic symbols emphasize feeling; artistic symbols are context-dependent — they only have meaning in the context of art.

Symbols in History

The earliest symbols represented beliefs about the Divine and its relation to human existence. Shamanic cultures today all unite religion, dance, drama, art, crafts, music, and economy in one ritual performance that symbolizes "first times": [179] the mythical period when the world was created. In ritual the past is dramatized as the "now" to influence the future: time is collapsed; everything is one whole. In tribal cultures, no one thing is symbolic of something else; all is symbolic of total existence.

Slowly cultures complicated the early "total" symbols into complex and hieratic systems. Each system included cultural meanings; e.g., hunting tribes created symbolic relations between, say, the times the bison rutted and the patterns of the stars. [405] This tradition continues: astronomical events are synchronized with the timing of ritual performances among Pueblo Indians and the Hopi today. In farming civilizations the signs of the zodiac were dramatized as particular gods and their actions had different levels of meaning: the performers expressed metaphoric meanings; they were enacted in the rituals of "the sacred marriage," "the ritual battle," initiation, "the scapegoat," etc.; and they were symbolic of the worlds of the stars, the gods, the seasons, human beings, the dead and the spirits. Ancient Near Eastern myths were always performed until the advent of writing at Ugarit split ritual and myth. When Homer's oral myths were created, they did not have the symbolic power of ritual. Yet they retained enough mythological power to be a symbolic model for classical tragedy and Western civilization.

From the 1st century A.D., the Church Fathers interpreted the Bible symbolically. Christ was dramatized as the *logos*: he combined all the archetypes, was polysemous, and was both the sender and the referent. Everyone acted "as if" he was Christ, *in imitatio Christi*. There were four symbolic meanings: the literal, allegorical, moral and anagogical. These were later explained by Dante, with reference to the Flight from Egypt, that "if we look at the letter it means the exodus of the sons of Israel from Egypt at the time of Moses; if we look at the allegory it means our redemption through Christ; if we look at the moral sense it means the conversion of the soul from the misery of sin to the state of grace; if we look at the mystical sense it means the departure of the sanctified spirit from the servitude of this corruption to the freedom of eternal glory." [156] This method "decoded" the Bible. Augustine said that natural things carried symbolic messages; with his knowledge of physics, geography, botany and mineralogy, he began the idea that classical knowledge was "a syncretistic encyclopedia": [173] all creatures had symbolic properties — often contradictory and with alternative meanings; e.g., the Lion was two things: Christ, because the lion conceals its trail with its tail just as Christ removes human sin through incarnation; and the Devil, because both he and the lion had hideous jaws. The medieval bestiaries, lapidaries and herbals had manifold meanings of symbol and allegory.

This symbolic mode finally collapsed before Aquinas' *Summae*: a strictly coded allegory for the Old Testament that eroded symbolic ambiguity. Its remnants in the Renascence were inherited by Shakespeare ("All the world's a stage") and his peers. The changes in Renascence visual art show a decrease in symbolism and a growth in allegory. The court of Elizabeth I had an excess of allegory and emblems which was carried to its logical conclusion with the Jacobean allegories of Ben Jonson's masques. [330]

From Descartes and Newton came the metaphor for the universe as a giant machine, while science was based on the quantification of distinguishable parts. The symbol, no longer scientific, moved to the domain of the arts. Thus the West lost the sense of unity given by the symbolic tradition, which continued in the East. From Kant and Romanticism, "art works" and "symbol" became parallel. Works of art were symbolic. Franz Schubert said: "The prototypes of the images and forms used by the oneiric, poetic, and prophetic idioms, can be found around us in Nature, revealing herself as a world of materialized dream, as a prophetic language whose hieroglyphics are beings and forms." [111] For Goethe, symbols are multi-dimensional and influence mental work, because "symbolisms transform the experience into an idea, and an idea into an image, so that the idea expressed by the image remains always active and unattainable and, even though expressed in all languages, remains unexpressible." [246]

For Romantics there are two kinds of aesthetic symbol: [173] coded messages in the form or structure; and messages implied by synaesthesia, association, increased awareness, and a sense of aesthetic transcendence. [150] The symbol is always ambiguous for Hegel, an analogue that hints at a wider meaning: "the Sphinx stands as a symbol for symbolism itself." He distinguished between the symbol, a mental concept or an object that is distinct from any context; and the aesthetic experience, or the mode in which the concept is expressed — a form of the sensuous or a representation.

In the 20th century symbolism was returned from art to mind as a whole by Freud who linked it to dream. Ricoeur says that symbols are not a code but are opaque, analogic and bound to language and culture; they tell us about our past and how we view the future. Thus a dramatist expresses a personal vision in vague symbols, without a pre-established code. The theatre work is ambiguous like all aesthetic "languages." At any one moment, anything can be a symbol. All depends on the "foregrounding" employed by the dramatist, actors and director. "The symbol is not a particular sort of sign. [It] is a textual modality, a way of producing and of interpreting the aspects of a text. . . . It is a modality of textual use." [173]

Jung & Symbols

In the playhouse or in schools, drama has symbolic contents, including archetypes (archaic types, or universal images). These contents are explicitly not codes but genuine symbols with ambiguous and inexhaustible meanings. Jung says they are empty but the audience fills them with meaning (and as Derrida shows, the dramatist allows for this in his writing). Jung was the first in the modern world to show the link of the quaternity to human ideas: that the notion of 4 is the fundamental structure of mental operations, metaphoric thought, symbolization in society, and the ideas expressed in dramatic acts. This notion accounts for why theatre scripts are continually structured around the eternal problems of existence (e.g., the *Oresteia, Hamlet* and *Six Characters in Search of An Author*, among others, focus on the tragedy of the human family) and why Freud used the structure of Sophocles' *Oedipus Rex* as an exemplar for the human mind. Jung points to the traditional figure of Christ as synonymous with psychic manifestations of the Self and proposes that "the one against three" is the quaternity within a mental structure that is a catalyst in the unification process — or, in alchemical terms, sparks "the spagyric birth." Symbols continually vacillate between 4 and 3: "Dr. Jung often observed that there is an unconscious tendency at work to round off (the Christian) trinitarian formula of the Godhead with a fourth element, which tends to be feminine, dark, and even evil." [317]

Symbolic Meaning

Symbolic meaning is imprecise and multi-faceted. It is structured by a culture so that people share it; yet individuals contribute to it, maintain, communicate, and change it. What does a symbol in drama mean? This is an issue of interpretation: a received meaning may not be the same as an intended meaning.

The form of a signifier gives specific qualities to the signified. Meaning is created, communicated and/or inferred according to whether it is conveyed by signs, metaphors, symbols and/or acts (drama/theatre/ritual). Signs convey a more limited meaning than symbols. In codes, from one sign we infer the meaning of another sign. Indexical signs convey meanings about that which is latent, such as a formula, diagram or drawing. Other signs, particularly aesthetic signs, convey meanings through a complexity of referents. Metaphors relate one thing to another through likeness; metaphoric meaning helps to define reality itself. Symbols can include the meanings of both signs and metaphors but they convey more meanings than either. Symbolic meaning is vague, has wide significance, and varies from culture to culture. Jung talks of some symbols whose meanings cross cultures and have deep human implications. The meaning conveyed by "acts" can include signs, metaphors and/or symbols, and when used dramatically the meaning shapes reality as we and others know it.

Sociocultural meanings are shared through symbols. Symbolic meanings may have "personal, subjective relevance and internalized normative value," but the shared sociocultural meanings of symbols are conveyed by acts that are "a communication currency." [447] Within social interaction and dramatic communication, symbolic meaning is highly complex. Symbols often have quite a simple form yet are multi-vocal in meaning (e.g., the cross, or the swastika). As signifiers, symbols synthesize a display of meanings, telescoping them into rich clusters. As communications, they have considerable economy and generalizing power. Specific social meanings are provided in cultural clusters through rituals and theatre; these can influence the symbols of the larger society in a strong or weak fashion. Theatre is effective in its period insofar as it can mix its symbols productively with those of the larger society.

Symbolic meanings are key factors in the way in which we construct reality in our minds, both personally as aesthetic fiction, as well as socially and dramatically as culture. [46] This construction of reality occurs because of two qualities of symbols:

1   *An aesthetic quality.* First, there is a "likeness" between symbolic form and its meanings: a perceptual continuity that patterns the relation. Second, there is an isomorphic relation between the quaternity structures of inner metaphors, dramatic acts and symbols.

2   *An (assumed) objective quality.* Shared cultural codes and symbols give the feeling that a "world" has an external existence. [447] Symbolic acts, such as those of drama and ritual, create a dynamic between these two qualities: the projection of the aesthetic quality into the world through action results in objective feed-back to mind and so provides symbolic meaning with the power of external reality.

For a number of contemporary scholars, notably anthropologists, symbolic meanings are polarized on a continuum. The nature of this continuum, however, can be described in different ways. One is that of Rappaport [505] who sees it in terms of the conceptual/experiential. Another is that of Victor W. Turner:

1   The normative and ideological which, as ritual symbols, contain organizational and moral meanings and principles. These tend to be grouped together as ideologies, or world-views. [115]

2 The affective and sensory which, as ritual symbols, contain physiological and biological meanings. Norms and values become saturated with emotions which, thereby, are ennobled. [589]

Symbolic meanings, says Turner, tend to have an autonomous existence of their own and, in adequate societal development, the interchange between symbolic poles must be balanced.

Symbolic Power

All forms of signification have power in the sense of

the ability either to maintain or to transform something in the face of inertia, resistance, or pressure. So understood, power has many forms: economic, political, rhetorical, inspirational, dramatic, symbolic. Power is the ability, in what ever form, either to move or to resist movement. Power is what energizes structures so that they become movements and processes. [259]

Power, implied in symbolic meaning, produces dramatic acts which construct reality. But these acts can only be effective if they are not seen as arbitrary: "What makes the power of words to command and order the world, is belief in the legitimacy of the words and of him who utters them, a belief which the words themselves cannot produce." [69] This power is controlled by the player who also has metaphor at his command. Both metaphor and symbol have power within their meaning. But whereas metaphor has the power of the double, symbolism has existential power due to its inherent ambiguity and the fact that it is performed.

Symbolic meaning is intrinsically ambiguous. This ambiguity accounts, at least in part, for the considerable ideological power of symbolic meaning: national flags, the insignia of political power, the sacred signifiers of religions; all have great emotional appeal to believers within specific acts. Ambiguity makes symbols useful within society: it is "a kind of bridge that allows us to run back and forth from one kind of meaning to another, until we take firm resolve to cross the bridge into new, and fixed, meanings." [170] Culture is a system of symbols and it has not been unknown for symbolic ambiguity to be used as a weapon of social control because [115] it both conceals and celebrates paradoxes. [589) This social control occurs in schooling, as McLaren has shown, and other contexts. Politicians can manipulate the ambiguity and paradoxes to control society: "'symbolic systems' fulfil their political function as instruments of domination (or more accurately, for legitimating domination) which help to make possible the domination of one class over another (symbolic violence)." [69] Through ambiguity, symbols become "powerful instruments in the hands of leaders and of groups in mystifying people for particularistic or universalistic or both purposes." [115] But the ambiguity of anti-structural ritual symbols can also propagate disorder through a surplus of signifiers:

> The bantering anti-signified of carnivalesque discourse is an insult to both the complementarity of ordinary speech and to the multi-signified of the serious ritual communication. It is also a statement in praise and a demonstration of the creative potential of human signification as opposed to its instrumental and representative use. Rather than "representing" something, discourse by means of a surplus of signifiers designates and celebrates itself. [24]

Nonsense (e.g., Edward Lear, Spike Milligan) or "topsy-turveydom" (e.g., Ben Jonson, Henry Fielding, W. S. Gilbert) uses symbolic ambiguity to communicate the forms of society — a paradoxical situation.

Christianity is made up of ambiguous symbols: the Virgin Birth, the God who was a Man, etc. It raises up the downcast and is a revolutionary faith; but when it turns the other cheek and renders unto Caesar, it is also counter-revolutionary. [389] Ambiguous symbolic meanings are inherent in the Mass. [448] Is the priest or Christ presiding? Are the bread and wine also the body and blood of Christ? A parallel situation occurs in the playhouse: the inherent ambiguity of the audience (the actual) juxtaposed with the performance (the illusion) is reflected by "the play within the play" that is, overtly or covertly, basic to Western theatre. But is Richard II meant to be a Christ figure? does Hal have two fathers, the real (Bolingbroke) and the false (Falstaff)? The symbolic meaning of the player is essentially ambiguous.

Symbolic ambiguity is inherent in the creation of the play and aesthetic worlds. It is paradoxical that these play worlds co-exist with the mundane world — that we live in both the fictional and the actual. Thus it is that the symbols of the ambiguous double — the mirror, the play within the play, the envelope in the pocket, the mask that covers the face, etc. — constantly reappear in the contemporary theatre.

Symbolic power assumes dramatic action. The relation of a symbol to its meaning goes beyond what can be pointed to or seen. It is not shown overtly in concrete experience. When symbols are used we find no actual object or action directly referred to except in the forms of the ideas of the relationship. As Gilbert Lewis has said, the qualities of the relationship are things which cannot be directly seen and described: "Human ideals and values and counter-values are pre-eminently the sort of things for which people require symbols, because they are insubstantial and abstract. They are hard to grasp and apprehend. But the values and ideals are felt as real, they have personal validity for the people who hold them." [388] Yet people are liable to take symbolic actions for the reality they stand for: e.g., instead of being a symbol they are a substitute for the action itself. Although from outside the society or culture we may consider them symbols, "for the actors they are not any longer." [388] To us the player may be acting symbolically but not to himself. He is occupied with thinking metaphorically and transforming it into action. If we, outside the action, choose to label it symbolic that is not his business.

Chapter 19
Dramatic Action

Action is always dramatic, overtly or covertly so. Action makes thought and learning social. Thinking/acting/learning are experientially "whole" although action is performative and generates the dramatic hypothesis:

> If I hypothesize my role as A, then my actions are Y.
> If I hypothesize my role as B, then my actions are Z.
> Thus my actions depend on how I hypothesize my role.

It is only with continual experience of the dramatic hypothesis that students can grasp abstract (logical) hypotheses. Knowledge of dramatic hypothesis is a *Knowing In* (that results in "thinking on the feet") while knowledge of abstract hypothesis is a *Knowing About*. The most obvious styles of dramatic action include play, dramatization, creative drama, improvisation, role play, life performances and theatre. But there are other existential actions which hinge upon dramatic qualities and we shall deal with four: creativity, language, learning and meaning.

Creativity

Just what is "creative" about creative drama? Much depends on what we mean by "creative." Behaviourism sees thinking as a chain of stimuli and responses that rely on habit, past experience and repetition. [379] But when a new thought is considered to be the interaction of a series of old ideas by trial-and-error, behaviourism cannot explain creative thought or acts. Gestalt approaches are more relevant to dramatic creativity. According to Wertheimer, parts and wholes inter-relate:

> There is *grouping*, *reorganization*, *structurization*, operations of dividing into sub-wholes and still seeing these sub-wholes together, with clear reference to the whole figure and in view of the specific problem at issue. . . . The process starts with the desire to get at the *inner-relatedness* of form and size. This is not a search for just any relation which would connect them, but for the nature of their intrinsic inter-dependence. . . . There is the feature of the functional meaning of parts. . . . The entire process is one consistent line of *thinking*. It is not an ad-sum of aggregated, piecemeal operations. No step is arbitrary, ununderstood in its function. On the contrary, each step is taken surveying the whole situation. [624]

This view is made contemporary by Rudolf Arnheim who speaks of the mind's activity as structuring significant perceptual information. Whole thought of this kind is promoted by spontaneous dramatic action. W. E. Vinacke distinguishes between realistic and imaginative thinkers: the former adhere to logical and scientific criteria, and are dominated by reason and facts; the latter allow inner currents to play with perceptual data, permit free experiment to explore hypotheses, suggestions, images and comparisons, and strive towards barely conceived goals. But creative thinkers switch and mix styles in their mental processes [598] and it is this flexibility of thought style that is encouraged by creative drama: choosing a thought-style to suit a problem.

In studies of the creativity used by specific artists [244] Stephen Spender and Ben Shahn describe their own preparation, the sudden emergence of a germ of thought (inspiration), and the re-working of material. Henri Poincaré uses a different vocabulary to describe the same patterns in mathematical creativity: conscious work, unconscious work, and the working out with skills. Patrick's research with artists revealed: preparation, incubation, illumination, and verification. In educational drama this process is spread out over time: the player works spontaneously and Patrick's creative pattern mostly happens before this.

In dramatic acts, creativity is processual: it is as much part of preparation as of spontaneous performance — recognized as an extension of the creativity of play by thinkers as far apart as Freud, Mead and Gadamer. Getzels and Jackson say, "It is almost as if creative adolescents experience a special delight in playful intellectual activity for its own sake." [243] This is closely related to intelligence: "thinking on the feet" is a creative and generic skill [139] of great value in later life to all students. It can lead to adult creativity in Brainstorming [624] and Synectics. In the latter, W. J. J. Gordon can say: "Synectics theory implies that not all play is creative but that all creativity contains play" and that "Conscious play, integrated with a desire for power over matter and pleasure at overcoming resistance, leads to technical innovations." [254] From the various studies in processual creativity, we can discern the following patterns:

Non-creative	*Creative*
Intelligence as measured by I.Q./"truth"	Intelligence as spontaneous response/perspectival "truth"
Independence/unruliness	Individuality/indiv. difference
Morbid withdrawal	Healthy solitude
Irresolution/indecisive	Ambiguity/paradox/delay of choice
Reliance on group/social collectivity	Acceptance of group only where applicable/community
Forced concentration/motive	Intrinsic concentration/motive
Recall of information	Discovering/knowing
Repetition (information as education objective)	Discovery (knowledge as education objective)
Strict rules/censorship	Adaptable rules/evaluation
Critical ("put down")	Appreciative (enjoyment)
Sentimental/stock responses	Honest/unique responses
Plain/realistic	Humorous/imaginative

Language

Dramatic action is the basis of language acquisition. After initial imitations, it is immediately upon "the primal act" that the child begins to develop language proper: from the surrounding noise he begins to distinguish certain sounds and, through imitation and play, identifies and reproduces them. *Speech is the sound of dramatic acts.* Language is not always linked to concepts — the deaf child organizes and classifies experience much like a hearing child — but "some of the most important concepts for the solution of problems — concepts of identity, similarity, comparison of magnitudes, spatial position, temporal sequence, causation and the like — are coded in the lexical and grammatical structure of a language. Nevertheless, many intellectual tasks can be performed without the use of linguistic codes." [101]

Words are signs without which much abstract thought would be impossible. Although many concepts are formed without language, words do symbolize the formation of a concept. If we present the child with a picture of a kangaroo, read descriptions of it, and indicate the word, "kangaroo," a concept may be formed. It will be formed more easily and will be remembered longer if we also play "kangaroos." With maturation, children form more concepts without words; and language becomes more closely linked to concept formation.

In English, the subject/predicate construction symbolizes the class of experience used in communication contexts. This kind of grammatical structure can help thinking beyond the point where language is used: its form permits the manipulation of complex concepts. Two approaches to this problem are "finite state grammar" and Chomsky's "phrase structure." "Content" words (nouns, verbs, adjectives, adverbs) are easier to learn than "functional" words (pronouns, conjunctions, prepositions) while learning plurals and other items means incorporating rules. [50]

Language is formed from speech yet teachers discourage their students from talking! *Talking is dramatic.* "Speech is life but writing is death," says Jacques Derrida, by which he means that dramatic and speech acts are the expressive media nearest to the self and, thus, they have the greatest effect upon learning. Language is more than response to, and production of, speech-decoding and encoding as Information Theory would have it. [286] This theory is essentially an extension of the general mathematical theory of probability; it has been of most use in electronic communication systems, but least when human subjects are involved. Behavioural approaches to language development are insufficient compared to dramatic strategies "by concretely re-enacting scenes from adult life, the child can grasp and identify with, if only partially, a style of life which he finds simultaneously alien, baffling, and attractive. Needless to say, there is a magical component in the dramatic play of young children, just as there is in the role-playing of older children and adolescents; but in both cases it is a magic that works." [109] Speech and reading, like drama, are based on identification. Writing is somewhat different.

The Sapir-Whorf Hypothesis indicates that "language is a guide to 'social reality'": [535] that the language we use conditions the way we look at the world, society and ourselves. For Whorf, language is a mould for our thought: "the shaper of ideas, the program and guide for the individual's mental activity, for his analysis of impressions, for his synthesis of his mental stock-in-trade." [631] The world appears different to people using different vocabularies, as it does if their perceptions, or their creations of fictions, differ. If the Innuit have many words for snow compared to the single English word, what do they see? And how do we see differently? If English speakers see in terms of things (nouns) while Navaho see the world as action (verbs), how can we understand one another? [138] and what were our play patterns whereby this difference came about? These are all questions that arise from Being "as if," from our fictional constructions of "how the world is."

Learning & Dramatic Experience

Learning is a change of the organism within experience. Learning results from transformation, an act that is overtly or covertly dramatic: it requires a dialogue between the learner and what is to be learned. Learning results in some kind of persistent change in behaviour, change that affects future patterns of action. There are two main kinds of learning:

1 *Social learning, and/or "learning to learn."*
   This is intrinsic and performative: *it changes who we are through what we do.* Mostly tacit and aesthetic, it is the ground for other learning; its affectivity helps the student's attitude to the Self.

2 *Conceptual and/or informational learning.*
   This is extrinsic and performative: *it changes what we can recall.* It is mostly explicit and cognitive: as the learning of specifics, it needs the "felt" quality of social learning to be persistent.

What kind of experience is this? Dewey, asked about his "learning by doing," replied, "consummatory experience." [167] "Consummatory" experience *for the learner* is dramatic, dialogic and *felt* (aesthetic). Aesthetic and learning experiences are unified in practice if theoretically distinct: the aesthetic refers to the quality of the experience — how it is felt; but learning is the outcome of experience and has (in most theories) no relation to how it is *felt.* [19] This is not so.

The teacher sets up situations which, while not overwhelming, move learners into new and persistent directions. Dramatic acts do so in two ways: they relate to the learner's needs, purposes, and intentions (e.g., in problematic situations); and they ensure that the learner is attracted by and totally involved in the activity (i.e. like play). To say "if a situation is an aesthetic one, it must have value for the individual independent of any subsequent event, experience or idea to which it might lead" [19] is to refer to its similarity to play. Dramatic and learning experiences both catch the learner's attention, because both contain the following elements: anticipation of expected outcomes in a problem/event, dedication to a task, and feelings of tension, release, and personal satisfaction. To accomplish these experiences, Donald Arnstine recommends the following teacher strategies:

1   to set up obstacles to learning that promote the discovery of ambiguities in anticipated situations;

2   to encourage curiosity and creativity;

3   to integrate drama with all other subject areas; and

4   to encourage students to value taste, creativity and imagination.

Differently, Howard Gardner talks of two major learning experiences:

A   *Direct Learning*
     The learner observes an adult activity and then imitates the actions performed by the model. In tribal societies spatial, bodily, and interpersonal knowings are emphasized in direct learning; similarly educational drama involves direct learning for the acquisition of performance skills in tribal ritual dramas. But in post-industrial societies direct learning is mostly used for practical skills (e.g., driving a car, sport, theatre education, etc.)

B   *Semi-Direct Learning*
     Instruction in a specific skill may occur outside the context in which that skill takes place. A small model may used for the learner's practice, e.g., in tribal cultures an initiate learns the constellations of the stars by using pebbles on the floor. With complex societies, learning occurs in contexts remote from the site of practice, e.g., schools. [19]

These two ways of learning, Gardner goes on to show, have three major variables:

a   *Media*. Various media (e.g., dramatic acts) are used to transmit knowledge in semi-direct, but not direct, learning.

b   *Sites*. Locations for learning vary between those on-site for direct learning, and those off-site for semi-direct (e.g., schools).

c   *Teachers.* Instructors vary: parents and grandparents usually
    of the same sex; members of the same caste or clan; siblings;
    and (in complex societies) a special class called "teachers."

The kinds of knowledge valued differs according to contexts. [19] In
tribal cultures, aesthetic qualities are inherent in learning. Complex
societies focus on linguistic, mechanical and logical knowledge while in
Western societies, unfortunately, aesthetic learnings are incidental.

Drama & Semiotics

Because most semioticians are linguists, they regard all works of art as
"texts." This also applies to "performatives" like dramatic acts. All
"texts" carry communications as signifiers. In spatial forms (e.g., art,
writing) the communication is repeatable, but in temporal forms (e.g.,
dramatic acts) it is not repeatable although it is recoverable. This applies to acts of learning. All learning entails work in the modes of both
thinking and action. [429] Dramatic learning is a way to so grasp ideas
that they are part of our inner Self: by transforming who we are in the
"as if," we come to deeply know the object of learning and our Self.
These acts, and the media that result, are signifiers and what is learned
is either:

A   signifier knowledge: learning that changes actions (social
    learning); or

B   signified knowledge: learning that changes knowledge and
    thinking (inner learning).

Both are vital. The teacher must find the appropriate balance. This
leads us to a number of basic issues:

1   Experiential dramatic learning uses more unconscious ele-
    ments than discursive learning. But conscious dramatic
    learning also exists.

2   It is not necessary for the player to know *how* he uses tacit
    knowledge in the dramatic mode. But it is necessary to know
    that it occurs. This is usually expressed, by creators and
    audience, as an increased control over emotion and feeling.

3   Dramatic learning is seen in the increased ability to give
    meaning to symbols and metaphors coded for dramatic
    purposes e.g., as *relations* and not as objects or things.

4   Dramatic learning improves feeling-response, in the oscillation
    between impulse and medium, [635] in choice, judgment, and
    imagining.

5   We are not necessarily able to distinguish between the
    multiple forms of tacit structures and dynamics. Categoriza-

tion, classification, and naming devices are discursive, rather than tacit, operations. Dramatic learning does not *necessarily* relate to the ability to describe events in verbal or written forms, although it may.

6   Dramatic learning demonstrates an increased ability to communicate tacit thought and feeling. Also for those who have mastered linguistic forms, dramatic learning can lead to perspectives on discursive issues.

7   Dramatic learning increases skills of creation and/or interpretation. "The skill of an artist, or rather his demonstration of a skill, becomes a message about his . . . unconsciousness. (But not perhaps a message from the unconscious.)" [38] But to create a "text," he has to learn a specific cultural code and context, both of which are in continual flux. This is achieved through re-play.

8   Dramatic learning is integrative and holistic. Consciousness is selective and partial but the "as if" is more integrative.

9   As dramatic learning grows it increases our ability to work with the double. This opens the way for alternatives; clarifies the message upon which our actions focus; and improves our ability to see the dramatic sign both as a formal analogue and as a function of human experience. The tendency to use the actual/fictional is so improved that it can lead us to an awareness of, and an ability to work with, meta-perspectives and paradoxes.

Coleridge said that we respond to fiction through "the willing suspension of disbelief." That is, *we respond to the imaginary world of play, art, theatre or text "as if" it really exists. But we do so in degrees. We learn fictionally as well as actually.* At the metaphorical level we learn that all objects within the fictional system can be felt as "real" whereas, from outside the system, they are not "real." The models and paradigms of religion, science, myth and ritual — as part of our culturally embedded knowledge — are constituent parts of metaphorical learning. But at the meta-dramatic level, fiction takes on the characteristics of the paradox. Dramatic learning leads to an understanding that fiction is the model of all meta-languages.

Studying Dramatic Acts

Those who wish to examine dramatic acts in educational drama, drama therapy and other practical fields, must make some basic decisions about method. Some may wish to use quantitative methods or a medical model. If so, they should realise that neither will tell them about dramatic acts per se: the first will answer the question, "How many . . . ?" while the second can only operate in physiological and cause-and-effect terms. The first question to be addressed is the nature of dramatic acts. Various models, all of which can be used, have been discussed in this book but perhaps the most useful for our purposes here is that of E. J. Furlong, who looks at the issue from three perspectives:

1 *In imagination* (the child playing at bears "in his head"):

   a day-dream;

   b directed imagination either from without (we picture events as directed by a novelist) or from within (events pictured in the novelist's imagination).

Each has five dimensions: the receptive state from relaxation to tension; content, or mental imagery; belief/disbelief; feeling; and degree of control.

2 *Supposal*:

   a plain supposal ("suppose you were a bear") which may be stimulated internally or externally, and may lead to In Imagination, With Imagination, or may not;

   b false supposal (to falsely believe there are bears around) which may be the result of In Imagination, With Imagination, dreams, hallucinations or illusions.

3 *With imagination* (the child acts "as if" he is a bear):

   This "is to act with freedom, with spontaneity . . . . it is to be original, constructive" with the qualities of creation and invention. [237]

There is a remarkable correspondence with Peter Slade's "projected play" (In Imagination) and "personal play" (With Imagination) although Furlong's typology is of imaginings and Slade's is of acts. The advantage of this model is that it views drama from the continuum of imagining/action.

Once a model has been chosen, a decision must be made as to whether the inquiry is to be descriptive or analytic.

Description

Descriptive methods are those which describe the "here and now" as we "live through" it: the observer describes what is seen in a number of ways. These can be anthropological, qualitative and/or phenomenological. I have described the first two elsewhere. [141]

Edmond Husserl describes the phenomenological method: the way things present themselves to mind by using "the phenomenological reduction": only immediate data are described and explanations of them are "bracketed out." What is left is pure consciousness: the Self (the individual's stream of consciousness), all perception, and human intentionality. With this method we can describe our experience of dramatic play in two ways: as a *player* or as an *observer*. Clearly the player cannot discuss the experience while experiencing it. But immediately afterwards, he can introspect and describe an event by "bracketing out" all attempts to explain it; he is left with both a tacit/embodied level and a consciousness of the event. He discovers the double, metaphorical structure of consciousness and a description. Thus it usually has at least two voices: the actual and the fictional. An observer's description is easier than that of the participant; notes and records can be taken during the dramatic event. Descriptions of the actual and fictional levels are made and compared for one of two purposes: to generate knowledge about the deep structures of the experience; or to heighten the consciousness of the observer about his own understanding of the event. A few accounts of dramatic events exist where the major perspectives include: the player's style of dramatizing, participation/distancing, cognitive/non-cognitive involvement, kinds of knowledge, depth of feeling, or degrees of concreteness, etc. More common are biographical accounts influenced by phenomenology; e.g., someone tells their "story."

Analysis

In order to analyse dramatic action, logic must be used: *criteria must be chosen whereby the analysis will be logical.* To be logical about dramatic actions and fictions was difficult earlier in this century: Russell like Ryle, Ayer and others thought that statements about fictions were logically false.

Modern logic grows from Ludwig Wittgenstein. He shows that there are differences in the logic of *Knowing In* and *Knowing About*. *Knowing In* the experience "here and now" only provides "a picture": it symbolically re-presents the truth and no evidence or reason changes that — it exists *ipso facto*. But *Knowing About* human actions occurs in two ways, through:

1   evidence — we know their causes through empirical science;

2   inductive, deductive, moral and interpretive reasons [52] in:

   *   the necessary criteria for judgment (e.g., sincerity/absorption with young children [557]);

   *   the context of the event (e.g., adolescents in rural Canada);

   *   the medium used (e.g., dramatic acts).

Wittgenstein is concerned with two kinds of logics:

A   Dramatic fiction is a context within which we think, a "game" where there is "play" between the forms of action and those of culture.

B   But talking about it is a context of discourse — a "language game" where the "play" is between descriptions of acts and the forms of culture.

To Wittgenstein, Being and "seeming" are entwined with the "games" of "play."

Put simply, modern logic varies with the frame of reference used: *actual and fictional worlds use different kinds of logic and require different kinds of criteria for analysis.* In the playhouse we grasp theatrical fiction from the view of either the player or the audience, comparing it with the meaning created between them. But the improviser uses two fictions: that realizable in the actual world (possible according to necessity) or that which is not (possible only in a fictional world). The observer in the classroom or the consulting room must acknowledge these distinctions in the logic used. Actual and fictional are not digital oppositions; each frames a world alternative to the other. Belief in dramatic fiction is more like a social imperative than a statement in classical logic.

What, then, is "truth"? There are two kinds of truth. *The truth of dramatic action hinges on the truth of imagining*: for Wittgenstein and many others, imagining is a species of thinking and what is important is how we interpret it. Being "as if" is the foundation of all creative acts for Arthur Koestler: linked to humour, it enables us to see two incompatible frames of reference at the same time — actual and fictional — which we interpret differently. The truth value of imagination, for Harold Rugg, occurs in "the transliminal mind" (between the conscious and unconscious) which, in the act, transforms two frames (feeling and verification) into "metaphoric thinking."

Truth for the observer is achieved by comparing what we know of the actual world with what we know of the play world. Ironically we can only know the actual through Being "as if." One curious twist to this idea are modern versions of Plato's "the great lie." Initially suggested in Jeremy Bentham's *Theory of Fictions*, it is developed by Hans Vaihinger: we must live in this world "as if" it is not illusory and we are not under sentence of death. Gilbert Ryle acknowledges that play is a form of thinking, and of a higher order than belief, but proclaims it a deceit. [129] In contrast, Louis Arnaud Reid said that unconscious feeling is part of knowing and so we use *"temporary absolutes"*: we assume a truth in order to operate in the "here and now" but we know it is not a permanent absolute. This is quite appropriate when "we are such stuff as dreams are made on."

Conclusion

This book has examined the intellectual background of educational drama: from a basis in educational thought (Part 1), it has addressed the effect of dramatic action on our inner psychological processes (Part 2) and on society's effect on them (Part 3). Finally, the mind as a whole (inner and outer) has been considered in dramatic terms.

There is no question of the need for all children and students to have the unique experience given by educational drama. Today's education has failed them just as it has failed to answer the changing needs of society. Western education has not effectively increased literacy and it is difficult to say it has produced "better" people: in this century we have probably killed more people than were ever alive before it. We perpetuate what worked in the past instead of trying to satisfy the needs of tomorrow. In a period of rapidly escalating change, to clutch at yesterday is almost like clinging to ancient history.

We require an education that does not simply try to catch up with the immediate past. Our students require learning that allows them to keep abreast of continual change; to be flexible and adaptable as circumstances alter; to develop good "practical knowledge" whereby they can easily recall procedures and, thereby, discover knowledge that is of use; and, above all, to be "person-oriented," for, however advanced our technical knowledge becomes, our students must always be able to negotiate well with others. Such are precisely the learnings promoted by educational drama. Continual activity in the Being "as if" is what educational drama is all about, for it asks with Bernard Shaw

> whether it is possible to change this monstrous fraud of child schooling into the beginning of the education that ceases only in the grave, and is the unending recreation of its subject.

Bibliography & References

Note: items listed below are often referred to in the text by square brackets, used particularly with direct quotations, but also with a few citations where there are difficulties of reference.

1. Abercrombie, M. L. J. "Small Groups." In B. M. Foss, ed., *New Horizons in Psychology*. Harmondsworth: Penguin, 1966.

2. Abraham, K. *Selected Papers on Psychoanalysis*. London: Hogarth, 1927.

3. Adland, D. E. *Group Drama*. London: Longman, 1964.

4. Adler, Alfred. *Social Interest: A Challenge to Mankind*. London: Faber and Faber, 1938.

5. Adolf, Helen. "The Essence and Origin of Tragedy." J. *Aesth. & Art Criticism*, X (1951): 112-125.

6. Alexander, Franz. "A Note on Falstaff." *Psychoan. Q.*, 2 (1933): 592-606.

7. —— . *Fundamentals of Psychology*. London: Allen & Unwin, 1949.

8. Alexander, Samuel. *Space, Time and Deity*. New York: Humanities Press, 1950.

9. Alford, Viola. *Sword Dance and Drama*. London: Merlin, 1962.

10. Allport, F. H. *Social Psychology*. Cambridge, MA: Riverside, 1924.

11. Altman, Leon L. "On the Oral Nature of Acting Out." *J. Am. Psychoan. Assoc.*, 5 (1957): 648-662.

12. Anand, Mulk Raj. *The Indian Theatre*. London: Dobson, 1950.

13. Anderson, G. L., ed. *The Genius of the Oriental Theater*. New York: Mentor, 1966.

14. Appleton, L. Estella. *A Comparative Study of the Play Activities of Adult Savages and Civilised Children*. Chicago: University of Chicago Press, 1910.

15. Aquinas, St. Thomas. *Summa Theologiae*. See *Philosophical Texts*, trans. T. Gilby. Oxford: Oxford University Press, 1951.

16. Aristotle. *Poetics*. Translated by Gerald Else. Ann Arbour, MI: University of Michigan Press, 1967.

17. Arlington, L. C. *The Chinese Theatre from Earliest Times until Today*. Shanghai, 1930.

18. Arnheim, Rudolf. *Visual Thinking*. Berkeley, CA: University of California Press, 1969.

19. Arnstine, Donald. "Aesthetic Qualities in Experience and Learning." In Ralph A. Smith, ed., *Aesthetic Concepts and Education*. Urbana, IL: University of Illinois, 1970: 21-44.

20. Assogioli, Roberto. *Psychosynthesis*. Harmondsworth: Penguin, 1976.

21. Augustine, St. *Confessions* and *The City of God*. London: Dent, 1921.

22. Aung, Maring Htin. *Burmese Drama*. Oxford: Oxford University Press, 1947.

23. Axline, Virginia M. *Play Therapy*. New York: Houghton, Mifflin, 1947.

24. Babcock, Barbara. *The Reversible World: Symbolic Inversion in Art and Society*. Ithaca, New York: Cornell University Press, 1978.

25. Bacon, Francis. "De Augmentis Scientiarum." In *Philosophical Works*, ed. J. M. Robertson. London: Routledge, 1905.

26. Bakhtin, M. M. *Speech Genres*. Austin, TX: University of Texas Press, 1986.

27. Baldwin, J. M. *Mental Development in the Child and Race*. London: Macmillan, 1895.

28. Balint, Edna. "The Therapeutic Value of Play in the School Situation." *The New Era*, 33, 10 (1952): 243-246.

29. Bamberger, Jeanne. "Where Do Our Questions Come From? Where Do Our Answers Go?" Paper presented at the American Educational Research Association Annual Meeting. San Francisco, CA (April 1979).

30. Bandura, A., D. Ross *and* S. A. Ross. "Imitation of Film-Mediated Aggressive Models." *J. Abn. Soc. Psych.*, 66 (1963): 3-11.

31. —— *and* R. H. Walters. *Social Learning and Personality Development*. New York: Holt, Rinehart & Winston, 1965.

32. Banton, Michael. *Roles*. London: Tavistock, 1968.

33. Barbu, Zevedei. "The Sociology of Drama." *New Society*, 2.2.67: 161-63.

34. Barret, Gisele. *L'expression dramatique: pour une théorie de la pratique*. Montreal: private edition, 1976.

35. —— . *Réflexions . . . pour les ensignants de l'expression dramatique . . . pratique, didactique, theorique*. Montreal: private edition, 1980.

36. —— . *Pédagogie de l'expression dramatique*. Rev. ed. Montreal: private edition, 1983.

37. Barthes, Roland. *Le plaisir du texte*. Paris: Seuil, 1973.

38. Bateson, Gregory. *Steps to an Ecology of Mind*. New York: Chandler, 1972.

39. —— *and* Margaret Mead. *Balinese Character*. New York: New York Academy of Sciences, 1942.

40. *Bearings of Recent Advances in Psychology on Educational Problems*. London Univ. Institute of Education. London: Evans, 1955.

41. Beech, H. R. "Personality Theories and Behaviour Therapy." In B. M. Foss, ed., *New Horizons in Psychology*. Harmondsworth: Penguin, 1966.

42. Bell, Charles. *Nervous System of the Human Body*. London: 1830.

43. Bender, L. *and* P. Schilder. "Forms as a Principle in the Play of Children." *J. Genet. Psychol.*, 49 (1936): 254-261.

44. Benedict, Ruth. *Patterns of Society*. London: Routledge, 1935.

45. Bentham, Jeremy. *The Theory of Fictions*. Ed. C. K. Ogden. New York: Harcourt, 1932.

46. Berger, Peter *and* Thomas G. Luckman. *The Social Construction of Reality*. New York: Doubleday, 1966.

47. Bergler, Edmund. "Psychoanalysis of Writers." In Géza Róheim, ed., *Psychoanalysis and the Social Sciences*, I. London: Imago, 1947.

48. Bergson, Henri. *Creative Mind*. Translated by M. L. Andison. New York: Philosophical Library, 1946.

49. Berkeley, George (Bishop). *A New Theory of Vision*. (1773). London: Dent, 1910.

50. Berko, J. "The Child's Learning of English Morphology." *Word*, 14 (1958): 150-177.

51. Berne, Eric. *Transactional Analysis in Psychotherapy*. New York: Grove, 1961.

52. Best, David. *Expression in Movement & the Arts*. London: Lepus, 1974.

53. ——. *Philosophy and Human Movement*. London: Allen & Unwin, 1978.

54. ——. *Feeling and Reason in the Arts*. London: Allen & Unwin, 1985.

55. Bettelheim, Bruno. *The Uses of Enchantment: The Meaning and Importance of Fairy Tales*. New York: Random House, 1975.

56. Bierstadt, E. H. *Three Plays of the Argentine*. New York: 1920.

57. Bion, W. R. *Experience in Groups*. London: Tavistock, 1963.

58. Blackham, H. J., James Britton *and* E. J. Burton. "A Theory of General Education." *The Plain View*, 13, 4 (1961).

59. Blattner, Adam *and* Ali. *Role Development: A Systematic Approach to Building Basic Skills*. San Marcos, TX: Blattner, 1985.

60. ——. *The Art of Play: An Adult's Guide to Reclaiming Imagination and Spontaneity*. San Marcos, TX: Blattner, 1985.

61. Bloomfield, Leonard. *Language*. London: Allen & Unwin, 1935.

62. Boas, Franz. "Introduction." *Handbook of American Indian Languages*, Part I. Washington, D.C., 1911.

63. Bolton, Gavin. *Towards a Theory of Drama in Education*. London: Longman, 1979.

64. ——. *Bolton at the Barbican*, ed. Warwick Dobson. London: National Association for the Teaching of Drama, 1983.

65. ——. *Drama as Education*. London: Longman, 1984.

66. Booth, David R. *Drama in The Formative Years*. Toronto: Ministry of Education, Government of Ontario, 1984.

67. ——. *Drama Words: The Role of Drama in Language Growth*. Toronto: Toronto School Board, 1987.

68. Boulding, K. E. *The Image*. Ann Arbor: University of Michigan Press, 1956.

69. Bourdieu, Pierre. *Outline for a Theory of Practice*. Cambridge: Cambridge University Press, 1977.

70. Bowers, Faubion. *The Japanese Theatre*. London: Peter Owen, 1952.

71. ——. *Theatre in the East*. London: Nelson.

72. Boyce, E. R. *Play in the Infants' School*. London: Methuen, 1938.

73. Brecht, Bertolt. *Brecht on Theatre*. Edited by J. Willett. London: Methuen, 1964.

74. Breuer, Josef *and* Sigmund Freud. *Studies in Hysteria*. London: Hogarth, 1936.

75. Brill, A. A. "Poetry as an Oral Outlet." *Psa. Rev.*, 18, 4 (1931).

76. ——, ed. *The Basic Writings of Sigmund Freud*. New York. Random House, 1938.

77. Brook, Peter. *The Empty Space*. Harmondsworth: Penguin, 1968.

78. Brown, J. A. C. *Freud and the Post-Freudians*. Harmondsworth: Penguin, 1961.

79. Brown, J. F. *Psychology and the Social Order*. New York: McGraw-Hill, 1936.

80. Brown, Radcliffe. *The Andaman Islanders*. Oxford: Oxford University Press, 1933.

81. Bruner, Jerome S. *On Knowing: Essays for the Left Hand*. Cambridge, MA: Harvard University Press, 1962.

82. ——. "Child's Play." *New Scientist*, April 1974.

83. Bruner, J., J. Goodnow *and* G. Austin. *A Study of Thinking*. New York: Wiley, 1956.

84. Buber, Martin. *I and Thou*. New York: Scribner's, 1958.

85. Burke, Kenneth. *A Grammar of Motives*. Berkeley, CA: University of California Press, 1945.

86. ———. *Language as Symbolic Action.* Berkeley, CA: University of California Press, 1965.

87. ———. "Dramatism." In *International Encyclopedia of the Social Sciences*, 7. New York: Macmillan, 1968.

88. Burns, Elizabeth. *Theatricality.* London: Longman, 1972.

89. Burton, E. J. *Teaching English through Self-Expression.* London: Evans, 1949.

90. ———. "The Place of Drama in Education Today. Living, Learning and Sharing Experience." In *Art, Science and Education.* Joint Council for Education Through Art, 1958.

91. ———. *British Theatre: Its Repertory and Practice 1100-1900.* London: Jenkins, 1960.

92. ———. *The Student's Guide to World Theatre.* London: Jenkins, 1963.

93. ———. *The Student's Guide to British Theatre.* London: Jenkins, 1964.

94. ———. "Drama as a First Degree Subject." Paper privately circulated, 1965.

95. ———. *Reality and "Realization." An Approach to a Philosophy.* London: Drama & Educational Fellowship, 1966.

96. Buytendijk, F. J. J. *Wesen und Sinn des Spiels.* Berlin, 1934.

97. Cameron, N. *and* A. Magaret. *Behaviour Psychology.* New York: Houghton, Mifflin, 1951.

98. Campbell, Joseph. *Masks of God.* 4 vols. Harmondsworth: Penguin, 1976.

99. Carr, H. H. "The Survival of Play." *Investigation Dept. Psychology and Education.* Boulder: University of Colorado Press, 1902.

100. Carroll, John B. "Language Development in Children." In Sol Saporta, ed.: *Psycholinguistics.* New York: Holt, Rinehart, 1961.

101. ———. *Language & Thought.* Englewood Cliffs, N.J: Prentice-Hall, 1964.

102. Cassirer, Ernst. *The Philosophy of Philosophic Forms.* Translated by W. Curtis, M. Swabey and R. Mannheim. 3 vols. New Haven, CN: Yale University Press, 1955-57.

103. Cervantes. *Don Quixote.* Translated by Thomas Shelton. London: Macmillan, 1908-23.

104. Chambers, E. K. *The Medieval Stage.* 2 vols. Oxford: Oxford University Press, 1903.

105. ———. *The English Folk Play.* Oxford: Clarendon Press, 1933.

106. Charles, Lucille H. "Growing Up through Drama." *Journal of American Folklore*, 59 (1946): 247-67.

107. Chen, Jack. *Chinese Theatre*. London: Dobson, 1949.

108. Chomsky, N. *Syntactic Structures*. The Hague: Mouton, 1957.

109. Church, Joseph. *Language & the Discovery of Reality*. New York: Random House, 1961.

110. Cicero. *De Republica*. Translated by Miller. London: Heinemann, 1947.

111. Cirlot, J. E. *A Dictionary of Symbols*. Translated by J. Sage. New York: Philosophical Library, 1962.

112. Cirilli, René. *Les prêtres danseurs de Rome*. Paris: Geuthner, 1913: 114.

113. Claparede, E. *Psychologie de l'enfant et pédagogie experimentale*. Translated by M. Louch & H. Holman. London: Longman, 1911.

114. Coggin, Philip A. *Drama in Education*. London: Thames & Hudson, 1956.

115. Cohen, Abner. *Two-Dimensional Man: An Essay on the Anthropology of Power and Symbolism in Complex Society*. London: Routledge & Kegan Paul, 1974.

116. Cohen, J. "Analysis of Psychological 'Fields.'" *Science News*, 13; 145-158.

117. Comenius, John Amos. *The Great Didactic*. See Jelinke, Vladimir, *The Analytic Didactic of Comenius*. Chicago: University of Chicago Press, 1953.

118. Cook, Caldwell. *The Play Way*. London: Heinemann, 1917.

119. Cornford, F. M. *The Origin of Attic Comedy*. Edited by T. H. Gaster. New York: Doubleday, 1961.

120. Courtney, Richard. *Drama for Youth*. London: Pitman, 1964.

121. ——— , ed. *College Drama Space*. London: Institute of Education, London University, 1964.

122. ——— . *Teaching Drama. A Handbook for Teachers in Schools*. London: Cassell, 1965.

123. ——— . "Planning the School and College Stage." *Education*: 9.4.65.; 725-728; 16.4.65.; 799-802; and 21.5.65: 1075.

124. ——— . *The School Play*. London: Cassell, 1966.

125. ——— . *The Drama Studio: Architecture and Equipment for Dramatic Education*. London: Pitman, 1967.

126. ——— . "Drama and Aesthetics." *British Journal of Aesthetics*, 8, 4 (1968): 378-86.

127. ——— . "On Langer's Dramatic Illusion." *Journal of Aesthetics & Art Criticism*, 29, 1 (Fall 1970): 11-20.

128. ——. "A Dramatic Theory of Imagination." *New Literary History*, 2, 3 (Spring 1971): 445-60.

129. ——. "Imagination & The Dramatic Act: Some Comments on Sartre, Ryle & Furlong." *Journal of Aesthetics & Art Criticism*, 30, 2 (Winter 1971): 11- 20.

130. ——. "Theatre and Spontaneity." *Journal of Aesthetics & Art Criticism*, 32, 1 (Fall 1973): 79-88.

131. ——. "Imagination and Substitution: The Personal Origins of Art." *Connecticut Review*, 9, 2 (May 1976): 67-73.

132. ——. "Making Up One's Mind: Aesthetic Questions About Children and Theatre." In Nellie McCaslin, ed., *Theatre for Young Audiences*. New York: Longman, 1978: 19-35.

133. ——. *The Dramatic Curriculum*. London, Ont.: Althouse Press, Faculty of Education, University of Western Ontario, 1980.

134. ——. "The Crux of the Curriculum: The Arts as Anthropocentrism." In Jack Condous, Janferie Howlett and John Skull, eds., *The Arts in Cultural Diversity*. Papers delivered at the 23rd World Congress, International Society for Education Through Arts UNESCO. Sydney, N.S.W.: Holt, Rinehart & Winston, 1980.

135. ——. *Re-Play: Studies of Human Drama in Education*. Toronto: OISE Press, 1982.

136. ——. "The Dramatic Metaphor and Learning." In Judith Kase-Polisini, ed.: *Creative Drama in a Developmental Context*. Papers delivered at the 1st International Research Conference, "Drama & Learning." Harvard University and OISE, Toronto. Lanham, MD: University Press of America, 1985: 39-64.

137. ——. "Indigenous Theatre: Rituals and Ceremonies." In Anton Wagner, ed., *Contemporary Canadian Theatre: New World Visions*. Toronto: Simon & Pierre, 1985: 206-15.

138. ——. "Islands of Remorse: Indian Education in the Modern Age." *Curriculum Inquiry*, 16, 1 (1986): 1-22.

139. ——. "Drama as a Generic Skill." *Youth Theatre Journal*, 1, 1 (Summer 1986): 5-27.

140. ——. "Mirrors: Theatrical Sociology/Sociological Theatre." *Proceedings*, International Conference on the Sociology of Theatre, 27-29 June 1986, University of Rome, Italy.

141. ——. *The Quest: Research & Inquiry in Arts Education*. Lanham, MD: University Press of America, 1986.

142. ——. *Dictionary of Developmental Drama*. Springfield, IL: Charles C. Thomas, 1987.

143. ——. *Drama Education Canada*. Sharon, Ont.: Bison Books, 1987.

144. ———. "On Dramatic Instruction: A Taxonomy of Methods." *Youth Theatre Journal*, 2, 1 (Summer 1987): 3-7.

145. ———. *Re-Cognizing Richard Courtney: Selected Papers in Educational Drama*, ed. David R. Booth and Alistair Martin-Smith. Markham, Ont: Pembroke Publishing, 1988.

146. ——— and Paul Park. *Learning in the Arts: Arts Education in the Elementary Schools of Ontario*. Research Report. 4 vols. Toronto: Ministry of Education, Government of Ontario, 1980.

147. ——— and Gertrud Schattner, eds. *Drama in Therapy*. 2 vols. New York: Drama Book Specialists, 1981.

148. ———, David R. Booth, John Emerson *and* Natalie Kuzmich. *No One Way of Being: Practical Knowledge of Elementary Arts Teachers in Ontario*. Research Report. Toronto: Ministry of Education, Government of Ontario, 1988.

149. Courtney, Rosemary. *Music and Language: Towards a Theory of the Influence of Aural Perception on Language Development and Reading*. Unpublished Ph.D. dissertation. University of Toronto, 1988.

150. Creuzer, G. F. *Symbolik and Mythologie der Alten Volker*. Leipzig-darmstadt: Leske, 1810.

151. Criste, Rita. Appendix C in Siks and Dunnington (see 583 below): 235-40.

152. Croce, Benedetto. *Aesthetic*. Translated by D. Ainslie. Reprint. London: Peter Owen, 1967.

153. Crutchfield, R. S. "Conformity and Character." *Am. Psych.*, 10 (1955): 191-198.

154. Curti, M. W. *Child Psychology*. London: Longman, 1930.

155. Dalrymple-Olford, E. "Psycholinguistics." In B. M. Foss, ed., *New Horizons in Psychology*. Harmondsworth: Penguin, 1966.

156. Dante Alighieri. *The Divine Comedy: Purgatory*, vol. 8. Harmondsworth: Penguin, 1955.

157. Darwin, Charles. *On The Origin of Species by Means of Natural Selection, or, The Preservation of Favoured Races in the Struggle for Life*. London: J. Murray, 1859.

158. Davidson, A. *and* J. Fay. *Phantasy in Childhood*. London: Routledge, 1952.

159. De Vega, Lope. In H. J. Chaytor, ed., *Dramatic Theory in Spain*. Oxford: Oxford University Press, 1925.

160. Del Sorto, J. *and* Corneytz, P. "Psychodrama as Expressive and Projective Technique." *Sociometry*, 8 (1944): 356-375.

161. Dennis, W. "Piaget's Questions Applied to Zuñi and Navaho Children." *Psych. Bul.*, 37 (1940): 520.

162. Derrida, Jacques. *Dissemination.* Translated by B. Johnson. Chicago: Chicago University Press, 1981.

163. Descartes, René. *The Philosophical Works of Descartes.* Translated by E. S. Haldance and G. R. T. Ross. 2 vols. Cambridge: Cambridge University Press, 1931.

164. Deutsch, F. "Mind, Body and Art." *Daedalus,* 89 (1960): 34.

165. Dewey, John. "Educational Principles." *The Elementary School* (1900).

166. ——— . *Art as Experience.* New York: Capricorn, 1934.

167. ——— . *Experience and Education.* New York: Macmillan, 1938.

168. Dobree, Bonamy. *Restoration Comedy.* Oxford: Oxford University Press, 1924.

169. Dollard, J., et. al. *Frustration and Aggression.* London: Routledge, 1944.

170. Duncan, Hugh Dalziel. *Symbols and Social Theory.* New York: Oxford University Press, 1969.

171. Durkheim, Emile. *Suicide.* London: Routledge, 1952.

172. Ebbinghaus, H. *Psychology: An Elementary Text.* Translated by M. Meyer. Boston: Heath, 1908.

173. Eco, Umberto. *Semiotics and the Philosophy of Language.* Bloomington, IN: Indiana University Press, 1984.

174. Edfeld, A. W. *Silent Speech & Silent Reading.* Stockholm: Almquist & Wiksell, 1959.

175. Edwards, Osman. *Japanese Plays and Play-Fellows.* London: Heinemann, 1901.

176. Ehrmann, Jacques, ed. *Game, Play and Literature.* Boston: Beacon, repr. 1971.

177. Einstein, Albert. *The World As I See It.* New York: Covici Friede, 1934.

178. Ekstein, R. *and* Seymour Friedman. "The Function of Acting Out, Play Action and Play Acting." *J. Am. Psychoan. Assoc.* 5 (1957): 581-629.

179. Eliade, Mircea. *The Sacred and the Profane.* New York: Harcourt, Brace, 1959.

180. Ellis, Henry. *Fundamentals of Human Learning and Cognition.* Dubuque, Iowa: William C. Brown, 1972.

181. Ellul, Jacques. *The Technological Society.* Translated by J. Wilkinson. New York: Knopf, 1964.

182. Emmett, Dorothy. *Rules, Roles and Relations.* London: Macmillan, 1966.

183. Empson, William. *Seven Types of Ambiguity*. London: Chatto & Windus, 1930.

184. Erickson, Erik. "Studies in the Interpretation of Play." *Genet. Psychol. Monog.* 22 (1940): 557-671.

185. ———. *Childhood and Society*. Harmondsworth: Penguin, 1965.

186. Evans-Pritchard, E. E. "The Dance." In *The Position of Women in Primitive Societies and Other Essays in Social Anthropology*. London: Faber and Faber, 1965.

187. Evernden, Stanley. "Drama in Schools." Private communication, 1966.

188. Fagan, Joen *and* Irma Lee Shepherd. *Gestalt Therapy Now*. New York: Harper & Row, 1971.

189. Fenichel, Otto. *The Psychoanalytic Theory of Neurosis*. New York: Norton, 1945.

190. ———. "On Acting." *Psychoan. Q.*, 15 (1946): 160.

191. Ferenczi, S. "Stages in the Development of the Sense of Reality." In *Sex in Psychoanalysis*. Boston: Badger, 1916.

192. Festinger, L. A. *A Theory of Cognitive Dissonances*. New York: Harper, 1957.

193. ———. "Informal Social Communication." *Psych. Rev.*, 57: 271-282.

194. ——— *and* K. Back. *Social Pressures in Informal Groups*. New York: Harper, 1950.

195. Feyerbend, Paul. *Against Method*. London: New Left Books, 1975.

196. Fink, Eugen. *Conversations with Husserl and Fink*. Ed. Dorian Cairns. The Hague: Nijhoff, 1976.

197. Finlay-Johnson, Harriet. *The Dramatic Method of Teaching*. London: Nisbet, n.d.

198. Firth, Raymond. *Symbols, Public and Private*. London: Allen & Unwin, 1973.

199. Flavell, J. H. *The Developmental Psychology of Jean Piaget*. New York: Van Nostrand, 1963.

200. Fleming, C. M. "The Bearing of Field Theory and Sociometry on Children's Classroom Behaviour." In *Bearings of Recent Advances in Psychology on Educational Problems*. London University. Institute of Education. London: Evans, 1955.

201. Flugel, J. C. *Man, Morals & Society*. London: Duckworth, 1945.

202. Fordham, Frieda. *An Introduction to Jung's Psychology*. Harmondsworth: Penguin, 1953.

203. Foulkes, S. H. *and* E. J. Anthony. *Group Psychotherapy*. Harmondsworth: Penguin, 2nd ed., 1965.

204. Frank, L. K. *Projective Methods*. Springfield, IL: Charles C. Thomas, 1948.

205. Frankfort, H. *and* H. A., J. A. Wilson and T. Jacobsen. *The Intellectual Adventure of Ancient Man*. Chicago: University of Chicago Press, 1946.

206. Frazer, J. G. *The Golden Bough*. 3rd ed. 12 Vols. London: Macmillan, 1907-15.

207. Freeman, Kathleen. *Ancilla to the Pre-Socratic Philosphers*. Oxford: Oxford University Press, 1948.

208. Freire, Paolo. *Education for Critical Consciousness*. New York: Seabury Press, 1973.

209. ——. *Pedagogy of the Oppressed*. New York: Seabury Press, 1974.

210. ——. *The Politics of Education: Culture, Power and Liberation*. South Hadley, MA: Bergin and Garvey, 1985.

211. —— and D. Macedo. *Literacy: Reading the Word and the World*. South Hadley, MA: Bergin and Garvey, 1987.

212. French, J. R. P., Jr. "Organised and Unorganised Groups under Fear and Frustration." *Univ. Ia. Child Welf.*, 20 (1944): 299-308.

213. Freud, Anna. "Introduction to the Techniques of Child Analysis." *Nerv. Ment. Dis. Monogr.*, 48 (1928).

214. ——. *The Ego and the Mechanisms of Defence*. London: Hogarth, 1936.

215. Freud, Sigmund. *Totem and Taboo*. London: Hogarth, 1913.

216. ——. *Psycho-Pathology of Everyday Life*. London: Benn, 1914.

217. ——. *An Outline of Psychoanalysis*. London: Hogarth, 1920.

218. ——. *Beyond the Pleasure Principle*. London: Hogarth, 1922.

219. ——. *Group Psychology and the Analysis of the Ego*. London: Hogarth, 1922.

220. ——. *The Ego and the Id*. London: Hogarth, 1922.

221. ——. "The Dynamics of Transference." *Collected Papers*, II. London: Hogarth, 1924.

222. ——. "Mourning and Melancholia." *Collected Papers*, IV. London: Hogarth, 1925.

223. ——. *Inhibition, Symptom and Anxiety*. London: Hogarth, 1927.

224. ——. *Civilization and Its Discontents*. London: Hogarth, 1930.

225. ——. *The Future of an Illusion*. London: Hogarth, 1930.

226. ——. *New Introductory Lectures in Psychoanalysis*. London: Hogarth, 1933.

227. ——— . *Moses and Monotheism*. London: Hogarth, 1939.

228. ——— . "Psychopathetic Characters on the Stage (1904)." *Psychoan. Q.*, 9 (1942): 459-464.

229. ——— . "Rumour." *Collected Papers*, V. London: Hogarth, 1950.

230. ——— . *Standard Edition of the Works*, IV. London: Hogarth, 1953.

231. ——— . "The Relation of the Poet to Day-Dreaming (1908)." In 230 above.

232. ——— . *Standard Edition of the Works*, VII. London: Hogarth, 1953.

233. ——— . *The Interpretation of Dreams*. London: Hogarth, 1955.

234. Friedman, Joel *and* Sylvia Gastel. "The Chorus in Sophocles' Oedipus Tyrannus." *Psychoan. Q.*, 2, (1950): 19.

235. Froebel, F. *The Education of Man* (1862).

236. Fromm, Erich. *Fear of Freedom*. London: Routledge, 1952.

237. Furlong, E. J. *Imagination*. London: Allen & Unwin, 1971.

238. Gadamer, Hans-Georg. *Truth and Method*. London: Sheed & Ward, 1975.

239. Galton, Sir Francis. *Inquiries into Human Faculty & Its Development* (1883). Reprint. London: Eugenics Society, 1951.

240. Gardner, Howard. *Frames of Mind*. New York: Basic Books, 1984.

241. Gaster, T.H. *Thespis*. Revised edition. New York: Doubleday, 1961.

242. Gentile, Giovanni. *Genesis and Structure of Society*. Translated by H. S. Harris. Urbana, IL: University of Illinois Press, 1966.

243. Getzels, J. W. *and* P. W. Jackson. *Creativity and Intelligence*. New York: Wiley, 1962.

244. Ghiselin, B., ed. *The Creative Process: A Symposium*. Berkeley, CA: University of California Press, 1952.

245. Giroux, Henry. *Theory and Resistance: A Pedagogy for the Opposition*. South Hadley, MA: Bergin and Garvey, 1983.

246. Goethe, W. "Maximen and Reflexionen." In *Werke*. Leipzig: Bibliographisches Institute, 1926.

247. Goffman, Erving. *The Presentation of Self in Everyday Life*. New York: Doubleday, 1959.

248. Goldman, Lucien. *Pour une sociologie du roman*. Paris: Gallimard, 1964.

249. Gomme, G. L. *Ethnology in Folklore* (1886).

250. Gomme, Lady Alice. *Traditional Games*. 2 vols. Reprint. New York: Dover, 1964.

251. Goode, Tony, ed. *Heathcote at the National*. London: National Association for the Teaching of Drama, 1982.

252. Goodnow, J. "A Test of Milieu Effects with Some of Piaget's Tasks." *Psych. Monog.*, 76 (1962): 1-22.

253. Gopal, Ram. *Indian Dancing*. London: Phoenix House, 1951.

254. Gordon, W. J. J. *Synectics*. New York: Harper, 1961.

255. Gough, H. G. "A Sociological Theory of Psychotherapy." *Am. J. Sociol.*, 53 (1948): 359-366.

256. Gowen, Herbert, H. *A History of Indian Literature from Vedic Times to the Present Day*. New York: Appleton, 1931.

257. Greimas, A-J. *Structural Semantics*. Translated by D. McDowell, R. Schleifer and A. Veilie. Lincoln: Nebraska University Press, 1983.

258. ——. *On Meaning: Selected Writings in Semiotic Theory*. Translated by P. J. Perron and F. H. Collins. Minneapolis: Minnesota University Press, 1987.

259. Grimes, Ronald L. *Beginnings in Ritual Studies*. Lanham, MD: University Press of America, 1982.

260. Gronbeck, V. *The Culture of the Teutons*. London: 1931.

261. Groos, Karl. *The Play of Animals*. Translated by E. L. Baldwin. London: Heinemann, 1898.

262. ——. *The Play of Man*. Translated by E. L. Baldwin. London: Heinemann, 1901.

263. ——. "Das Spiel als Katharsis." *Zeitschrift Pedagogie* (1914).

264. Guha-Thakurta, P. *The Bengali Drama, Its Origin and Development*. London: Kegan Paul, 1930.

265. Guthrie, E. R. *The Psychology of Learning*. New York: Harper, 1935.

266. H.M.S.O. *Handbook for Teachers in Elementary Schools*. (1937).

267. ——. *The Story of a School* (1950).

268. Haaga, Agnes. "Recommended Training for Creative Dramatics Leaders." In Siks and Dunnington (see 583 below): 198-208.

269. Haas, Robert Bartlett *and* J. L. Moreno. "Psychodrama as a Projective Technique in H. H. and J. L. Anderson, eds., *An Introduction to Projective Techniques & Other Devices for Understanding the Dynamics of Human Behaviour*. Englewood Cliffs, NJ: Prentice-Hall, 1951.

270. Hadamard, J. *The Psychology of Invention in the Mathematical Field*. Reprint. New York, Dover, 1954.

271. Hadfield, J. A. *Dreams and Nightmares*. Harmondsworth: Penguin, 1954.

272. ———. *Childhood and Adolescence*. Harmondsworth: Penguin, 1962.

273. Hall, Edward T. *The Hidden Dimension*. New York: Doubleday, 1966.

274. Hall, G. Stanley. *Youth*. New York: Appleton, 1916.

275. Hampden-Turner, Charles. *Radical Man: The Process of Psycho-Social Development*. New York: Doubleday, 1981.

276. Hanson, N. R. *Patterns of Discovery: An Inquiry into the Conceptual Foundations of Science*. Cambridge: Cambridge University Press, 1958.

277. Hardiston, O. B., Jr. *Christian Rite and Christian Drama in the Middle Ages: Essays in the Origin and Early History of the Drama*. Baltimore: The Johns Hopkins University Press, 1965.

278. Harrison, Jane E. *Themis*. Cambridge: Cambridge University Press, 1912.

279. Havemeyer, L. *The Drama of Savage Peoples*. New Haven: Yale University Press, 1916.

280. Hayes, Cathy. *The Ape in Our House*. New York: Harper, 1951.

281. Heathcote, Dorothy. *Sydney Lectures*. Ed. Graham Scott (1975). Sydney, N.S.W.: University of Sydney, n.d. See also: Goode, above; Johnson and O'Neill, Wagner, below.

282. Hegel, G. W. F. *Philosophy of Right*. Translated by T. M. Knox. Oxford: The Clarendon Press, 1942.

283. Heidegger, Martin. *Being and Time*. Translated by J. Macquarrie and E. Robinson. New York: Harper, 1962.

284. Heisenberg, Werner. *Physics and Beyond: Encounters and Conversations*. New York: Harper & Row, 1971.

285. Hellersberg, E. F. "Child's Growth in Play Therapy." *Am. J. Psychother.*, 9 (1955): 484-502.

286. Henle, Paul, ed. *Language, Thought & Culture*. Ann Arbor, MI: University of Michigan Press, 1958.

287. Herbert, E. L. "The Use of Group Techniques in the Training of Teachers." *Human Relations*, 14 (1961): 3.

288. Hesiod. *Works and Days; Theogony; The Shield of Heracles*. Translated by R. Lattimore. Ann Arbor, MI: University of Michigan Press, 1977.

289. Hodgson, John *and* Martin Banham, eds. *Drama in Education*. 3 vols. London: Pitman, 1972, 1973, 1975.

290. Hofstadter, Douglas R. *Gödel, Escher, Bach: An Eternal Golden Braid*. New York: Basic Books, 1979.

291. Hoijer, Harry, ed. *Language in Culture*. Chicago: University of Chicago Press, 1954.

292. Holmes, Edmond. *What Is and What Might Be*. London: Constable, 1911.

293. Holt, E. B. *Animal Drive*. New York: Williams & Norgate, 1931.

294. Homans, George C. *The Human Group*. London: Routledge, 1951.

295. Horace. *Art of Poetry*. Translated by T. A. Moxon. London: Dent, 1934.

296. Horney, Karen. *The Neurotic Personality of Our Time*. New York: Norton, 1937.

297. ———. *New Ways in Psychoanalysis*. New York: Norton, 1939.

298. ———. *Our Inner Conflicts*. New York: Norton, 1945.

299. ———. *Neurosis and Human Growth*. London: Routledge, 1951.

300. Hourd, Marjorie L. *The Education of the Poetic Spirit*. London: Heinemann, 1949.

301. ———. "Some Reflections on the Significance of Group Work." *New Era*, 42 (1961): 1.

302. ——— and Gertrude E. Cooper. *Coming into Their Own*. London: Heinemann, 1959.

303. Howarth, Mary R. *Child Psychotherapy*. New York: Basic Books, 1964.

304. Hughes, A. G. *and* E. H. *Learning & Teaching*. 3rd rev. ed. London: Longman, 1962.

305. Huizinga, Johan. *Homo Ludens—A Study of the Play Element in Culture*. Boston: Beacon, 1955.

306. Hull, E. M. *Folklore of the British Isles*. London: Methuen, 1928.

307. Hume, David. *Treatise on Human Nature*. 2 vols. London: Dent, 1911.

308. Hunningher, B. *The Origin of the Theatre*. New York: Hill and Wang, 1961.

309. Hunt, David E. "Demystifying Learning Style." *Orbit*, 16, 1 (February 1985): 3-6.

310. Hunter, I. M. L. *Memory*. Rev. ed. Harmondsworth: Penguin, 1964.

311. Husserl, Edmond. *Cartesian Meditations*. Translated by D. Cairns. The Hague: Nijhoff, 1960.

312. Irwin, Eleanor C. "Play, Fantasy and Symbols: Drama with Emotionally Disturbed Children." In Richard Courtney and Gertrud Schattner, eds., *Drama in Therapy*, vol. 1. New York: Drama Book Specialists, 1981: 111-26.

313. Isaacs, Susan. *Intellectual Thought in Young Children*. London: Routledge, 1930.

314. ———. *Social Development in Young Children.* London: Routledge, 1933.

315. Jackson, L. *and* K. M. Todd. *Child Treatment and the Therapy of Play.* London: Methuen, 1946.

316. Jacques, E. *The Changing Culture of a Factory.* London: Tavistock, 1951.

317. Jaffe, Aniela. "Symbolism in the Visual Arts." In Carl Jung, ed., *Man and his Symbols.* New York: Dell, 1968.

318. James, William. *Principles of Psychology,* I. Reprint. New York: Dover, 1950.

319. Jennings, Sue, ed. *Dramatherapy: Theory and Practice for Teachers and Clinicians.* London: Croom Helm, 1987.

320. Johnson, David Read. "Dramatherapy and the Schizophrenic Condition." In Richard Courtney and Gertrud Schattner, eds., *Drama in Therapy,* vol. 2. New York: Drama Book Specialists, 1981: 47-66.

321. Johnson, Liz *and* Cecily O'Neill, eds. *Dorothy Heathcote: Collected Papers in Educational Drama.* London: Hutchinson, 1984.

322. Johnstone, Keith. "Acting (Possession, Trance, Hypnotism and Related States): An Interview with Keith Johnstone" by Zina Barnieh. *Discussions in Developmental Drama,* 4 (February 1973): 3-8.

323. ———. *Impro: Improvisation and the Theatre.* London: Faber and Faber, 1979.

324. ———. "Theatresports." *Canadian Theatre Review,* 23 (Summer 1979): 27-31.

325. Jones, Ernest. *Hamlet and Oedipus.* London: Gollancz, 1949.

326. ———. "Psychoanalysis and Anthropology." In *Essays in Applied Psychoanalysis,* II. London: Hogarth, 1951.

327. ———. "Psychoanalysis and Folklore." In *Essays in Applied Psychoanalysis,* II. London: Hogarth, 1951.

328. ———. *Sigmund Freud: Life and Work.* London: Hogarth, 1953-7.

329. Jones, Roger S. *Physics as Metaphor.* New York: New American Library, 1982.

330. Jonson, Ben. *The Complete Masques.* Edited by Stephen Orgel. New Haven: Yale University Press, 1969.

331. Jung, C. G. *The Psychology of the Unconscious.* New York: Mead, 1916.

332. ———. *Contributions to Analytical Psychology.* New York: Harcourt, Brace, 1928.

333. ———. *Modern Man in Search of a Soul.* New York: Harcourt, Brace, 1933.

334. —— . *Introduction to a Science of Mythology*. London: Routledge, 1940.

335. —— . *The Integration of the Personality*. London: Routledge, 1940.

336. —— . *Two Essays on Analytical Psychology*. *Collected Works*, VII. London: Routledge, 1958.

337. —— . *Psychology and Religion*. *Collected Works*, XI. London: Routledge, 1958.

338. —— and C. Kerenyi. *Essays on a Science of Mythology: The Myths of the Divine Child and the Divine Maiden*. New York: Harper & Row, 1963.

339. Kabuki Theatre. Washington, D.C., Japanese Embassy, 1954.

340. Kahn, C. H. *The Art and Thought of Heraclitus*. Cambridge: Cambridge University Press, 1979.

341. Kalidasa. *Works*. Translated by A. W. Ryder. Reprint. London: Dent, 1951.

342. Kalvodova-Sis-Vanis. *Chinese Theatre*. China: Spring Books, n.d.

343. Kant, Immanuel. *On Education*. Translated by A. Churston. London: K. Paul, Trench, Trubner, 1899.

344. Kanzer, Mark. "Contemporary Psychoanalytic Views of Aesthetics." *J. Am. Psychoan. Assoc.*, 5 (1957): 514-524.

345. —— . "Acting Out, Sublimation and Reality Testing." *J. Am. Psychoan. Assoc.*, 5 (1957): 663-684.

346. Kaprow, Allan. "Statement." In Michael Kirby, ed., *Happenings*. New York: E. P. Dutton, 1965: 44-52.

347. Kardiner, A. *The Individual and His Society*. New York: Columbia University Press, 1939.

348. Keith, A. Berriedale. *The Sanskrit Drama in its Origin, Development, Theory and Practice*. Oxford: Oxford University Press, 1924.

349. Kincaid, Zoe. *Kabuki: The Popular Stage of Japan*. London: Macmillan, 1925.

350. King, Nancy. *Giving Form to Feeling*. New York: Drama Book Specialists, 1975.

351. Kingsley, H. L. *The Nature & Conditions of Learning* (1946).

352. Kirby, E. T. *Ur-Drama: The Origins of Theatre*. New York: New York University Press, 1975.

353. Klein, Melanie. *The Psychoanalysis of Children*. London: Hogarth, 1932.

354. —— , Paula Heimann, Susan Isaacs *and* Joan Riviere. *Developments in Psychoanalysis*. London: Hogarth, 1952.

355. Kluckhorn, C. *and* D. Leighton. *The Navaho*. Cambridge, MA: Harvard University Press, 1948.

356. Koestler, Arthur. *The Sleepwalkers*. New York: Macmillan, 1959.

357. —— . *The Act of Creation*. London: Macmillan, 1964.

358. Kohlberg, Lawrence. *Recent Research in Moral Education*. New York: Holt, Rinehart & Winston, 1978.

359. Kolb, D. A. *Learning Style Inventory*. Boston, MA: McBer & Company, 1976.

360. Koste, Virgina Glasgow. *Dramatic Play in Childhood: A Rehearsal for Life*. Lanham, MD: University Press of America, 2nd ed., 1987.

361. Kris, Ernst. "On Preconscious Mental Processes." *Psychoan. Q.*, 19 (1950): 542-552.

362. —— . *Psychoanalytic Explorations in Art*. London: Allen & Unwin, 1953.

363. Kubie, L. S. *Neurotic Distortion of the Creative Process*. Kansas: University Kansas Press, 1958.

364. Kuhn, Thomas S. *The Structure of Scientific Revolutions*. Chicago: Chicago University Press, 1970.

365. Laban, Rudolf. *Modern Educational Dance*. London: Macdonald & Evans, 1948.

366. Lacan, Jacques. "The Function of Language in Psychoanalysis." In Anthony Wilden, *The Language of the Self*. Baltimore: John Hopkins University Press, 1968.

367. Laing, R. D. *The Divided Self*. Harmondsworth: Penguin, 1965.

368. Lakoff, George *and* Mark Johnson. *Metaphors We Live By*. Chicago: Chicago University Press, 1980.

369. Lampert, Magdalene. "Teaching About Thinking and Thinking about Teaching." *Journal of Curriculum Studies*, 16 1 (Jan.-Mar., 1984): 1-18.

370. Landau, J. M. *Studies in Arab Theatre and Cinema*. Pittsburgh: University Pennsylvania Press, 1957.

371. Landis, Joseph C., ed. *The Dybbuk and Other Great Yiddish Plays*. New York: Bantam, 1966.

372. Landy, Robert J. "The Use of Distancing in Psychotherapy." *The Arts in Psychotherapy*, 10, 3 (1983): 175-85.

373. Langer, Susanne K. *Feeling and Form*. New York: Scribner's, 1953.

374. Lazarus, Moritz. *Die Reize des Spiels*. Berlin, 1883.

375. Lazier, Gil. "Scientific Research in Theatre." In Stanley S. Madeja, ed., *Arts and Aesthetics: An Agenda for the Future*. St. Louis, MD: CEMREL, 1977: 148-63.

376. Lazlo, Ervin. *Introduction to Systems Philosophy.* New York: Harper & Row, 1972.

377. Leach, Edmund. "Anthropological Structuralism and Artistic Communication." In Malcolm Ross, ed., *The Arts: A Way of Knowing.* Oxford: Pergamon Press, 1983.

378. Lebel, Jean-Jacques. "On The Necessity of Violation." *The Drama Review*, 13, 1 (T41, Fall 1968): 89-105.

379. Lee, Harry B. "The Values of Order and Vitality in Art." In Géza Róheim, ed., *Psychoanalysis and the Social Sciences*, II. New York: International University Press, 1950.

380. Lee, Joseph. *Play in Education.* New York: Macmillan, 1915.

381. Leeper, R. "Cognition Processes." In S. S. Stevens, ed., *Handbook of Experimental Psychology.* New York: Wiley, 1951.

382. Lehman, Harvey C. *and* Paul A. Witty. *The Psychology of Play Activities.* New York: Barnes, 1927.

383. Leibnitz, G. W. *Philosophic Writings.* Edited by M. Morris. New York: E. P. Dutton, 1934.

384. Lesser, Simon O. *Fiction and the Unconscious.* Boston: Beacon, 1957.

385. Lévi-Strauss, Claude. *Structural Anthropology.* Translated by M. Lagton. New York: Harper & Row, 1976.

386. Lewin, K. *Principles of Topological Psychology.* New York: McGraw Hill, 1936.

387. ———. *Resolving Social Conflicts.* New York: Harper, 1948.

388. Lewis, Gilbert. *Day of Shining Red: An Essay in Understanding Ritual.* Cambridge: Cambridge University Press, 1980.

389. Lewis, I. *Social Anthropology in Perspective.* New York: Penguin, 1976.

390. Lewis, J. H. *and* T. R. Sarbin. "Studies in Psychosomatics: the Influence of Hypnotic Stimulation on Gastric Hunger Contractions." *Psychosom. Med.*, 5 (1943): 125-131.

391. Lewis, M. M. *Infant Speech: A Study in the Beginnings of Language.* Rev. ed. New York: Humanities, 1951.

392. Linton, Ralph. *The Cultural Background of Personality.* London: Routledge, 1947.

393. Locke, John. *Philosophic Works.* Translated by J. A. St. John. 2 vols. London: G. Bell & Sons, 1883.

394. Lombard, Frank Alanson. *An Outline History of the Japanese Drama.* London: Allen & Unwin, 1929.

395. Lovell, K. "A Follow Up of Some Aspects of the Work of Piaget and Inhelder into the Child's Conception of Space." *Brit. J. Ed. Psych.*, 29 (1959): 104-117.

396. ——. "A Follow Up Study of Inhelder and Piaget's The Growth of Logical Thinking." *Brit. J. Psych.* (1961): 52.

397. Lowen, Alexander. *Biosynthesis.* Harmondsworth: Penguin, 1976.

398. Lowenfeld, Margaret. *Play in Childhood.* London: Gollancz, 1935.

399. ——. "The World Pictures of Children." *Brit. J. Med. Psychol.*, 18 (1938), 65-101.

400. Lowenfeld, Viktor *and* W. Lambert Brittain. *Creative and Mental Growth.* New York: Macmillan, 6th ed., 1975.

401. Malinowski, B. *Sex and Repression in Savage Society.* London: Kegan Paul, 1927.

402. ——. "The Problem of Meaning in Primitive Languages." In Ogden, C. and I. A. Richards: *The Meaning of Meaning.* London: Routledge, 10th ed., 1949.

403. Mandelbaum, D. G., ed. *Edward Sapir: Culture, Language and Personality.* Berkeley, CA: University of California Press, 1957.

404. Maritain, Jacques. *Creative Intuition in Arts and Poetry.* New York: Pantheon, 1953.

405. Marshack, Alexander. *The Roots of Civilization.* New York: McGraw Hill, 1972.

406. Marx, Karl *and* Friedrich Engels. *Manifesto of the Communist Party.* Chicago: C. H. Kerr, 1951.

407. ——. *Das Kapital.* Translated by E. and C. Paul. 2 vols. London: Dent, 1930.

408. Maslow, Abraham H. *Motivation and Personality.* New York: Harper & Row, 1954.

409. May, Rollo. *Love and Will.* New York: Norton, 1964.

410. ——, Ernest Angel *and* Henri F. Ellenberger, eds. *Existence.* New York: Simon & Schuster, 1958.

411. McCarthy, Bernice. *The 4Mat System: Teaching to Learning Styles with Right/Left Mode Techniques.* Barrington, IL: EXCEL, Inc., 1981.

412. McCarthy, D. "Language Development in Children." In L. Carmichael, ed., *Manual of Child Psychology.* New York: Wiley, 1946.

413. McCaslin, Nellie. *Theatre for Young Audiences.* New York: Longman, 1982.

414. ——. *Creative Dramatics in the Classroom.* (1968). Rev. ed. New York: Longman, 1989.

415. McDougall, William. *Introduction to Social Psychology.* London: Methuen, 1908.

416. McLaren, Peter L. *Cries from the Corridor.* Toronto: Methuen, 1980.

417. ——. *Schooling as a Ritual Performance: Towards a Political Economy of Educational Symbols and Gestures.* London: Routledge & Kegan Paul, 1986.

418. ——. *Life in Schools: An Introduction to Critical Pedagogy in the Foundations of Education.* New York: Longman, 1988.

419. McLeod, John. *A Survey of Drama in Post-Primary Schools.* Melbourne, Australia: Education Department, Government of Victoria, 1985.

420. ——. *Drama Is Real Pretending.* Melbourne, Australia: Education Department, Government of Victoria, 1988.

421. McLuhan, H. Marshall. *Understanding Media: The Extensions of Man.* New York: Bantam, 1968.

422. Mead, George, H. *Mind, Self and Society.* Chicago: University of Chicago Press, 1934.

423. Mead, Margaret. *Coming of Age in Samoa.* New York: Morrow, 1928.

424. ——. *Sex and Temperament in Three Primitive Societies.* London: Routledge, 1935.

425. Mearns, Hughes. *Creative Power.* New York: Doubleday, 1929.

426. Mednick, S. A. *Learning.* Englewood Cliffs, NJ: Prentice-Hall, 1963.

427. Menzies, I. E. P. "A Case Study in the Functioning of Social Systems as a Defence against Anxiety: a Report on the Study of the Nursing Service of a General Hospital." *Human Relations*, 13 (1960): 2.

428. Merrell, Floyd. "Of Metaphor and Metonymy." *Semiotica*, 3/4, 31 (1980): 289-307.

429. ——. *Semiotic Foundations: Steps Toward an Epistemology of Written Texts.* Bloomington, IN: Indiana University Press, 1982.

430. Mill, John Stuart. *Utilitarianism.* London: Dent, 1910.

431. Miller, David, ed. *Popper Selections.* Princeton: Princeton University Press, 1985.

432. Miller, G. A. *Language and Communication.* New York: McGraw-Hill, 1951.

433. Miller, N. E. *and* J. Dollard. *Social Learning and Imitation.* London: Kegan Paul, 1945.

434. Mitchell, Elmer D. *and* S. Bernard Mason. *The Theory of Play.* Rev. ed. New York: Ronald Press, 1948.

435. Miyake, Shutaro. *Kabuki Drama.* New York: Japan Travel Bureau, 1948.

436. Money-Kyrle, T. E. "Varieties of group formation" in Géza Róheim, ed., *Psychoanalysis and the Social Sciences*, II. New York: Int. Univ. Press, 1950.

437. Montaigne, Michel de. "Customs" and "Education of Children." In *Essays*. London: Dent, 1910.

438. Moore, G. E. *Principia Ethica*. Reprint. Cambridge: Cambridge University Press, 1968.

439. Moreno, J. L. *Psychodrama*, I. New York: Beacon House, 1946.

440. ———. *Psychodrama*, II. New York: Beacon House, 1959.

441. ———. *Who Shall Survive?* Translated by H. Lesage and P. H. Maucarps. New York: Nerv. Dis. Pub. Co., 1934.

442. Morgan, Elizabeth. *A Practical Guide to Drama in the Primary School*. London: Ward Lock, 1968.

443. Morris, Ben. "How Does a Group Learn to Work Together?" in W. R. Niblett: *How and Why do we Learn?* London: Faber and Faber, 1965.

444. Mowrer, O. H. *Learning Theory and Personality Dynamics*. New York: Ronald, 1950.

445. ———. *Learning Theory and the Symbolic Processes*. New York: Wiley, 1960.

446. Mulcaster, Richard. *Elementarie*. See S. S. Laurie, *Studies in the History of Educational Opinion from the Renaissance*. New York: Humanities Press, 1968.

447. Munn, Nancy. "Symbolism in a Ritual Context: Aspects of Symbolic Action." In John J. Honigmann, ed., *Handbook of Social and Cultural Anthropology*. Chicago: Rand-McNally, 1973: 597-612.

448. Murphy, Gardner. *Personality: A Biosocial Approach to Origins & Structure*. New York: Harper, 1947.

449. Murray, Gilbert. In Jane E. Harrison: *Themis*. Cambridge: Cambridge University Press, 1912.

450. ———. *Aeschylus, the Creator of Tragedy*. Oxford: Oxford University Press, 1940.

451. ———. In T. H. Gaster: *Thespis*. Rev. ed. New York: Doubleday, 1961.

452. Neill, A. S. Summerhill. New York: *Hart*, 1960.

453. ———. "A Play in Ten Acts by a Boy of Nine." In Hodgson and Banham, vol. 2 (see 289 above): 121-24.

454. Newman, James R. *The World of Mathematics*. New York: Simon & Schuster, 1956.

455. Newton, Robert G. *Acting Improvised*. London: Nelson, 1937.

456. Nicoll, Allardyce. *History of English Drama*. 5 vols. Cambridge: Cambridge University Press, 1923-46.

457. ———. *Masks, Mimes and Miracles*. London: Harrap, 1931.

458. ———. *The Development of the Theatre*. London: Harrap, 1948.

459. ———. *Theatre and Dramatic Theory*. London: Harrap, 1962.

460. Noddings, Nell *and* Paul J. Shore. *Awakening the Inner Eye: Intuition in Education*. New York: Teacher's College Press, Columbia University, 1984.

461. Nunn, Percy. *Education: Its Data and First Principles*. London: Arnold, 1920.

462. O'Connor, N. *and* B. Hermelin. *Speech & Thought in Severe Subnormality*. Oxford: Pergamon, 1963.

463. O'Farrell, Lawrence. "Making it Special: Ritual as a Creative Resource for Drama." *Children's Theatre Review*, 33, 1 (1984): 3-6.

464. O'Neill, Cecily, A. Lambert, R. Linnell *and* J. Warrwood. *Drama Guidelines*. London: Heinemann, 1976.

465. Opie, Iona *and* Peter. *The Lore and Language of School-Children*. London: Oxford University Press, 1959.

466. ———. *Children's Games in Street and Playground*. London: Oxford University Press, 1969.

467. Ordish, T. F. "Folk Drama." *Folk-Lore* (2): 314 et. seq.; (4): 149 et. seq.

468. Ornstein, Robert. *The Psychology of Consciousness*. San Francisco: W. H. Freeman, 1972.

469. Ortega Y Gasset, José. *Towards a Philosophy of History*. New York: Norton, 1941.

470. Osborn, A. F. *Applied Imagination*. New York: Scribner, 1957.

471. Osgood, Charles E. *Method and Theory in Experimental Psychology*. Oxford: Oxford University Press, 1953.

472. ———. "Psycholinguistics, in Sigmund Koch, ed., *Psychology: A Study of a Science*, VI. New York: McGraw-Hill, 1963.

473. ——— *and* J. Jenkins. "Psycholinguistic Analysis of Decoding and Encoding." In Osgood and Sebeck (see 474 below).

474. ——— *and* Thomas A. Seboeck. *Psycholinguistics: A Survey of Theory & Research Problems*. Baltimore: Waverley, 1954.

475. Paivio, A. *Imagery and Verbal Processes*. New York: Holt, Rinehart & Winston, 1971.

476. Parsons, Talcott. *The Social System*. London: Tavistock, 1952.

477. Patrick, C. *What is Creative Activity?* New York: Philosophical Library, 1955.

478. Patrick, G. T. W. *The Psychology of Relaxation*. New York: Houghton, Mifflin, 1916.

479. Peacock, James A. *Rites of Modernization: Symbolic and Social Aspects of Indonesian Proletarian Drama.* Chicago: Chicago University Press, 1968.

480. Peirce, C. S. *Collected Papers*, 8 vols. Cambridge, MA: Harvard University Press, 1931, 1958.

481. Peller, Lili E. "Libidinal Development as Reflected in Play." *Psychoanalysis*, 3 (Spring 1955): 3-11.

482. Pepper, Stephen C. *World Hypotheses.* Berkeley, CA: University of California Press, 1942.

483. Perls, F. S. *Gestalt Therapy Verbatim.* Lafayette, CA: Real People Press, 1969.

484. Phillpotts, B. S. *The Elder Edda.* Cambridge: Cambridge University Press, 1920.

485. Piaget, Jean. *Language & Thought of the Child.* New York: Harcourt, Brace, 1926.

486. ———. *Play, Dreams and Imitation in Childhood.* Translated by C. Gattegno and F. M. Hodgson. London: Routledge & Kegan Paul, 1962.

487. Pirandello, Luigi. *Six Characters in Search of an Author.* Translated by F. May. London: Heinemann, 1954.

488. Plato. *Dialogues.* Translated by B. Jowett. Oxford: Oxford University Press, 1871.

489. ———. *Laws,* in *Dialogues* (see 488 above).

490. ———. *The Republic.* Translated by A. D. Lindsay. London: Dent, 1935.

491. Plotinus. *The Enneads.* Translated by S. MacKenna. 3rd rev. ed. New York: Philosophical Library, n.d.

492. Polanyi, Michael. *Personal Knowledge: Towards a Post-Critical Philosophy.* Chicago: University of Chicago Press, 1958.

493. Popovich, James, E. "Development of Creative Dramatics in the United States." In Siks and Dunnington (553 below).

494. Popper, Karl R. *The Philosophy of Karl Popper.* 2 vols. LaSalle, IL: Open Court Publications, 1974 (see also Miller, above).

495. Pound, Ezra *and* Ernest Fenollosa. *The Classic Noh Theatre of Japan.* New York: Knopf, 1917.

496. Price-Williams, D. "Crosscultural Studies." In B. M. Foss, ed., *New Horizons in Psychology.* Harmondsworth: Penguin, 1966.

497. Progoff, Ira. *Jung's Psychology and Its Social Meaning.* London: Routledge, 1953.

498. Propp, Vladmir. *The Morphology of the Folk Tale.* Austin, TX: University of Texas Press, 1968.

499. Querat. *Les jeux des enfants*. Paris, 1905.

500. Quintillian. *Institutes of Oratory, or Education of an Orator*. Translated by J. S. Watson. London. G. Bell, 1910-13.

501. Rabelais, François. *Gargantua and Pantagruel*. London: Dent, 1908.

502. Raglan, Lord. *The Hero*. London: Methuen, 1936.

503. Rank, Otto. *Trauma of Birth*. New York: Harcourt, Brace, 1929.

504. —— . *Will Therapy* and *Truth and Reality*. New York: Knopf, 1947.

505. Rappaport, Roy A. *Ecology, Meaning and Religion*. Richmond, CA: Atlantic Books, 1979.

506. Read, Herbert. "The Limitations of a Scientific Philosophy." In *Art, Science and Education*. London: Joint Council for Education through Art, 1958.

507. Reaney, M. Jane. "The Psychology of the Organised Group Game." *Psych. Rev. Monog. Supp.* 4, 1916.

508. —— . *The Place of Play in Education*. London: Methuen, 1927.

509. Reich, Wilhelm. *Character Analysis*. New York: Organs Institute, 1945.

510. Reid, Louis Arnaud. "Feeling and Understanding." In Ralph A. Smith, ed., *Aesthetic Concepts and Education*. Urbana, IL: University of Illinois Press, 1970: 45-76.

511. Reik, Theodor. *A Psychologist Looks at Love*. New York: Rinehart.

512. —— . *Masochism in Modern Man*. New York: Grove Press, 1957.

513. Reisman, David. *The Lonely Crowd*. New Haven: Yale University Press, 1953.

514. Rescher, Nicholas. *Conceptual Idealism*. Oxford: Blackwell, 1973.

515. Richardson, J. E. "An Experiment in Group Methods of Teaching English Composition." In *Studies in Social Psychology of Adolescence*. London: Routledge, 1951.

516. —— . "Teacher-Pupil Relationship as Explored and Rehearsed in an Experimental Tutorial Group." *New Era*, 6-7, 44 (1963).

517. Rico, Gabriele Lusser *and* Mary Frances Claggett. *Balancing the Hemispheres: Brain Research and the Teaching of Writing* (1980).

518. Ricouer, Paul. *Rule of Metaphor: Multidisciplinary Studies of the Creation of Meaning in Language*. Translated by R. Czerny and others. Toronto: University of Toronto Press, 1975.

519. Rivers, W. H. R. *Conflict and Dream*. London: Routledge, 1921.

520. Robinson, E. S. "The Compensatory Function of Make-Believe Play." *Psych. Rev.*, 1920: 429-439.

521. Róheim, Géza. "Psychoanalysis of Primitive Cultural Types." *Int. J. Psa.* 13, 1932: 197.

522. ———. *The Riddle of the Sphinx.* London: Hogarth, 1934.

523. ———. "Psychoanalysis and Anthropology." *Psychoanalysis and the Social Sciences*, I. London: *Imago*, 1947.

524. ———. "Psychoanalysis and Anthropology." in Sandor Lorand, ed., *Psycho Analysis Today.* London: Allen and Unwin, 1948.

525. ———. *Origin and Function of Culture.* London: Hogarth.

526. ———. "The Oedipus Complex, Magic and Culture." *Psychoanalysis and the Social Sciences*, II. New York: International University Press, 1950.

527. Rosenblatt, Bernard S. "A Theory of Curriculum for Theatre Education at the Elementary Grades." *Children's Theatre Review*, 33, 2 (1984): 11-15.

528. Roth, Henry Ling. *The Natives of Sarawak and British North Borneo.* London, 1896.

529. Rousseau, Jean-Jacques. *Émile.* Translated by Foxley. London: Dent, 1917.

530. Rugg, Harold. *Imagination: An Inquiry into the Sources and Conditions That Stimulate Creativity.* New York: Harper & Row, 1963.

531. Ryle, Gilbert. *The Concept of Mind.* New York: Harper & Row, 1949.

532. Seaburg, Dorothy I. *and* Rene Zinsmaster. "What Can Teachers Learn from Directors in the Performing Arts?" *Elementary School Journal*, 72, 4, January 1972: 67-75.

533. Sabathchandra, E. R. *The Sinhalese Folk Play and the Modern Stage.* Colombo: Ceylon University Press, 1953.

534. Sachs, Hanns. *The Creative Unconscious.* Cambridge, MA: Sci-Art, 1942.

535. Sapir, E. "Conceptual Categories in Primitive Language." *Science*, 5, 1931: 578.

536. Sarbin, Theodore R. "Role Theory." In Gardner Lindzey, ed., *Handbook of Social Psychology*, I. Cambridge, MA: Addison Wesley, 1954.

537. Sartre, Jean-Paul. *Being and Nothingness.* Translated by H. E. Barnes. New York: Washington Square, 1963.

538. Schechner, Richard. *Essays on Performance Theory: 1970- 1976.* New York: Drama Book Specialists, 1977.

539. ——— *and* Mady Schuman, eds. *Ritual, Play and Performance: Readings in the Social Sciences/Theatre.* New York: Seabury Press, 1976.

540. Schiller, Friedrich. *Essays, Aesthetical and Philosophical.* London: Bell, 1875.

541. Schneider, Daniel E. *The Psychoanalyst and the Artist.* New York: International University Press, 1950.

542. Schutz, Alfred. *The Phenomenology of the Social World.* Translated by G. Walsh and F. Lehnert. Evanston, IL: Northwestern University Press, 1967.

543. Schuyler, Montgomery. *A Bibliography of the Sanskrit Drama, with an Introductory Sketch of the Dramatic Literature of India.* New York: Columbia University Indoiranian Series, No. 3, 1906.

544. Schwartz, Emanuel K. "A Psychoanalytic Study of the Fairy Tale." *Am. J. Psychother.*, 10 (1956): 740-762.

545. Scott, A. C. *The Classical Theatre of China.* London: Allen and Unwin, 1957.

546. Sears, R. R. "Identification as a Form of Behavioural Development, in D. B. Harris, ed., *The Concept of Development.* Minneapolis: University of Minnesota, Press, 1957.

547. Seashore, Carl. *Psychology in Daily Life.* New York: Appleton, 1916.

548. Ely, John. *In Context: Language and Drama in the Secondary School.* London: Oxford University Press, 1976.

549. Segal, Hanna. *Introduction to the Work of Melanie Klein.* London: Heinemann, 1946.

550. Shannon, Charles E. "The Mathematical Theory of Communication." *Bell System Technical Journal*, July-October 1948: 379-423; 623-656.

551. Siks, Geraldine Brain. *Creative Dramatics: An Art for Children.* New York: Harper & Row, 1965.

552. ——— . *Drama with Children.* New York: Harper & Row, 1977.

553. ——— and Brian Hazel Dunnington, eds. *Children's Theatre & Creative Dramatics.* Seattle: University of Washington, 1961.

554. Skinner, B. F. *The Behaviour of Organisms.* New York: Appleton, 1938.

555. ——— . *Verbal Behaviour.* New York: Appleton, 1957.

556. Skinner, Colin. *The Black Box.* Victoria, B.C.: play privately circulated, 1970.

557. Slade, Peter. *Child Drama.* Edited by Brian Way. London: London University Press, 1954.

558. Slavson, S. R. *Recreation and the Total Personality.* New York: Association Press, 1948.

559. Smilansky, Sarah. *The Effects of Sociodramatic Play on Culturally Deprived Children.* New York: Wiley, 1968.

560. Solomon, Joseph C. "Therapeutic Use of Play." In H. H. and G. L. Anderson, eds., *An Introduction to Projective Techniques & Other Devices for Understanding the Dynamics of Human Behaviour.* New York: Prentice-Hall, 1951.

561. Southern, Richard. *The Seven Ages of the Theatre.* London: Faber and Faber, 1962.

562. Soven, Margot. Developing Paragraph "Intuition": A Spiral Approach (ED229749) 1979.

563. Spariosu, Mihai. *Literature, Mimesis and Play.* Tübingen: Gunter Narr Verlag, 1982.

564. Spence, Lewis. *Myth and Ritual in Dance, Game and Rhyme.* London: Watts, 1947.

565. Spencer, Herbert. *The Principles of Psychology.* New York: Appleton, 1873.

566. Spinoza, Benedict. *The Works.* Translated by R. H. M. Elwes. 2 vols. New York: Dover, 1951.

567. Spolin, Viola. *Improvisation for the Theatre.* Evanston, IL: Northwestern University Press, 1963.

568. —— . Theatre Game File. St. Louis, Mo: CEMREL, 1970.

569. Sprott, W. H. *Human Groups.* Harmondsworth: Penguin, 1958.

570. Stanislavsky, Constantin. *Creating a Role.* New York: Theatre Arts Books, 1961.

571. Stekel, Wilhelm. *Autobiography.* New York: Liveright, 1950.

572. Sterne, Lawrence. *Tristram Shandy.* Edited by J. A. Work. New York: The Odyssey Press, 1940.

573. Sullivan, H. S. *Conceptions of Modern Psychiatry.* Washington, D.C.: White, 1947.

574. Suttie, Ian. *The Origins of Love and Hate.* London: Penguin, 1935.

575. Sutton-Smith, Brian. "In Search of Imagination." In Kieran Egan and Dan Nadaner, eds., *Imagination and Education.* New York: Teacher's College Press, Columbia University, 1988: 3-29.

576. —— and Gil Lazier. "Psychology and Drama." *Empirical Research in Theatre,* I, 1 (Summer 1971): 38-46.

577. Tarachow, Sidney. "Circuses and Clowns." In Géza Róheim, ed., *Psychoanalysis and the Social Sciences,* III. New York: International University Press, 1951.

578. Taylor, D. W., P. C. Berry *and* C. H. Block. "Does Group Participation When Using Brainstorming Facilitate or Inhibit Creative Thinking." *Yale Univ. Industr. Admin. Psych. Tech. Rep.,* 1957.

579. Thorndike, E. L. *Psychology of Arithmetic.* London: Macmillan, 1922.

580. Tiddy, A. *The Mummers' Play*. Oxford: Oxford University Press, 1923.

581. Tille, A. *Yule and Christmas*. London: Black, 1899.

582. Tinbergen, N. *The Study of Instinct*. Oxford: Oxford University Press, 1951.

583. Todorov, Tzvetan. *Symbolism and Interpretation*. Translated by C. Porter. Ithaca, NY: Cornell University Press, 1982.

584. Tolkien, J. R. R. *Tree and Leaf*. London: Allen & Unwin, 1964.

585. Tolman, E. C. *Purposive Behaviour in Animals and Men*. New York: Century, 1932.

586. Thomas, Vincent, ed. *Creativity in the Arts*. Englewood Cliffs, NJ: Prentice-Hall, 1964.

587. Turkewych, Christine *and* Niccolina Divito. "Creative Dramatics and Second Language Learning," *TESL Talk*, 9, 3 (Summer 1978): 63-70.

588. Turner, Ralph H. "Role-Taking Process Versus Conformity." In Dennis Brissett and Charles Edgley, eds., *Life as Theater: A Dramaturgical Sourcebook*. Chicago: Aldine, 1975: 109-22.

589. Turner, Victor W. *The Forest of Symbols: Aspects of Ndembu Ritual*. Ithaca, NY: Cornell University Press, 1967.

590. ——— . *From Ritual to Theatre: The Human Seriousness of Play*. New York: Performing Arts Journal Publications, 1982.

591. Tylor, E. *Primitive Culture*. 2 vols. London: Murray, 1871.

592. Tyson, Moya. "Creativity." In B. M. Foss, ed., *New Horizons in Psychology*. Harmondsworth: Penguin, 1966.

593. Urena, P. H. *Literary Currents in Hispanic America*. Cambridge, MA: Harvard University Press, 1945.

594. Vaihinger, Hans. *Philosophy of "As If."* Translated by C. K. Ogden. Reprint. London: Kegan Paul, 1966.

595. Valentine, C. W. "The Psychology of Imitation with Special Reference to Early Childhood." *Brit. J. Psych.*, 2 (1930): 105-132.

596. Van Gennep, Arnold. *Rites of Passage*. Chicago: Chicago University Press, 1960.

597. Verissimo, E. *Brazilian Literature—An Outline*. New York: Macmillan, 1945.

598. Vinacke, W. E. "The Investigation of Concept Formation." *Psych. Bul.*, 48 (1951): 1-31.

599. Viola, Ann. "A Clarification of Terms." In Siks and Dunnington (see 583 above): 8-12.

600. Von Bertalanffy, Ludwig. *Robots, Men and Minds*. New York: George Brazillier, 1967.

601. Vygotsky, L. S. *Thought & Language*. Translated by E. Hanfmann & G. Vakar. New York: Wiley, 1962.

602. Wagner, Betty Jane. *Dorothy Heathcote: Drama as a Learning Medium*. Washington, D.C.: National Education Association of the United States, 1976.

603. Walder, Robert. "The Psychoanalytic Theory of Play." Translated by Sara A. Bonnet., *Psychoan. Q.*, 2 (1933): 208-224.

604. Waley, Arthur. *The No Plays of Japan*. London: Allen & Unwin, 1922.

605. Walters, R. H. *and* R. D. Parke, in L. P. Lipsitt and C. C. Spiker, eds., *Advances in Child Development and Behaviour*, II. New York: Academic Press, 1965.

606. Wangh, Martin. "The Scope of the Contribution of Psychoanalysis to the Biography of the Artist." *J. Am. Psychoan. Assoc.*, 5 (1957) : 564-575.

607. Ward, Winifred. *Creative Dramatics*. New York: Appleton, 1930.

608. —— . *Stories to Dramatics*. Nashville, TN: Children's Theatre Press, 1952.

609. —— . "Let's Pretend." *Junior League Magazine*, 60 (Feb. 1953).

610. —— . *Playmaking with Children*. New York: Appleton, 2nd. ed., 1957.

611. —— . "Creative Dramatics in Elementary and Junior High Schools." In Siks and Dunnington (see 583 above).

612. Warren, Bernie. *Using the Creative Arts in Therapy*. Cambridge, MA: Brookline, 1984.

613. Watson, P. C. "Reasoning." In B. M. Foss, ed., *New Horizons in Psychology*. Harmondsworth: Penguin, 1966.

614. Watts, A. F. *The Language and Mental Development of Children*. London: Harrap, 1944.

615. Way, Brian. *Development Through Drama*. London: Longman, 1968.

616. —— . *Audience Participation: Theatre for Young People*. Boston: Walter H. Baker, 1981.

617. Weininger, Otto. *Play and Education: The Basic Tool for Early Childhood Education*. Springfield, IL: Charles C. Thomas, 1979.

618. —— . *Out of the Minds of Babes: The Strength of Children's Feelings*. Springfield, IL: Charles C. Thomas, 1982.

619. —— . "Just Pretend: Explorations of the Use of Pretend Play Teaching Handicapped and Emotionally Disturbed Children." In Judith Kase-Polisini, ed., *Creative Drama in a Developmental Context*. Papers delivered at 1st International Research Conference, Harvard and OISE, Toronto. Lanham, MD: University Press of America, 1985: 3-32.

620. ——. "'What If' and 'As If': Imagination and Pretend Play in Early Childhood." In Kieran Egan and Dan Nadaner, eds., *Imagination and Education*. New York: Teacher's College Press, Columbia University, 1988: 141-52.

621. Weissman, Philip. *Creativity in the Theater*. New York: Basic Books, 1965.

622. Welsford, Enid. *The Fool*. Cambridge: Cambridge University Press, 1925.

623. ——. *The Court Masque*. Cambridge: Cambridge University Press, 1927.

624. Wertheimer, Max. *Productive Thinking*. New York: Harper, 1945.

625. Wexberg, Erwin. *Individual Psychology*. New York: Cosmopolitan, 1929.

626. White, R. *and* R. Lippit. "Leader Behaviour and Member Reaction in Three 'Social Climates.'" In D. Cartwright and A. Zander, eds., *Group Dynamics*. London: Tavistock, 1960.

627. White, Robert W. "Motivation Reconsidered: The Concept of Competence." *Psychology Review*, 66 (1959): 297-333.

628. Whitehead, A. N. *and* Bertrand Russell. *Principia Mathematica*. Cambridge: Cambridge University Press, 1910.

629. Whiting, J. W. M. "Sorcery, Sin and the Superego." In M. R. Jones, ed., *Nebraska Symposium on Motivation*. Lincoln: University of Nebraska Press, 1959.

630. ——. "Resource Mediation and Learning by Identification." In I. Iscoe and H. W. Stevenson, eds., *Personality Development in Children*. Austin: TX: University of Texas, 1960.

631. Whorf, B. L. *Collected Papers in Metalinguistics*. Washington, D.C.: Dept. of State, 1952.

632. Wickham, Glynne. *Early English Stages*. 3 vols. London: Routledge, 1959.

633. Wiles, John *and* Alan Garrard. *Leap to Life?* Rev. ed. London: Chatto & Windus, 1965.

634. Winnicott, D. W. *Playing and Reality*. Harmondsworth: Penguin, 1974.

635. Witkin, Robert W. *The Intelligence of Feeling*. London: Heinemann, 1974.

636. Wittgenstein, Ludwig. *Tractacus Logico-Philosophicus*. Trans, D. F. Pears and B. F. McGuiness. New York: Humanities Press, 1929.

637. ——. *Philosophical Investigations*. Translated by G. E. M. Anscombe. New York: Macmillan, 1953.

638. Wise, Arthur. *Speech Communication*. London: Longman, 1959.

639. Woltman, Adolf G. "The Use of Puppetry as a Projective Method in Therapy." In H. H. and G. L. Anderson, eds., *An Introduction to Projective Methods and Other Devices for Understanding the Dynamics of Human Behaviour.* New York: Prentice-Hall, 1951.

640. ———. "Concepts of Play Therapy Techniques." *Am. J. Orthopsychiat.,* 25 (1955): 771-783.

641. Wood, Walter. *Children's Play and Its Place in Education.* London: Kegan Paul, 1913.

642. Woolf, Rosemary. *The English Mystery Plays.* Berkeley: University of California Press, 1972.

643. Yajnik, R. K. *The Indian Theatre: Its Origins and Later Development under European Influence, with special reference to Western India.* London: Allen & Unwin, 1934.

644. York, Eleanor Chase. "Values to Children from Creative Dramatics." In Siks and Dunnington (see 583 above).

645. Young, Karl. *The Drama of the Medieval Church.* 2 vols. Oxford: Oxford University Press, 1933.

646. Zimmer, Heinrich. *The King and the Corpse.* New York: Bollinger XI Series, Pantheon, 1948.

647. Zucker, A. E. *The Chinese Theatre.* London: Jarrolds, 1925.

648. Zung, Cecilias. L. *Secrets of the Chinese Drama.* London: Harrap, 1937.

Index